The Stay-at-Home Mom's Guide to
MAKING MONEY FROM HOME

LIZ FOLGER

The Stay-at-Home Mom's Guide to

MAKING MONEY
from HOME

Revised 2nd Edition

Choosing the Business That's Right For You
Using the Skills and Interests You Already Have

PRIMA PUBLISHING
3000 LAVA RIDGE COURT • ROSEVILLE, CALIFORNIA 95661
(800) 632-8676 • www.primalifestyles.com

PRIMA PUBLISHING and colophon are trademarks of Prima Communications Inc., registered with the United States Patent and Trademark Office.

Library of Congress Cataloging-in-Publication Data
Folger, Liz
The stay-at-home mom's guide to making money from home / Liz Folger.
p. cm.
Includes bibliographical references and index.
ISBN 0-7615-2149-6
Home-based businesses—Management. 2. Self-employed women. 3. Mothers—Employment. I. Title
HD62.38 .F65 1999
650.14'085'2—dc21   99-048742

00 01 02 03 HH 10 9 8 7 6 5 4 3 2
Printed in the United States of America

How to Order

Single copies may be ordered from Prima Publishing, 3000 Lava Ridge Court, Roseville, CA 95661; telephone (800) 632-8676. Quantity discounts are also available. On your letterhead, include information concerning the intended use of the books and the number of books you wish to purchase.

Visit us online at www.primalifestyles.com

To my dad, W. H. McKay

Contents

Acknowledgments

First, I want to thank my husband for his encouragement and support throughout this project. The guy has read this book more times than anybody should be allowed. None of the superlative adjectives can adequately define him. To my parents, Bill and Doris McKay, for their continued support. I'm grateful to Bambi Dingman, my mentor, for suggesting I give writing a try. A big thanks to Bonnie Hearn, my writing teacher, for enlightening me on the art of focus; to my online writing teacher, Blythe Camenson; and to Mary Anne Hultgren, my mother-in-law, and her red pen.

Last and in no way least, I want to thank everyone who allowed me to interview them for this book. The profiles in this book are what have made it so popular. Without these work-at-home moms relenting to my hours of interviewing, *The Stay-at-Home Mom's Guide to Making Money from Home* would have never been possible. I thank each one of you from the bottom of my heart! You have taught me, and every person who reads this book, more than you will ever know.

INTRODUCTION

A Few Words from Liz Folger

✦

You are never given a wish without also being given the power to make it come true.
—Richard Bach

You'VE PURCHASED THIS book because you want to make a difference in your life and in the life of your family. Maybe you've worked your 40+ hours a week and are tired of spending so little time with your family and are looking for a different way to make money. Or you're a stay-at-home mom who would like to make some extra cash. Whatever your reason for picking up this book, I'm here to tell you this: You can do anything you set your mind to. And I'll tell you why.

When I had completed an earlier edition of this book and had sent it off to the editors, I was, how shall I put it, beside myself. Writing a book was not a longtime passion of mine, nor did I have the English major to

back me up. As a matter of fact, I didn't even have a college degree. I simply liked the subject of moms working at home, wanted to be a work-at-home mom myself, and looked around for a book on the subject so I could learn how to make this goal a reality.

Unfortunately, I couldn't find such a book. So I decided to write it myself. I couldn't think of a better way to learn how to work at home than to interview successful work-at-home moms and compile their information and other resources into a book. So that's exactly what I did.

After sending my manuscript off to the publisher, I called my writing teacher Bonnie Hearn. I had taken a writing class from her through an adult-learning school when I lived in Fresno, California. I learned so much from her and she had, in more ways than one, become my writing mentor.

I immediately told Bonnie, "I did it. I finished the book, on time, and mailed it off to the publisher." And do you know what she said to me? "Liz, you've written a book, you can do anything now." I don't think anyone has ever told me those words before. I can't even tell you how good I felt about myself when she said that to me.

And you know, you don't have to write a book to get to that point.

In case you're like me and have never been told those beautiful words before, I'm taking matters into my own hands and I'll tell you myself:

Whatever your goals, dreams, and ambitions, you can accomplish them. You can do anything you set your mind to. That is, if you really want it badly enough.

The Stay-at-Home Mom's Guide to
MAKING MONEY FROM HOME

PART ONE

Home Business Basics

CHAPTER ONE

Deciding to Start Your Own Home Business

✦

There is no shortage of opportunities for resourceful women.

—Barbara Sher, author of *Wishcraft*

I REALLY WANT to stay home with my kids and start a home business so I can help contribute to the family's finances, but I don't have a clue where to start."

If you've thought or even spoken those words, you're not alone. Many women get up early, get the kids dressed, drop them off at day care, drive in rush-hour traffic, and arrive at work exhausted, thinking, "There has to be a better way."

If this sounds familiar, I have just appointed myself the good news fairy. Yes, there is a better way—that is, if you really want it and are prepared for some hard work ahead. You'll be making some

trades—some good (trading commuting for working in your pajamas) and some not so good (trading paid health insurance and retirement benefits for providing your own). This book isn't about wild dreams; it tells you truthfully how you can stay home with your kids and make some money while doing something you really enjoy.

Women today are put into a difficult situation. We're made to feel we have to work, bring in that second income, and raise good, upstanding children. If we don't, we're failures. And when the family goes to hell, the mother takes the blame. Neighbors shake their heads and sigh, "She never spent any time with those kids or her husband. She was always working. No wonder that family is so screwed up."

If we do decide to stay home with our kids, we're blamed for wasting our education. "How hard can that be, really? She probably just sits in front of the television all day." If you stay at home, however, you're more than aware of all the responsibilities you have to juggle.

Choosing to work at home can be a tough financial decision. I love the Spanish proverb that says, "A rich child often sits in a poor mother's lap." Sometimes we lose sight of our priorities and forget where our true wealth lies. If you try to make everyone happy, you're going to come out on the losing end. A home business is a perfect solution. You can stay home with your kids and do something for yourself, all at the same time.

What Are You Really Earning?

I F YOU'RE working at a regular job right now, you're probably torn between bringing in a second income yet wanting to be home with your kids. One frustrated mother decided to sit down and figure out just how much she was making after having to fork out for child care, taxes, and other amenities because of her job. She discovered that the nanny she had hired to watch her kids was making the same amount she was—only the nanny was the one spending all the time with

her kids. Finding a way to work from her home soon became top priority.

Here's something else to think about: The $40,000 your husband makes and the $25,000 you make do not add up to $65,000 a year. In the book *Two Incomes and Still Broke?* (Times Books, 1996), author Linda Kelley points out, "It's not how much you make, but how much you keep." If you think you may be earning less than your paycheck shows, read Kelley's book. You may have expenses that you are not considering. Child care, commuting costs, meals out, vehicle maintenance, federal and state taxes, and social security can all eat up your hard-earned cash.

Even more eye opening is the following list of costs a normal working mother accrues. This list was compiled by Larry Burkett in *Women Leaving the Workplace* (Moody Press, 1995).

1. Child-care costs: about $300 per month for one child and $450 per month for two. This figure does not include lost wages when a child is sick, additional medical expenses associated with group child care, or the additional fees that always seem to be associated with children's groups (gifts, trips, etc.).

2. Transportation costs: $250 per month, including car payments, maintenance, and gasoline costs.

3. Work-related clothing costs: estimated cost about $50 per month.

4. Additional eating-out costs: estimated at $80 per month. As most working mothers know, there is a fatigue factor that comes along with managing a home and job. This is often manifested in hurried meals, eating out a lot, or ordering in pizzas.

5. Miscellaneous expenses: $70 per month.

Obviously there may be other expenses (such as hiring a maid), but when you add these all up, the total is a minimum of $750 (but probably closer to $900). Don't forget that all these costs, except for child care, are paid with after-tax dollars, and the additional earnings of a working wife may push the family into a higher tax bracket.

If we assume that the median income of a working mother is $14,500, then that means a net return of slightly more than $300 per month. Based on a 40-hour workweek, a working mother nets around $2 per hour for her time.

If that same working mother used her services at home to reduce the family's food bills and shopped at discount stores and garage sales, it is quite possible she would net more savings for her family than the income she generates.

Once you figure out your own financial situation, you may find that you don't need that second income after all—at least not one that is earned outside your home. And you can come home to be with your kids and work at a business that you love, instead of one that you have to go to and where you may be unappreciated and underpaid.

When Is the Best Time to Start Your Home Business?

THIS IS a complicated question," says Carole Sinclair in *Keys for Women Starting and Owning a Business* (Barrons, 1991). But she answers it quite simply: "If the business is a good option for you, then it's the right time . . . and waiting for the perfect time may mean that you never start." If this is something that you want to do, then do it. Don't put it off until your kids are in school, have graduated, or until you're laid off from work. You may never find the perfect time to start a home business, just as you never find the perfect time to have children. The biggest mistake you can make on the road to self-employment is to never take the first step.

It's Not All or Nothing

THERE IS no one right way to start a home business. Everybody's situation is different. My goal is to show you the many different avenues you can take. If, in the end, you feel that the financial burden would be too much for you if you were to suddenly quit your job to start a business from home, then don't do it that way. Think about starting your home business part time. Find a way that you can work on your new business a few hours a week. Ever heard the phrase, Better keep your day job? Writers and artists hear it all too often. As you start your business, read as many books as you can find on your particular business, talk to people in similar types of businesses, and slowly work at getting the customers you need. Eventually, you'll get to the point where you can quit your full-time job and continue full time with your home business.

The Ideal Situation: Start Learning About Your Business Before You Start a Family

MANY MOMS, myself included, find themselves pregnant and say, "Hey, wait a minute, I think I want to stay home with this baby. What can I do for work?" Ideally, if you want to start a home business, you should get the business experience you need *before* you have kids. Let's look at the profession of medical transcription, for instance. The pay is great and the job is one you can do from home. But it takes a while to become competent at it. You need to take some medical terminology classes at your local community college and receive on-the-job training at a hospital or a doctor's office. If at all possible, decide what type of business you want to start and get the training

you need so your business is off the ground before you have your babies.

Two sisters, Elizabeth Bartel-Poole and Kristen Castiglione, are co-owners of From Molly's Doghouse, a business that sells homemade gourmet dog biscuits. They started their business because they both knew that once they started having children, they would want to stay home with them. They say, "We absolutely love dogs and we want them to live happy, healthy lives. In researching whether this would be a good business to start, we found some amazing facts about spending and pets." Their inventory has now grown to include colorful dog mats, totes, bandannas, and a dry dog-biscuit mix. They sell their products through mail order as well as wholesale to pet shops and gourmet stores, and they also publish a newsletter. This business has worked out wonderfully for them, and Kristen is now expecting her first baby.

Unfortunately, we're not all as well organized as these two sisters. So if you already have some kids of your own, read on.

The Pros and Cons of Self-Employment

IF YOU'RE thinking of starting a new endeavor, the first thing to do is write out a list of pros and cons. Why do you want to start a home business? What are the pros and what are the cons for you? This will help you record your dreams and fears in black and white so you can deal with them one by one.

Before you get out your own paper and pencil, take a look at this list of what other moms have said:

PROS

- The flexibility to attend your child's games, plays, and school events.

- The possibility of making more money.

- More self-confidence.

- No more dreading asking for time off when your child is sick.

- The thrill of knowing your service really helped someone.

- Your kids learn a healthy work ethic from seeing you work.

- Your kids know what your job is and that they can be a part of it.

- You aren't torn apart when you have to drop your child off at day care.

- Strangers aren't raising your kids.

- You gain independence in running your own business.

- Fewer miles on the cars.

- Spend less money on clothes, gas, and car maintenance.

- You can work with your cat on your lap.

- You can work on your business if you can't sleep at night.

- You can take your kids on outings when everyone else is at their 9 to 5 jobs.

- You can wear whatever you want to work.

- You don't have to deal with difficult co-workers or bosses.

- You can create your own schedule and make your own hours.

- You can have a baby and not be criticized for it.

- You can accept only the work you want to.

- You have the freedom to start a business that you love.

- You can hold tea parties in the middle of the day with your daughters.

- "If the kids forget to take something with them to school I can take it to them. I don't know how we would do this if I was an hour and a half away." (Marilyn Rowland, indexer)

- "When I have the flu, I can go upstairs and crawl in bed. I can take my calls up there and nobody has any idea that I'm in bed." (Suzette Trimmer, owner of a nanny-finding service)

- "I'm not totally exhausted like I was when I was commuting three hours a day." (Marilyn Rowland)

- "I can fit my work schedule into my family's instead of vice versa." (Melody Upham, soapmaker)

- "I don't have to answer to anybody. I can put my children first without having someone say, 'What do you mean you won't be here on time?'" (Rebecca Bostick, architect)

- "I am able to be more involved with my children's education." (Karen Potter, child-care provider)

CONS

- It's all on your shoulders.

- There's no one to run to if your computer breaks down. You are the one who has to fix it or be able to find someone quickly who can.

- Payments are sometimes few and far between.

- You're never really away from your work. You're in business 24 hours a day.

- Because you work for yourself, some people may not see your business as a real job.

- The isolation.

- Paid vacations are a thing of the past.

- You can have sick days, but you aren't going to get paid for them. If anything, you will be losing money.

- You have to pay for health insurance and figure out your retirement savings yourself.

- "There's nobody to pass the buck to. No one taking care of taxes and pensions. Usually the corporate world does that for you." (Suzette Trimmer)

If You've Always Been at Home

IF YOU'VE always been at home, you've probably been asked, "So what do you do for a living?" When you say, "Oh, I stay home with my kids," the response is often a polite but patronizing, "Oh, how nice." Once these people stop pitying those of us who do decide to stay home, they'll find out that some of the stay-at-home moms used to be lawyers, doctors, and engineers. Others, like myself, had to put off their education because of family responsibilities.

Another complaint I hear from moms who stay home is that they feel they don't have any outside projects to call their own. It's a case of the low-self-esteem blues. Becoming self-employed is a way to do something for yourself, and being successful can make your self-esteem rise to new heights. Then when someone asks what you do, you can proudly say, "I stay home with my kids and I also run an extremely successful business."

I Want to Be Rich

SOME PEOPLE get the silly notion in their heads that running a home business will make them millionaires practically overnight. It is true that people who work for themselves can make more than the average person who works for someone else. In fact, the average home-based income is $50,000 a year—about $25,000 more than the average employee makes. But this isn't something that will happen instantly.

Whatever you do, don't start your business because you need to make tons of money fast. A business takes time. There are no easy roads to riches. In *Home Business Happiness* (Alive, 1996), by Cheri Fuller, Rick Warren is quoted as saying, "Things that last usually require more time and determination than usual. An oak tree takes sixty years to grow, while a mushroom only takes six hours of growth. Do you want your business to have the stability of an oak tree or a mushroom?" Don't get discouraged. It probably won't take sixty years for your business to turn a profit, but it will take time.

Whatever business you decide to start, choose it because you love it, not because you think you're going to make a bushel of money. If you love something, you are more apt to stick with it when things get tough. And trust me, there will be tough times.

How you make your money is much more important than how much money you make. Finding a better way of life may be more important than how much money you contribute to the family every month. Your home business may not make you rich, but it will keep you in the environment where you want to be. You can't put a price on watching your baby's first step—on just being there for your kids.

CHAPTER TWO

How to Avoid Scams

◆

He that maketh haste to be rich shall not be innocent.
—Proverbs 20:20

THE ADS YOU have just read are real. You can find them in reputable magazines and newspapers on a daily basis. Before you begin looking for the perfect business, it's a good idea to learn how to stay clear of the scammers who are just waiting for your call.

Financial obligations can be tough, and many moms want the opportunity to stay home yet still earn money. Because of this, moms have become a big target for work-at-home scams. It's been estimated that $40 billion a year is lost to scams in the United States alone. It's estimated that 6 million people answer classified ads each year regarding money scams. These ads practically jump off the page, grabbing at our fantasies and checkbooks. They all sound too good to be true, and they are.

Plain and simple, scams appeal to our greedy side. I think just about everybody would love to make millions of dollars without having to lift a finger (a reason scams do so well). I can't tell you how many times I have seen those ads and wondered, "Maybe this one is the big moneymaker." This is usually when my husband arrives on the scene and gives me his *Home Improvement* impersonation: "I don't think so, Liz."

We simply don't want to admit these ads are lying to us. We really want to believe that we could be making easy money by assembling crafts or stuffing envelopes as our children play at our feet. When we see the same ads over and over again, we become convinced they have to be true. If these companies were dishonest they would have been put out of business long ago, right? Wrong.

It is very difficult to catch scammers. Usually they advertise out of state and have

HOW TO SPOT A SCAM

Have you ever had to pay money to a future employer when you gave the company your application? Have you ever seen a legitimate job application that asked you to submit $5 or $10 if you wanted to get the job? Of course not. Legitimate businesses make money from what they sell, not from people trying to get jobs. Here's a typical scam ad:

Important Notice: $1,500 weekly working from your location. No experience necessary. Flexible hours! No gimmicks! Serious individuals only. Call 1-800-555-5555.

This ad is a great example of a scam. The amount of money it promises you is on the first line. It uses a lot of exclamation marks and promises "no gimmicks" (its explanation of why it sounds too good to be true). A work-at-home scam will usually promise you at least one of the following:

- Big money in a short amount of time.
- Guaranteed markets and a huge demand.
- No experience necessary.
- You could practically run the business in your sleep.
- You will only need to work a couple of hours a week and you'll still make hundreds of dollars.
- Your business will not fail.

HOW TO SPOT A REAL JOB

Real jobs are easy to spot: They don't promise you the moon and the stars. Here's an ad for a real job:

> **Part-time secretary needed for an institutional equity analyst. Must have excellent word-processing skills (Word 6.0, Excel, Lotus) and be able to handle pressure. Will do travel arrangements, phones, filing, word processing, etc. . . . Fax résumé and salary requirements to: 1-800-555-5555.**

- It tells you exactly what the job requires.
- It tells you for whom you'll be working.
- It wants to check out your credentials.
- It's not asking for money.
- It doesn't promise anything but a job.

---

a pack of lawyers working for them. This means that if you were to take them to court, you'd have to travel to the state their company resides in, costing you more money than you'd try to win back from them in court. Worse, most scammers who are put out of business simply start another one under a new name. Scammers aren't stupid, and neither are you. In this chapter we'll look at some ways to spot scams and steer clear of them.

Common Scams

MOST SCAMS work by mailing you some free information—but in order to get started, you're going to have to send the company some green stuff. Once you

send them money, you'll find out that the business is totally different from what was advertised. Beware: Once you get on a scammer's mailing list, you'll soon become inundated with lots and lots of proposals for making money at home. Just trash the ad. Better yet, use it to line your birdcage or start a fire in your fireplace.

To avoid a scam, you have to first be familiar with it. Let's look at some of the common work-at-home scams that you will find in newspapers and magazines. I'll tell you how they work—or better, how they don't.

ENVELOPE STUFFING

To be blunt, the only thing you will be stuffing in an envelope is your money. This ad usually promises that for just a "little fee" it will give you the "secrets" on how you can make hundreds of dollars stuffing envelopes from home. It sometimes will say "free supplies." Don't let that fool you into thinking you won't have to pay that fee to get started.

Only after you send the company your cash do you find out that you aren't being offered a job. You'll simply be sent a letter telling you to place the same envelope-stuffing ad in a magazine or to send the ad to friends and relatives. You make money when other people respond to your ad—and then you're a scammer, too.

CRAFT ASSEMBLY

This one sounds easy enough, right? Especially if you like crafts or sewing. But it's not that simple. Usually the company will require that you buy all your equipment and supplies from it—sewing machines, sign makers, and so on. This is how the company makes its money. Then, after you purchase the needed equipment and assemble your products, you send them in and wait for a check. The company may accept your first batch of work, but the second time around it will find your work unacceptable. What's even more discouraging is that you're never told what part of your work was unsatisfactory. This way you have no idea how to fix the problem. No matter how good you are or how many times you redo your work, it will never be up to the company's standards.

VENDING MACHINES

Here you are promised all the help and support you need to get your business running, but too often the support is nonexistent. You are given phone numbers of other so-called happy vendors who can tell you what a moneymaker this business is. The people you call are not happy vendors, of course, but part of the whole scheme. Once you invest your money, which is often thousands of dollars, you find out there isn't really much of a market for your machines after all. Time and again I have heard from people who have invested in vending machines, and they just can't find anyone who will let them put them in their stores. It's a lot more work than is stated in the sales letter. Recently, the Federal Trade Commission (FTC) put a vending company out of business because the company was giving phony references to potential buyers and made false claims.

COUPON CLIPPING

With this scam, sometimes you have to pay a fee for the information you need to get started. Once you receive your information, you are told that you will receive a percentage, usually 10 percent, of the cash value of the coupons that you clip. The cash value of a coupon is actually $1/20$ of a cent, not the 25 cents or 50 cents you're led to believe. So while you think you're sending the company $3,000 worth of coupons, which would average about $300 for you, in actuality you would receive only around $15. To make it worse, you usually won't get paid until your account reaches $20. Some companies are really picky about the coupons you send them. They don't like getting the same coupon twice. So you can't go out on Sunday morning and buy all the Sunday papers.

Some of these ads tell the story of a church group that got together and raised money clipping coupons. This makes you feel that it has to be a legitimate business if a church is involved. This is exactly what they want you to think. See, I told you these scammers aren't stupid.

COMPILING MAILING LISTS

As with the envelope stuffing, you pay for the information to get started. You will then be told you need to place an ad the company provides for you and that you will have to pay for this ad. It will look much like the ad you answered. Once someone responds to your ad, you can sell that address to the company for around 50 cents. The company then sends the addressee an opportunity to do what you're doing. Just remember that your name will be associated with the ad. If someone has a problem, guess who he or she will come looking for? Depending on where you live, it can cost anywhere from $20 to $50 a week to run an ad. That's $80 to $200 a month! Say you get fifty people who respond at 50 cents a name per month. You make a whopping $25 that month. Yet it cost you between three to eight times that to place the

ad. This is a big-time loser job. Again, the only person making money is the scammer.

USING ANOTHER COMPANY'S PRODUCTS FOR MAIL ORDER

While this setup isn't illegal, you need to ask yourself why the company is boasting about how much money you will make selling their items—why don't they just do it themselves and cut out the middleman so they could keep more of the profit? Think of the mail-order companies that are successful, such as L. L. Bean. I don't think they would ever allow someone else to ship their merchandise.

The company will supply you with the camera-ready ads, but you have to pay to have them placed. Barbara Brabec, in *Home-made Money* (Betterway Publications, 1994), explains it best: "What mail-order beginners do not realize is that catalog mailings may yield only a 1/2 to 1 percent order response— which is only 5 to 10 orders for every 1,000 pieces mailed. And that is if the list is good. . . ." Most of the time you will find the merchandise supplied is very cheap, and you probably won't be getting any repeat customers.

READING BOOKS

For a small fee, you will be given the information you need to get started reading books or movie scripts. However, if and when you do finally receive your instruction guide, you find that you still have not secured a job. The guide simply explains that you need to contact publishers directly and offer to read manuscripts. This takes persistence and determination. You must also realize that most publishers use in-house staff to read books and scripts.

900 NUMBERS

As with most "start your own business" ads, ads for 900 numbers promise that you'll make a barrelful of money with an investment of only a few hundred dollars. But that isn't really the case, as Robert Mastin explains in *900 Know-How* (Aegis Publishing Group, 1996). Stay away from companies that pressure you to sign now, say they'll do all the advertising for you, and imply you will make tons of money overnight. If the 900-number industry is beckoning you, please read Mastin's book first and forget the phony (no pun intended) ads.

RESPONDING TO 800 NUMBERS, 900 NUMBERS, AND 809 NUMBERS

If an ad gives you a toll-free number to call and then asks you to call a 900 number, just stop right there. That 900 number is going to cost you! If this company were legitimate, why would it charge you a very expensive phone call to give you its information? Because this is how the company is making money. The 900 number will tell you that you need to send the company a SASE for a job application. In return you get the application—along with a phone bill for the 900 number, which may cost you between $15 and $100. Not long ago the federal government passed a law stating that 900 numbers could not be used for the sale of employment information. The 900 numbers form of scam should thus be seen less and less.

The 809 number scheme is even worse. This number is located in the Caribbean, so it doesn't have the regulations that numbers do in the United States. There won't be any warning that you are being charged big bucks for the bogus phone call. You'll just get a large phone bill at the end of the month. The call can cost you $25 dollars or more a minute, and the representatives do their best to keep you on the phone for as long as possible.

"I'VE MADE A MILLION DOLLARS, AND SO CAN YOU"

You've seen these full-page ads featuring successful people standing by their fancy cars or sitting at an imposing desk. The ad copy explains how they were going into debt, and how the whole family was living in someone's dark basement, but then they found this wonderful business that is making more money than they know what to do with. And because they are so kind, they want to tell you how you can do the same. Sure they do.

First, ask yourself this: "If they had such a great idea that is making tons of money, why would they share any of this with me?"

These people usually are selling a course. In this course you are instructed to do just as they have done. Supposedly, you will be taught the secrets of mail order and before long (probably overnight), your mailbox will be overflowing with money.

Now, I must admit, I fell for this scam a few years ago in my quest for the perfect business. I paid about $300 for a folder full of nothing. Well, the material had plenty to say, but none of it helped me get started. As a matter of fact, I sent the whole thing back. Fortunately, the company returned my money. You may not be so lucky.

Is It Multilevel Marketing or an Illegal Pyramid Scheme?

Here are some key points that separate a legal multilevel marketing business from an illegal pyramid scheme. In a multilevel marketing scheme:

- Your income is based on selling products, not on recruiting others into the business.

- You'll make a good amount of sales, not just one or two a year.

- Start-up fees are minimal. If start-up fees are substantial, that's a big red flag that the company is not legal.

- The parent company will buy back all unsold goods if you decide to quit the business. If it won't, beware!

- The company you work for shouldn't be making money off you, but rather with you.

Mystery Shopping

I'd first like to mention that "mystery shopping" can be a legitimate form of employment. Unfortunately, due to the many mystery shopping scams out there, it's important to draw a distinction between the scams and those companies who are on the up and up.

For those of you unfamiliar with how mystery shopping works, here's a short description. Mystery shoppers are used by market researchers. You are given various assignments to pose as a customer visiting retail shops, restaurants, motels, and so forth. As the "customer," you review many things, such as how you are treated, if your questions are answered thoroughly and politely, if the place of business is clean, and so on. After the visit you fill out a report on your experience and mail it off.

The bottom line when trying to figure out if a mystery-shopping job is a scam or not is this: You should never have to pay a company a filing fee or for information to work for them. The scam can come in many forms. Having to call an 809 or 900 number would be your first tip-off that you should have nothing to do with the company. Some companies will ask for a "registration deposit." This will supposedly cover the cost of setting your file up, and so on. However, the company fails to tell you that most (legitimate) mystery shopping positions cost you nothing to start.

Medical Billing

Medical billing is another legitimate business that moms are running from home. Unfortunately, if you're thinking of starting such a business, there is a good chance you could become a victim of a scam. For some reason many stay-at home moms, when searching for a home business, think about starting this business because of the exceptional income potential. I'll admit when I was first looking for a home business I looked into medical billing. My suggestion is to really research this business. Also read the profile on medical billing in this book. The FTC has brought charges against several medical billing companies for overstating potential earnings, saying they will supply you with leads—later you will find out they are false leads—and failing to provide key pre-investment information that the law requires.

One hook some medical billing companies may use to lure you in is this: A company will state there is a new law that all claims have to be filed electronically, all you'll need to do is buy some very expensive software from the company. This is a lie. There is no such law.

If a company tells you no experience is needed, and it will provide you with the clients, run! As the FTC explains, "If you have no experience in medical billing, please do not fall for these sales ploys. Software will not make you a medical biller. Education and more education is how you will learn." The FTC has found that few entrepreneurs who purchase a medical billing business opportunity are able to find clients, start a business, and generate reviews, let alone earn a substantial income and recover their investments. The FTC states, "Competition in the medical billing market is very strong among a number of large and well-established firms."

Online Scams: Get Rich on the Internet

IT'S A fact that the Internet is becoming a very popular place for people to spend their time and money. With all these people zipping around on the information superhighway, you should be able to make tons of money. Just put up a Web site, sell something—anything, it really doesn't matter—and you'll soon be a millionaire. If only it were really that easy. As with any business, you have to spend time and money on it to make it a success. Actually getting people to come to your site, like it enough to browse it, and even come back on a regular basis takes time. Never fall for an ad promising that for a small fee of $40, $75, or $150 you'll learn how to make millions of dollars in just a few days doing business on the Net. I've had a Web site for more than three years now, and I'll be the first to tell you how much time, work, and money is involved when you are running a successful Internet site. For more information about making money on the Net, please read chapter 11.

CHAT ROOMS AND MESSAGE BOARDS

Chat rooms can be a great resource for work-at-home moms to get together and network. However, there are chatters who will try to sell to the room their "great" business opportunity, and if you don't sign up with his or her company right that second, you'll be missing out on so much money. You are called crazy if you don't take them up on such an offer. Once again, never be forced into making a decision to join a business opportunity. If you ever find yourself in this

type of situation, leave the chat room immediately.

I've been hosting message boards for about five years now. Over and over again I've seen people set themselves up to be scammed with such posts as,

Help, I'm disabled and need to pay rent this month, tell me how I can work from home!

Or,

I just had my first baby and the thought of going back to work and putting her in day care breaks my heart. I so desperately want to work at home. E-mail me with your ideas.

I can just see these people's e-mail boxes filling up with so many scams it scares me. I would highly recommend if you are looking for a home business, don't post these types of messages. Each person who responds to you with a business opportunity will sound perfect. "Easy money, excellent pay, NO

HOW TO CHECK OUT A COMPANY

- Call the Better Business Bureau (BBB) in the state where the business resides. Call information to get the number. It may cost you some change to find out if the company is legitimate, but it could save you lots of money down the road. You can also find the BBB on the Internet at http://www.bbb.org/council/main/index.html.

- Before you sign anything or hand over any money, have an attorney check everything over. Sure it will cost you a few bucks, but in the end it may save you a bunch.

HOW TO REPORT A SCAM

- Call your local state attorney's office.

- Call the Better Business Bureau in the city or state of the scammer.

- Call your local consumer protection agency.

- Call the National Fraud Information Center at 1-800-876-7060. You can also find it on the Internet at http://www.fraud.org/.

- If you received the information by mail, call your local post office and report the scammer.

- If you have a consumer problem or complaint, write to the Federal Trade Commission. Although the agency cannot act to resolve individual problems, it can act when it sees a pattern of possible law violations. Write to Correspondence Branch, Federal Trade Commission, 6th Street and Pennsylvania Avenue, N.W., Washington, D.C., 20580, or call 202-326-2418. You can also find the Web site at http://www.ftc.gov/.

EXPERIENCE NEEDED—just send me $59.95 and I'll tell you how to start making money NOW!"

Scammers feed on desperation. The more desperate you are, the easier you become a target.

BULK E-MAIL

Suppose you come across an online opportunity where you are told you can make money sending bulk e-mail by purchasing bulk e-mail lists and spamming (sending unsolicited e-mail) software. You should be aware of the strict spamming laws that are now enforced. You could be out of business and out of money very quickly running this type of business.

According to the FTC, "More often than not, bulk e-mail offers appeared to be fraudulent, and if pursued, could have ripped off unsuspecting consumers to the tune of billions of dollars."

CHAIN LETTERS VIA E-MAIL

This is the same old concept, e-mail style. You are usually told this is a legal operation (it's not). You are to send money to the top mailing address on the list (you of course add your name to the bottom of the list) and send the e-mail to several of your friends (or

HOW TO KNOW YOU'RE ABOUT TO GET SCAMMED

- You have an uneasy feeling about this so-called work-at-home job. Trust your instincts. How many times have you had an uneasy feeling when you put your application in at the local retail store? You may not have wanted the job, but you didn't have to wonder if it was a scam.

- You are pressured to make a decision now. "Listen, lady, this is a once-in-a-lifetime chance, just give me 50 bucks to prove it. Don't think about it, just do it." If you hear that sort of spiel, get out immediately. Hang up the phone or throw the letter away.

- It sounds just a little too good to be true. It is.

- It's a "secret plan" to make a million dollars. If it's so secret, why are they sharing this great idea with you? Why don't they just keep their great idea to themselves so they can make even more money?

- There are lots of CAPITAL LETTERS and exclamation marks in the ad!!!!!!!

- The job requires no skills or knowledge of the business.

- The ad claims the easiest and quickest way to make money is to start this particular business.

- The envelope and letterhead are printed poorly.

- You see no sign of a return address or phone number.

- There is no money-back guarantee.

- They want you to send cash only. Please don't ever send cash. For one thing, it's hard to prove that you actually sent it. A lot of scammers make their money in small quantities.

- You see a lot of personal testimonies, but they never identify the person so you can check with them.

- You are required to pay a fee for instructions or merchandise before they tell you how the program works.

you can buy a bulk e-mail list). Once again, this is illegal. People on the Net have had it up to the brim with unsolicited e-mail and will go out of their way to report a spammer.

For more information about scams on the Internet, check out Scambusters (www.scambusters.com) and The Better Business Bureau (www.bbb.org/).

Don't Lose Your Self-Confidence to a Scam

ONE REASON I hate scams is because they do a search-and-destroy mission on your self-confidence. When you pay your hard-earned cash for the information you need to get started, you may feel a little hesitant about your decision. Your husband may not like the idea of your spending money on such a foolish venture. It takes a big commitment on your part to go through with it. Whether it's assembling crafts or stuffing envelopes, you soon realize that the whole

thing was a mistake. Your family may tease you or make you feel stupid for falling for such a scheme. Even if they're supportive, you may say harsh words to yourself. You figure that working from home isn't really possible, just as everyone told you. Finding the courage to try out your own business idea becomes more difficult than ever.

Making money in a hurry is a fantasy. Even if you can find people who will immediately buy your products or service, you may have to wait for payment. Once you do get paid, most likely that money will just have to go right back into the business. Talk to business owners, and they will tell you it takes time to build a client base and make a profit.

My Humble Advice

DON'T PICK a business because of all the so-called wealth you will be making. It's practically impossible to start a business overnight and be making oodles of

ONLINE RESOURCES

Scambusters is a comprehensive site for those who want more information on how to stay clear of scammers. It also has a newsletter you can sign up to receive for free. Check them out at http://www.scambusters.com.

I have created a Web site (www.bizymoms.com) for work-at-home moms, which includes a section on scams (www.bizymoms.com/scams.html). You will also find a link to the scam board, where you can ask questions about particular companies and their legitimacy.

money by the next day. It takes months and even years to start turning a good profit. And if in those first few months you hate what you're doing, there's a good chance you won't want to continue your business into the coming years. Just remember it takes time and hard work to become financially successful. Pick a business because you know in your heart that this is your dream job, the job that allows you to spring from your bed every morning and proclaim to the world, "I get to go to work today!"

Finding the Right Business for You

✦

Everyone must row with the oars she has.

—English proverb

I CAN'T TELL you how many times I've heard someone say, "I want to start a home business, but I don't know what I want to do." I've even said that myself, as you can see from the long list of home business ideas I've thought of establishing. It's so sad that many people, like myself, forget what it is we enjoy doing. I have a question for you that might help you solve this dilemma: What was it that you enjoyed doing when you were between the ages of 8 and 12?

Me? I enjoyed writing poetry. I would even illustrate my poems. That was something I loved to do. When I was assigned to write a poem in school, it wasn't work, it was fun. But somewhere between diagramming sentences and finding no real encouragement or direction with my creative writing, I lost what it was I really enjoyed.

If you can't remember that far back, ask your friends and relatives what type of child you were. Look at old pictures. What were you doing in the pictures? Were you the clown? The bookworm? Could you usually be found in the garden? Playing with an animal? In the kitchen dreaming of being the world's best chef? Drawing and coloring? Always wanting to play school and you had to be the teacher?

This is a great way to remember what it was that you enjoyed doing. It may sound a little silly, but give it a try and see what you can come up with. This just may be your key to what type of home business you should start.

In *No More "Nice Girl"* (Bob Adams, 1993), author Rosemary Agonito says, "I've come to realize over the years how important it is to work through our childhood experiences to achieve self-understanding. Who we are, why we made our particular life choices, how our daily actions and responses to the world are shaped, and most important, where we are headed—these secrets lie buried in childhood, waiting to be uncovered." I really believe in my heart that our true interests start at a young age. If you were lucky, you were encouraged in these interests and excelled. Many, however, were told, "You can't make a living at that. Why don't you try this?"

When I ask people what it is they enjoy doing, they often reply, "I don't know." How very sad that we live in a society that makes us forget what it was we wanted to do and forces us to work in jobs we often dislike.

Now, what kind of business could you start at home? That is a question only you can answer. But what better time than the present to start something you really like doing?

She Must Be Crazy, She Actually Likes Her Job

THE THOUGHT that you actually like your job can make others shake their heads and tell you right to your face that you're a complete wacko (they're just jeal-

ous). But what's really crazy is that many of us don't put the two together—our specific interest and how to make money at it.

Maybe you graduated from high school and went to college because that's what everyone else was doing. You received your degree in whatever and worked wherever, not really liking it but feeling stuck there. For some women, the only time they found out what it was they liked to do was when they decided to stay home and raise their children. What makes you tick has always been a part of you. You may have forgotten it exists, but it's there inside of you waiting to be discovered once more.

No Skills? Think Again

YOU MAY be saying to yourself, "This home business idea sounds great, but I don't have any skills." Everyone has skills. If you're a mom, you have skills, believe me.

Sometimes, as mothers, we tend to forget that once upon a time we had another life and we did things we enjoyed. Don't let having kids stop you from having a life. Find an area of interest and reserve a few hours a week for yourself. If it would help, start to attend classes at your local adult-learning school or college. Find a mentor or start apprenticing with someone. Maybe you feel the lack of education would hinder you. Well, if you have your own business, you're the boss. Nobody can tell you that they're not going to hire you because you don't have a degree.

You may have been doing something all your life that you could turn into a business. Teachers become tutors, secretaries become desktop publishers and word processors, stay-at-home moms become bookkeepers, and nurses become writers for various health publications. The possibilities are unlimited. However, don't get hung up on doing something because you have been doing it a long time. Do it only if it's something you really want to do.

Service Businesses

WHEN YOU'RE thinking about the business you would like to start, keep in mind that service-oriented businesses are the simplest to start. More than half of the businesses that are run by women are service businesses, such as word processing, accounting, bookkeeping, and calligraphy. Why? Because there is little or no inventory, which means less money that you have to pay out of your pocket to get your venture started. You will also find that people who do not have the time or knowledge to do a particular task themselves will pay someone else to do it for them. Which means you. Count on it: If you love it and you're good at it, there will be a demand for your business.

Computer Jobs

PLEASE REMEMBER this: A computer isn't going to magically make a business for you. Don't discourage yourself by thinking that because of the booming computer industry, the only way you can possibly make money in your home is by using a computer. If you enjoy working with a computer, then you may be an ideal candidate for starting a business as a word processor or newsletter publisher. If you can type a zillion words a minute but hate it, then don't do it. Only start a computer-oriented business because you love it. A computer is great for keeping in touch with other work-at-home moms (WAHMs) and keeping track of tax records, but it doesn't have to be the focus of your business.

Make a List

I'VE HEARD from many a mom, and have experienced myself, the frustrations of not knowing what business to start. You need to set a goal you can dream about and eventually reach. Right now, get a piece of paper, a pen, and a timing device. Give yourself five minutes and start writing down home business ideas that interest you. I know you have thought of them. Don't let that pen leave the paper; just start brainstorming and see what appears.

More Questions to Ask Yourself

IF YOU'RE still drawing a blank on what business you would like to start, answer the following questions:

1. What do you enjoy doing? Write it down, no matter how silly or unbusiness-like it may seem to you. For example:

   - I enjoy reading.
   - I like spending time with my family.
   - I love to hike.
   - I like to play on the Internet.
   - I enjoy the subject of home businesses.

2. List all your hobbies.

3. It's the weekend, and you have two full days to do whatever you want. What are you going to do? Backpack, visit friends, read the whole time, go horseback riding?

4. When you visit the bookstore, what sections do you usually find yourself in? The how-to section, cooking, humor, astronomy?

5. If you could get your degree all over again, what would it be in?

6. Is there an area you know a lot about and excel in? You'll start a great business and have more credibility if you operate within your own area of expertise.

7. Is there something you do that people compliment you on and have asked you to help them with? This is a key point. Carol Milano, author of *HERS* (Allworth Press, 1991), says, "Sometimes women realize that what they've been doing as favors to friends—like pet training or party planning—is actually a viable service to sell to others."

8. What interests do you have that could be a hot business in the next few years? Take the area of geriatrics. With the aging of the baby boomers, more and more services catering to the elderly are becoming popular. With the Internet becoming more mainstream, there is a demand for people who can design a Web site. Candles are becoming a billion-dollar-a-year industry. I would suggest you read current articles by Faith Popcorn, a major trend spotter. Also read up-to-date small- and home-business magazines, which often publish stories on soon-to-be-hot businesses.

9. As you read through your lists, are there subjects that keep coming up again and again? If so, take three interests that you really like doing and consider all the different ways you could expand them. Don't be surprised if one of these ideas jumps off the page and gives you a great big hug. Here's an example.

   If your area of interest is plants, you could:

   - Sell fresh herbs to local restaurants.
   - Sell herbs and flowers to nurseries.
   - Start a plant service for offices.
   - Become a landscaping consultant.

   Now write some of your own.

My area of interest:

- _____
- _____
- _____
- _____
- _____
- _____

Have Fun!

HAVE YOU found a few ideas that really sound like a lot of fun? *Fun* is the key word here, because if it sounds like torture you probably won't stay in the business long. Start researching each idea that interests you. Is there already a business similar to your idea, and if so, how is it doing? If there are no such businesses, why not? Have you found a gold mine of an idea, or have other people tried that business and failed? If so, why? Was there no market, or was the owner just not cut out to do that sort of business? It may feel like I'm interrogating you, but in the end, if you take the time to answer all these questions, your business will shine that much brighter.

Don't become depressed if ideas aren't coming fast and furious. It may take a period of soul searching and research to come up with the perfect home business for you. A great book for helping you figure out what it is you enjoy doing is called *The Artist's Way* (Tarcher/Putnam, 1992) by Julie Cameron and Mark Bryan. Just keep reading all you can on self-employment and talk to other home business owners. This may take some time, so be patient and enjoy your search.

Setting Yourself
Up for Success

✦

There are risks and costs to a program of action.
But they are far less than the long-range risks and costs of comfortable inaction.
—John F. Kennedy

DO YOU HAVE what it takes to make a success of a home business? Self-motivation is one of the biggest factors in success. Pat Curry, a freelance writer, says it best: "Time management is a big issue and you have to be self-motivated to work at home. Some people ask, 'How do you get motivated to work when you're at the house?' Well, I feel the need to pay the bills is really motivating."

You're also going to need a lot of determination; you'll need to be resourceful, to like to take risks, and to be able to spot opportunities that others miss. You should be able to work alone and handle stress without going completely crazy. It helps to be organized (I

tend to fail in this category, but you can't be everything), disciplined, decisive, flexible, energetic, as well as able to refocus your attention easily from family interruptions back to your work. You will also need a lot of patience.

Although it sounds as if you have to be Superwoman, take heart—help is available. If you feel you're lacking in any of these areas, you will probably be able to gain at least some of what you need from classes, seminars, and correspondence courses. Explore courses in time management, starting a small business, and others offered through the business department of your local community college. You can also buck up your confidence and self-motivation by making sure you know everything there is to know about your business before you plunge in. Why set yourself up for failure when you can set yourself up for success?

I could here give you a test to see if you have what it really takes to start a home business, but to be quite frank, when I have taken those tests, I checked the answers I figured would make me look like I would make a great entrepreneur. This isn't really cheating, it's proof of self-motivation. I know that if you really want to start your own business, you can do it. And to make sure you succeed, you need to do the groundwork.

Do the Research

IT'S EASY to set yourself up to fail with the excuse, "Well, I just didn't know what I was getting myself into," but there's no reason to do this. Don't put a cent into your business until you've thoroughly researched everything involved. Give yourself a good six months to research and write up a killer business plan (see chapter 5) before you actually start your business. The library is a great place to start. Read everything you can about home businesses in general and the specific business you want to start. If you have narrowed down your business idea, become great friends with your librarian. Librarians are in the information business and can give you a long list of helpful books and other information. Librarians will amaze you with what they know and their ability to find things.

Research Your Market

Market research is another way to determine if there actually are people out there who are interested in what your business has to offer. "Market research" may sound imposing, but you can find this information on an informal level. Gather together a group of people you think may be interested in using your service or product. Ask them what they would pay and what they would or wouldn't like to see in the business you are describing. Ask them to be as honest as possible.

You might try testing the market to see what kind of reaction you get. For example, you could offer your service free to a volunteer organization or sell your product at a charity auction. Then get people's reactions. What do they think of your service or product? Would they be interested in purchasing something like that on a regular basis?

Find a Niche

ANOTHER WAY to guard against failing in your business choice is to fill a need. Many businesses are started by people who needed a particular product or service, couldn't find anyone who offered it, and decided to take matters into their own hands. If you feel a need for a certain product or service, chances are that other people feel the same way. For example, a number of moms in different parts of the country have started a kid taxi service with their minivans. They saw that parents were having a tough time combining work with getting their kids from school to soccer practice, day care, or other activities, and back home again. In some cases this business has grown from one minivan to a whole fleet.

Take Small Steps

IT'S EASY to say you're going to start a home business. Every day you say, "I'll get started tomorrow." The whole thing can seem pretty overwhelming. But you can take small, painless, and even fun steps toward getting your business off the ground by developing your plan of action. It's easy to come up with excuses not to begin. But if you really want to make this work, give yourself an official starting date (be realistic) and circle it on your calendar. From that day on, do something every day to make that dream into a reality. For example:

- Contact your local adult-learning school or community college to find out about business or tax classes.

- Find out the cost of a business license.

- Talk to potential customers and see what they think of your idea.

- Go to the library and read everything you can on starting a home business.

Overcome Your Fears

ARE YOU ready to leave your present position but afraid to embark on a new adventure? That is a normal feeling. The truth is, starting anything new is scary. It's much easier to keep everything the same and complain about it than it is to go out there where you have never gone before and try to change your whole life.

Fear has struck every mom who has started her own business. Successful women may seem problem-free, but in the beginning they had their share of apprehension and uncertainty. The moms profiled in this book were all once right where you are now. They thought starting a home business was an ideal idea. But at some point each had to say, "Here it goes, I'm leaving the comfort of my own job and trying something new that may not make a whole lot of money. Can I do it?" Still, they left their comfort zone and forged ahead. As you'll read in the profiles in part II, it was worth it. They say, "It wasn't easy." "I was scared." "We had to scrimp, but we made it and it's worth it, and I don't ever see myself working for anyone else again."

Find a Mentor

WHAT MOTHER hasn't called her friend around dinnertime because she hasn't a clue what she should make? What mother hasn't talked to her friends about the way young Fred has this nasty habit of biting strangers (and no, we're not talking about the family dog)? What mother hasn't called her friend to ask for advice on finding a sitter, how to talk to her child's teacher, or where to find low-cost kids' clothing? This

QUESTIONS TO ASK A BUSINESS OWNER

Find someone in a business similar to yours, but one you won't be competing with. Ask her if she has time to answer a few questions. Here are some questions to get you started:

- How long have you been in business?
- Why did you start this particular business?
- What would you do differently if you had to do it all over again?
- What skills are needed for this type of business? Do I need a specific degree or training?
- What is the hardest thing about this business?
- What do you feel are the most important skills required for success?
- What do you like most about your business?
- What do you detest?
- How much money should I set aside to start my business?
- Is this a seasonal business?

is all a form of mentoring—getting advice from someone who's been there—and it works.

Ever heard of the "good old boys network"? Basically, it's just a bunch of guys helping other guys make it to the top. Now you can join the "good old WAHMs network." Check out one of the work-at-home-moms' organizations (see the resources in the back of this book for ideas). Go online and talk to other self-employed mothers and ask for help and advice. This is no time to believe that because this is the business you want to start, you should know everything already—quite simply, you don't. Just

admit it and start asking questions. If you can find a woman who is willing to become your mentor, count yourself very lucky. Listen to what she has to say and watch her as she works. Glean as much knowledge as you can.

Don't Be Afraid to Change Course

YOU MAY have heard the scary statistics that 80 to 90 percent of all businesses fail in the first year, and 95 percent fail in five years. That is downright depressing. Here's my advice: Don't let these statistics stop you in your tracks.

I would much rather tell you the good news: Fewer home businesses fail, because you don't have to pay rent on office space or pay employees. Usually, a home business starts out part time, and the family isn't relying solely on income from that business to survive. If your first attempt at a business doesn't work out, you don't have to toss it altogether. As I know from my own experience, it's easy to redirect your business into another channel. A good example of this is my famed personalized children's book business. Once I figured out that it wasn't for me, I made the transition into a writing career. I had the computer and the motivation, so all I really needed to buy were some stamps and envelopes to send my submissions to magazines and newspapers.

Here is what author Barbara Sher says in *Wishcraft* (Ballantine Books, 1979): "One of the most harmful misconceptions in our society is that you've got to figure out what you want and then you have to stick to it. This attitude is one of the things that makes it so hard to get into action. . . . If a goal isn't serving you, you are free to change it."

Ways to Avoid Failing

WHATEVER YOU do, don't let a man tell you that because you're a woman, your business is prone to failure. Male- and female-owned businesses fail at about the same rate and for all the same reasons. One big reason is not enough money—realizing too late that it will take a whole lot more of the green stuff than you thought to get your new endeavor started. Another big reason is lack of management ability. You may not be able to do everything yourself, but this doesn't mean you have to fail. If you don't know how to do something, or you know how to do it but you just don't want to, ask for help or hire it out. You'll end up saving money, time, and quite possibly the business.

These are the steps you need to follow to make your business happen:

- Ask yourself what it is you want to accomplish with this business.

- Research, research, research.

- Find out who your competition is and find out how they run their business.

- Make sure you know what makes your business unique.

- Write up a business plan (see chapter 5 for advice).

- Do something you love and know how to do.

- Make sure there's a market for your service or product.

Overcome Obstacles

INEVITABLY, YOU will encounter a few obstacles. I know those darn ads you read make you think starting a home business is the easiest thing in the world, but it's not. It's much easier to sit and daydream about becoming self-employed than to actually take that dream and make it a reality.

Some of the typical obstacles you may encounter could include family members who are not supportive or friends and relatives who think you're crazy for leaving your secure job and don't mind telling you so. You may find out that the business equipment you need will cost much more than you expected, or you may discover that zoning laws will affect how you conduct your business. Low self-confidence can be a killer. Thoughts such as, "Well, I just don't know enough yet to start my business," or, "I'll just wait until I finish my degree," can make you feel like the whole home business idea is way out of your reach.

Being an adult beginner is not an enjoyable experience. Although you think you should know everything in your particular field, chances are you still have things to learn. Don't feel foolish asking for help. Just accept the fact that you're a beginner. Learn from your mistakes, but don't quit your business over them.

Are you willing to work for it? Do you want to start a home business so bad you can taste it? Don't let obstacles become a reason for giving up on what you truly want. Just look at your small children for inspiration. When your kids started to walk, did you ever see them fall down and say, "Man, I just

can't do this; I'm no good. I've tried to walk at least a hundred times. Mom and Dad don't fall down. What is my problem? I think I'll just give up." No, those little babies just keep at it until they're walking everywhere.

At some point, you're going to come up against a roadblock, but that isn't a good reason to chuck the whole idea. You're just going to have to find a new way to get around it. Don't let obstacles be a reason for giving up on what you really want for yourself. As my husband says, "Everything a worm can do to an apple, you can do to a roadblock."

Women are blessed with more roles than we know what to do with. Between being an attentive mom, a supportive wife or partner, and a businesswoman, you may feel at times you have bitten off more than you can chew. Whatever you do, don't give up.

Get Encouragement from Friends

SAD BUT true, some of your well-meaning friends may try to discourage you from getting started; that's just the way it goes. But that is no reason not to share your new idea. Instead of keeping it to yourself, make your friends part of your success. Call a meeting, but disguise it as a potluck or a tea. Tell your friends that you know they have a lot of talents among them, and you'd love to hear their stories and suggestions. They aren't as likely to say you're going to fail if they have helped you in just a small way in planning your business. More likely they will want you to succeed.

Don't Start Without a Plan

ALTHOUGH YOU may be most afraid of failing, if you can start a good business that has a niche all its own or run a better business than the one down the street, you may have the opposite problem. Believe it or not, you could have more business than you planned for. But that's another story. Right now, when you're revved up to begin, is the time to make your business plan. And that's the subject of the next chapter.

CHAPTER FIVE

Creating Your Business Plan

✦

Make no little plans. Make the biggest one you can think of,
and spend the rest of your life carrying it out.

—Harry S. Truman

WHEN I STARTED my first business I didn't have a solid, well-thought-out business plan. I threw together a rough one that I used to apply for a bank loan (which I didn't get, by the way), but I didn't have one like I am providing for you. If you take the time to research and answer all these questions, you will have a much clearer idea of what your expenses will be, who your potential customers are, and who your competition is.

A good business plan will also help you figure out approximately what your business will cost to get off the ground. You don't want to guess at this! It's often a good idea to speak with an accountant or an attorney about what it will take to start up your business. Knowing your costs will help you decide what you're going to charge. Keep in mind that women tend to undervalue their services dramatically. One mother confessed to me that what she charges by the hour now is three times more than what she charged when she started just a short time ago.

Most businesses fail because they don't have a clearly spelled-out business plan. Don't make that mistake! Fill out the information as accurately as possible. The more questions you can answer now, the fewer surprises you'll encounter down the road. A well-researched plan not only helps you define your goals, it is also a document you can present to a loan officer or other potential loan source.

Business Plan

READ THROUGH the business plan before you begin answering questions. Undoubtedly, you will find that there are questions you can't answer. That's where you'll need to do more research. You may want to contact a small business counselor or another mom with a home business for advice. Chapters 6, 7, and 8, which cover the topics of money, legalities, and marketing in more depth, may also help you find some answers. Once you have finished these chapters, go back and finish filling in the blanks.

What Is My Business?

1. What is my business exactly? Explain in one or two sentences. (If you can't describe your business in a couple of sentences, rethink your business and focus your idea.)

    _____

    _____

    _____

    _____

2. Am I selling a product or providing a service?

    _____

    _____

    _____

3. Is my particular business needed? List the reasons why.

    _____

    _____

    _____

    _____

4. Where do I see my business being in one year? In three years? In five years? (Be as specific as possible.)

    _____

    _____

    _____

    _____

Start-up Costs

1. How will I fund my business? (Include loans, credit cards, and personal savings. If you're using any sort of loan, remember to figure in finance charges.)

    _____

    _____

_____

_____

2. What equipment will I need to purchase to start my business (computer, car, sewing machine)?

_____

_____

_____

_____

How much will it cost? $_____

3. What office supplies will I need (letterhead, business cards, envelopes, paper, etc.)?

_____

_____

_____

_____

How much will each item cost? (Don't forget printing costs.) $_____

4. What permits and licenses will I need?

_____

_____

_____

_____

_____

What will they cost? $_____

5. What organizations should I join to help my business grow (local chamber of commerce, women's entrepreneurial groups, local WAHM groups)?

_____

_____

_____

_____

_____

How much are the membership fees? $_____

6. What trade publications will help me in my home business (crafting, accounting, computing magazines; WAHM publications)?

_____

_____

_____

_____

What are the subscription fees? $_____

7. What insurance will I need (health, liability, etc.)?

_____

_____

_____

_____

Total cost: $_____

8. What miscellaneous costs remain (factor in higher phone and utility bills)? $ _____

Marketing

1. How would I describe my target customer? (Include sex, age, occupation, and income bracket.)

_____

_____

_____

_____

_____

2. What publications does my target customer read?

_____

_____

_____

_____

_____

3. What type of organizations does my target customer belong to?

_____

_____

_____

Should I join these organizations? If so, what will it cost? $ _____

4. What is the best way to reach my potential customer without having to place an ad (write a press release, teach a class/seminar, write a column for the local paper)?

_____

_____

_____

_____

5. If I place an ad, which publications will be best?

_____

_____

_____

_____

How much will it cost? $ _____

6. Will I make my own ads or have someone help me?

_____

_____

_____

_____

_____

How much will it cost? $ _____

7. Will I create my own Web site or hire someone to do this? Do I need a Web page at this time? If not, what other ways can I advertise on the Internet?

_____

_____

_____

_____

_____

How much will it cost? $ _____

8. How else can I advertise (flyers, brochures, a sign on the side of my car)?

_____

_____

_____

_____

_____

What are the costs? $ _____

Competition

1. What other businesses will I be competing with?

_____

_____

_____

_____

_____

2. Have similar businesses failed? Why?

_____

_____

_____

_____

_____

3. What makes my business different from my competitor's business? (Include price, quality, unique services, and so on.)

_____

_____

_____

_____

_____

4. How does my competitor get customers?

_____

_____

_____

_____

_____

5. How much is my competitor charging? $ _____

6. How well is my competitor's business doing? Why?

_____

_____

_____

_____

_____

Day Care

1. Will I need day care? (If yes, continue through question 3.)

_____

How many days a week and for how many hours?

_____

2. Will I hire someone to come into the house or will I use outside day care?

_____

How many days a week and for how many hours?

_____

What will it cost? $ _____

3. Can a family member or friend provide free day care?

_____

Home Office

1. Is there a room in the house where I can set up an office?

_____

2. If I need to fix up a room to make it an office, how much will it cost?
   $ _____

Miscellaneous

1. What will my working hours be?

_____

_____

_____

_____

_____

2. Will my customers come to the house, or will I deliver my service or product?

_____

_____

_____

_____

_____

3. Will I need to use a car in my business?

_____

_____

_____

_____

_____

How much will it cost? $ _____

4. Will I place my product in craft malls, fairs, or galleries?

_____

How much will this cost? $ _____

5. If I'm selling a product, from whom will I buy my supplies?

_____

_____

_____

_____

_____

6. How much money do I need to make each month to help the family survive? $ _____

Each year? $ _____

What's the Cost of Doing Business?

Add up costs in all sections of this plan.

1. What are my total costs? $ _____

2. How much money do I have to put into the business to get it off the ground (supplies, equipment, advertising, etc.)? $_____

3. What are my ongoing costs (utilities, day care, marketing, etc.)? $_____

4. What should I charge to cover my costs and make a profit? $_____

Need Help?

A BUSINESS PLAN isn't a one-time deal. You need to pull your business plan out regularly and make changes. As your business grows, you will encounter new problems and puzzles for which you will need to find solutions. If filling out this plan gave you more questions than answers, call your local Small Business Development Center or the Service Corps of Retired Executives program (SCORE) for help. (SCORE is a Small Business Administration–sponsored group of volunteer business consultants. These people will help you out not only with the legal aspect of your business, but also with just about everything else. They can tell you what you need to get your business going and where to go get it. And all their help is free.) Both offer free assistance and have a lot of wonderful knowledge to share (see the resources in the back of this book).

CHAPTER SIX

Money

✦

The two most beautiful words in the English language are "Check enclosed."
—Dorothy Parker

O NCE YOU'VE FOUND the business of your dreams, you'll need to find a way to finance it. I wish I could tell you it will be easy and you will get customers immediately, but that probably won't be the case. Things will be tight for a while, and you'll have to make a few sacrifices. If you have had to quit your job to get your business started, you're not going to have a lot of excess change sitting around the house.

It's natural to underestimate the cost of getting a business going. We half expect that by the evening of the first day we open for business, we should have more money than we know what to do with. Then reality sets in. On Mrs. Fields's opening day, she made $75 selling her cookies.

The loan she had taken out was $50,000. If you find your business making money right away—and this does happen—be sure you put that money back into the business and pay off any debts that you have.

Bank Loans

M ANY OF the women I interviewed for this book started their businesses with very little money. Most used $100 or less. Crazy as it sounds, my advice is to start your business without a loan. The key is to begin small and use the resources you already have. I estimate that the average cost to start a business from home ranges from $50 to $2,000. Banks are not fans of giving out such small business loans. In fact, most of them will not give out a business loan smaller than $100,000.

However, banks do offer personal loans. If you need certain equipment for your business, such as computer or photography equipment, you could use a personal loan to purchase it. Your best bet is to go with a secured personal loan (secured loans are backed by something of value that you own, such as a car or property). As of this writing, the interest rate on a secured loan runs about 11 percent. There are unsecured personal loans available, but their interest rate is around 17 percent, close to what credit cards charge. You usually have about two years to pay these loans back. Banks can be particular about what you use your personal loan for. In fact, some banks will not give you a personal loan if it's for business purposes.

The reality of getting a bank loan involves a substantial amount of paperwork, lots of phone calls, and possible rejection. The main qualifier for any type of loan is your credit history. No matter how great a business idea you have, you're not going to get a loan if you have a past credit history that is shaky. And if you are granted the loan, you will have to pay that loan back, even if your business doesn't continue in the direction you thought it would.

When looking into loans, use your community resources. Call your local chamber of commerce. If it has a women's group, all the better. See if it has any suggestions on business loans. Call the Small Business Administration or SCORE agency in your area. If you live near a college or university, you can usually find a Small Business Development Center. Its whole mission is to help you get your business started, and it may have some financing answers for you. Many states and towns have programs for women who are looking for seed money to start a business. Any one of these organizations may be able to answer questions or refer you to additional sources.

Additional Lending Resources

- Women's Business Center: http://www.onlinewbc.org/docs/finance/index.html

- National Association of Women's Business Owners: http://www.nawbo.org/nawbo/nawbostart.nsf

- Advancing Women: http://advancingwomen.com/wk_entrwomfin.html

- Colorado Business Bank: http://www.cobizbank.com/

Personal Loans

WHEN I started my first home-based business selling personalized children's books, I took a loan from my parents. I do not recommend this route. My business failed, and I still owe a lot of money to my parents. They were really good about it, but I still felt sick about the whole thing. When it comes to loans from family and friends, I don't advise it.

Believe it or not, there may be individuals who would love to finance your business. Why? They may want to use the loan as a tax deduction, or they may just like a good risk. Where can you find these wonderful people? Use your networking skills. You just never know who knows whom. If you let everyone know you're looking for money to start your business, you just may get a bite.

If you do opt to accept financing from another party, even if it is from your parents or a friend, spend the time (and money, if necessary) to draw up a contract stating exactly how much the loan is, the rate of interest being charged, and the payment schedule. Having these key points set down on paper can help prevent bad feelings or legal complications.

Using Your Own Money

TWO COMMON ways to self-finance a home business include charging start-up costs to a credit card or dipping into the family savings. Some of the women profiled in this book used credit cards to start their business, because, quite frankly, it was their only option. Most of what they purchased totaled under $1,000, but be aware that credit card interest rates can be higher than the interest rates on some types of loans. Be sure to explore other financing options first and use your credit card as a last resort. Put a limit on how much you charge and stick to it.

One of the women I interviewed used her family savings to start her business. She

set a limit on how much she would spend. If the business wasn't sustainable after that money was gone, she said she would look into doing something else. Fortunately, the business took off and that wasn't a problem. If you have the money, my advice would be to use it to start your business. That way you won't have to worry about paying back a loan or paying off a credit card debt.

Create a Separate Business Account

START A special account for your business and keep it separate. You may find this really tempting, but don't dip into the business account for reasons other than business expenses. Your money will soon be used up if you're spending it on groceries or rent. You may feel guilty if the family funds are low and you have some money in your business account, but if you keep withdrawing it to pay for food and clothing your dream will soon be gone. A credit card that is used only for business purposes is also a nice way to keep track of your expenses. Separate accounts also make figuring out taxes much easier.

What to Charge

BEFORE YOU can figure out what to charge for your service or product, you need to figure out all your costs, including everything from letterhead to phone bills to gasoline. These costs are very much a part of what it takes to produce or do an actual service. Don't guess how much it takes to run your business.

I always recommend that if you're trying to price a service or product that is very similar to others on the market, find out what the other businesses are charging. To find out this information, pose as an interested customer. That's another reason why I love the Internet. Finding out what competitors charge has never been easier. Many times you can find their pricing information right on their Web site.

I have to admit, the whole pricing thing can get confusing. Let's say you made this beautiful widget—it didn't take you all that long to make and the materials you used are practically free. Everyone who sees it is in awe. When people ask the cost of what you are selling, you tell them the price, and they get this stunned look and say, "That's it?" What do you do in this situation? Well, if I were you, I'd raise your price until people stopped saying, "That's it?"

Now, let's say you make this painstakingly time-consuming craft. The materials can only be bought from a small tribe in Africa. So of course, you have to charge BIG money. The only problem is, no one buys it, because who in his or her right mind would pay that type of money for such a simple-looking product? Then it's time to figure out another way to make this product, or you may take it one step further and decide to make something else.

One crafter, Beth Fisher, shares the formula she uses for pricing her handcrafted items:

Cost of materials (at what I pay for them wholesale) + Time (at minimum wage) = Cost of item

Cost of item x 10% overhead = Wholesale price

Wholesale price x 30% markup = Retail price

Beth explains, "I've found that this is the fairest way to price my items, both for me and for my customers. People in our area expect you just to take the cost of materials and double it for the retail price, but since I hand-crochet and bead most of my items, the only way to get paid for my time is the above method."

Missi White is the owner of "Secretary to Go: You Only Call When You Need Me," an "off-site secretarial service providing for your on-site needs." Missi started this business when, after working 12 years as a secretary, she left to become a stay-at-home mom. However, she still had employers asking her to do various projects because they knew she did such wonderful work.

The pricing dilemma hit Missi as well. "I was still apprehensive about charging 'too much' for such services. One particular client of mine is a small architectural firm that operates as a nonprofit ministry to churches and seminaries. I never wanted to charge much more than the employer had paid me as an employee." Missi's extremely support-ive husband urged her to charge almost five dollars more per hour than the firm had paid her. Missi says, "I felt guilty and approached the issue very gingerly. They were in a des-perate situation and gladly paid 'whatever you need to charge'! I remained the sole sec-retary for that firm, working with an off-site arrangement for nearly nine months!"

Missi had another former employer call her in desperate need of her skills. As she would have to go into his office and work around her carpool schedule and obtain baby-sitting for her preschooler, she accounted for baby-sitting costs and added those to her fee as well. "Again, I felt apprehensive," says Missi. "I gingerly told him my fee (which was double what he had paid me when I was on his payroll) and he said, 'Fine . . . what-ever you need to charge. I need help and I wanted YOU'."

I think Missi sums up nicely the feel-ings you get when deciding what to charge. "So . . . while I know that I am a fabulous secretary because I adhere to the rules of the old school—loyalty, hard work, and thinking ahead of the game—I sometimes think I am being presumptuous and taking advantage of a desperate situation to charge the fees that I do. I have learned I am very low priced for the market in my area. I am learning that when someone SEEKS ME OUT, they really want ME!!! And I do not have to work for them, so I can charge to make it worth my time. The next time I get a request for serv-ices, I will be reprinting my fliers and raising my rates. You get what you pay for, and I know I can give the quality work I am charg-ing for!"

Many times as work-at-home moms we tend to undercharge. Guilt is a big factor when deciding what to price. However, if you know in your heart that you are providing the type of service or product that can't be found on every street corner and that you are being pursued because of your skills, don't forget to add all of your costs into your rates. You'll feel so much better about yourself—and you'll make more money.

Make sure you know your exact costs. When you're trying to determine what to charge, keep the following ideas in mind:

- Factor in all your expenses.
- Get paid for your time.
- Make your prices competitive—do the research.
- Make a profit.

STRATEGIES FOR COMPETITIVE PRICING

Huge companies pay big money to find the "perfect" price the consumer will pay. Your home business budget isn't the same as that of a huge company (as you may have already noticed). Haley Peter wondered what to charge for her quilt repairing and finishing business called A Stitch in Time. For many years it was just a hobby, until recently when she decided to turn it into a business. Haley explains, "I came across the problem of pricing my services. So what I finally did was to make up survey forms. I asked my customers, other quilters, friends, family, and anyone else I could find [to] take a few minutes to answer my questionnaire." She basically asked them what they thought was a fair price for her quilting service. After Haley got all of the surveys back she added up the prices for each service and divided the total by the number of surveys (averaging), and voilà, she had her prices!

Here are some tips to help you figure out pricing:

- Talk to other entrepreneurs in your business to find out what they charge. (Different areas of the country vary greatly.)

- Call local businesses similar to yours and find out what they charge. Then charge just a little bit less.

- Get online. There are many business forums where people get together and talk about their businesses. Ask for advice on pricing or any other question.

- Contact organizations associated with your business. They often have lists of the current prices to charge for your service.

- Be bold: Ask potential clients what they would be willing to pay and where they buy similar products or services.

Getting Paid

REMEMBER THE work-at-home scams discussed in chapter 2? The ads that say if you start this particular home business today, you'll have to carry home all your checks in large canvas bags tomorrow morning? Think again. After all the time you put into finding the perfect business, starting it, and finding clients, making sure you have the best product or service available is only half of the battle. There's a good chance you'll need to bill your clients for the work you've done for them. To make sure you don't wait and wait for your check to arrive in the mail, here are a few steps to speed up the process:

- **Sign a contract.** Have a price list or a contract available for your clients. This way customers know what they are getting, how much they are going to pay, and when it will be ready. Nobody can get confused or say, "Hey, wait a minute, you didn't say that," because it's all there in black and white. This works especially well in a service-type business. The books *The Contract and Fee Setting Guide for Consultants and Professionals* (Wiley, 1990), by Howard L. Shenson, and *301 Legal Forms and Agreements* (EZ Legal Books, 1993), compiled by Mario German, give some excellent examples of sample contracts.

- **Require half now and half later.** One way to avoid no payment at all is to ask for half of your money up front.

- **Give a discount for prepayment.** It may only be a discount of 5 percent, but for some people, it'll be a deal they can't resist.

- **Be persistent.** If someone owes you money, don't give up. Be persistent with phone calls and sending bills. If all else fails, go with the next suggestion.

- **Hire a collection agency.** This isn't fun, and you may find you won't recoup all of your costs. However, this may be the only solution in some situations.

CHAPTER SEVEN

Insuring Your Success

✦

Happiness has many roots, but none more important than security.
—E. R. Stettinius

YOU'VE JUST SIGNED up with the company of your dreams. You can make as much money as you like, come to work at any time, and leave at any time. But there is just one problem with this company. No benefits. No health insurance, no 401(K) plans, no dental insurance—nothing.

Well, that's sort of how it is when you decide to start your own business. The fear of no benefits keeps many a mom from working at home. So what do you do? Do you give up your dream of doing what you really want in life because you feel you cannot pay for your own health or disability insurance, only to regret later that you should have followed your dreams?

One work-at-home mother, who would like to remain anonymous, explains, "I am single right now, with three children (who are insured through their dad). I do not have health insurance, it is outrageous!!! I save through my savings account . . . too afraid to invest, but getting the courage to try. I am going to start an IRA for myself next year." Do you have similar feelings? Are these feelings keeping you from starting a home business?

This chapter includes information on many types of insurance. Although you may not need all of it, it is a good idea to know what is available and how insurance can actually work in your favor.

Health Insurance

IF YOU are married, you may already be covered by your spouse's health insurance. If not, you're going to have to do some research to find a plan that isn't going to cost you an arm and a leg.

Many of the businesses that you can run from your home, such as indexing, word processing, and architecture, have their own central organizations. Sometimes these organizations have health insurance plans that you can pay into. In the event you don't have one of these central organizations to join, you'll need to start the task of looking into other options.

Tina Kampman recently found out how hard it really is to become insured. She says, "I recently had to go through the exercise of trying to purchase our own health insurance. This was not a pleasant experience. There are a lot of plans, but if you have one thing wrong with you, they will turn you down. Many of the plans have pre-existing condition clauses, which are onerous."

However, Margaret Lyon of Lyon Graphics has found buying health insurance to be not so bad. "I buy my own health insurance. . . . Considering that I don't see the doctor often, it seems expensive to pay close to $100 a month for health insurance, but if I am in an accident or get very ill, I have the security of knowing that I am covered," says Margaret.

Another work-at-home mom, Emma S. McDonald, owner of Beginning Teachers'

Tool Box (www.inspiringteachers.com), has found an insurance agent who specializes in self-employed group plans. She says, "My son and I are the only two on the policy, and it costs me about $200 a month, which isn't bad. We are located in Texas, but I'm sure that each city probably has someone who can do the same thing." She believes the average work-at-home mom can find good insurance that isn't $400 to $600 a month.

Two insurance companies that offer low-cost health insurance are Alliance for Affordable Health Care (1-800-733-2242) and National Association for the Self-Employed (1-408-377-7780).

Additional Insurance Companies

- Aetna: http://www.aetna.com/aeindex.htm, or call 1-860-273-0123

- Blue Cross/Blue Shield: http://www.bluecares.com/

- HealthAxis: http://www.healthaxis.com/cgibin/laslink/home, or call 1-888-470-2121

- For additional health insurance companies, visit http://www.ic-links.com/9810lh.html

Disability Insurance

DISABILITY INSURANCE probably isn't the first insurance that pops into your mind when you are thinking about self-employment. However, when you hurt yourself and are unable to work, you'll wonder, "Why didn't I sign up for disability insurance?"

"Disability insurance is often overlooked by people, but it's very important for financial security," explains Kampman. "A typical WAHM would be much more likely to be disabled than to die. Disability insurance protects your income. For more information about this, read the book *Make the Most of Your Money* [Simon & Schuster, 1997], by Jane Bryant." You can often get disability insurance through your local provider.

Saving for Your Retirement

SAVING IS hard enough, but being self-employed and saving for retirement is even trickier. Janice M. Boyles is saving for the future. "I think this is tough for everyone. It's hard to determine if that need for future savings will suddenly appear next week, next month, at college time, or retirement time." While Janice's husband has a retirement plan, she has always felt the need for her own method of savings for emergency situations. So Janice joined American Express's savings/retirement program, whereby you can contribute the amount you want to save by having it charged monthly on your credit card. Janice explains, "That money is set aside for you at a certain percentage. You can't withdraw any for at least eight years without a penalty. The interest rate is fairly good, and you can increase your contribution at any time."

Believe it or not, there are IRAs in which the self-employed can invest. That's what Kampman is able to do. "I fund retirement through my IRA-SEP, which sole proprietors are entitled to establish. It is a great way to save pre-tax dollars and is based on the amount of business you do, not your income like a regular IRA. So, we can put away quite a bit every year if we want to."

Special Insurance for the Home-Based Worker

IF CUSTOMERS will be coming into your house, you may need to make some adjustments to your insurance policy. You don't want to have to go out of business because someone slips on your icy sidewalk and decides to sue you for everything you don't have. Talk to your current provider and explain the situation. Your provider can give you a good idea of what you're going to need (your homeowner's policy will not cover this). Talk to your insurance agent and have him or her write up a policy on business insurance for home use (also known as business liability insurance). The average cost for this is $500 annually, but shop around for the best price. Although this might seem high, it is nothing compared with what a person could sue you for if he or she is hurt doing business on your property.

If you are in the business of creating information or a product that can affect people down the road, you might want to look into liability insurance. CPAs, attorneys, bookkeepers, and software makers are good candidates for this type of insurance. You are looking at a minimum of $2,500 to $5,000 for a policy. This amount will pay your claims, and the expense of defending yourself. Even if the suit is groundless, it can cost you thousands of dollars in defense costs. Being insured could easily save your business if you were ever sued.

Lynn Chapman, owner of Lynn's Handmade Herbal Soaps (www.snowcrest.net/lynnsoap/), almost gave up on the idea of starting her own soap-making business because she had such a difficult time finding liability insurance she could afford. When Lynn finally found a premium she could afford, she paid about $900 a year. The good news is, now it's easier than ever to find a policy. Lynn has since gone with another company (to find more information about this company visit www.rlicorp.com) and now pays around $250 a year. When and if you need this type of insurance for your business, Lynn recommends finding an association or a guild that is related to your business. Contact the association to see if it offers help or knows of an agency that can help you. Also join listservs on the Internet that talk about your particular home business. (A listserv is a group of people with the same interests who e-mail each other with their questions and suggestions.)

Insuring Your Equipment and Software

YOU WILL also want to insure any special business equipment, so that in case of fire, theft, or other types of damage, you are covered and can get a replacement without any interruption in business. You may also want to check out Safeware, which is a computer insurance company. A policy covering $2,000 to $5,000 of computer equipment costs approximately $69 a year. It covers physical damages that are done to your hardware, software, printer, and scanners through fire, power surges, accident, theft, and so on. Call Safeware (1-800-848-3469) for more information.

If you tend to have a substantial amount of business information on your computer's hard drive and one day out of the blue it crashes—of course it crashes after you've just entered thousands of addresses—you could very well want to cry right there on the spot. However, if you are carrying what's called electronic data processing insurance, you won't be nearly as upset. This policy covers hardware, software, and cost of reconstruction. You can check to see if you can get this carried under a home business policy. If not, you may have to get a commercial policy to cover this. Just ask your insurance agent what your best option is.

If There's a Will, There's a Way

FOLLOWING YOUR dreams is never the easy choice. Don't discount the self-employed life simply because you feel you can't afford it. Research and talk with other self-employed individuals. Talk with other work-at-home moms to find out what insurance they carry and who their provider is. Networking is key when looking for the correct insurance for you and your business.

Keeping Your Home Business Legal

◆

If you fail to plan, you plan to fail.

—Old proverb

WHENEVER YOU START a home business, whether big or small, you'll have to deal with legal issues. Don't think that you're too small for local authorities to bother with. You don't want to be put out of business because you just never got around to checking the zoning laws or getting a business license.

Taxes

NO MATTER how small your business is, the government is very interested in it. So don't forget about ol' Uncle Sam around tax time—which for many home-based businesses means paying tax installments four times a year.

Victoria Phillips, a home-based accountant, offers some pointers.

When getting started, I think it's very important you keep your bookkeeping in very good order. Some of the better bookkeeping I've seen done is where people have separate checking accounts and separate credit cards for their business. It's very important if you do use a credit card that you keep it separate for business. That way you can use that interest easier in your business.

Either do your accounting on the computer or do a one-write system (when you write the check it's entered into your check register). I find this to be the most valuable tax information because when you take it to an accountant, they can find all these items that are deductible because you have been keeping such good records. If it's all a jumbled mess, it's very difficult for an accountant to sort out the stuff that's deductible.

Make sure you reconcile your checkbook. Keep your receipts, then you want to make sure you find a good accountant. Someone who is willing to listen to what you have to say. Here's the biggie: Make sure you pay your taxes. Don't mess around with the IRS. If you owe the IRS money, pay them.

RECOMMENDED BOOKS

- *Minding Her Own Business: The Self-Employed Woman's Guide to Taxes and Recordkeeping* (Adams Media, 2000), by Jan Zobel, E.A.

    In an easy-to-understand format, you'll learn everything you need to know to stay out of trouble with the IRS.

RECOMMENDED ACCOUNTING SOFTWARE

For the following software, check out the company Web sites for free demos or 30-day free trials. Find the software that suits you the best before you buy.

- Quicken: http://www.intuit.com
- Microsoft Money: http://www.microsoft.com/moneyzone

- M.Y.O.B.: http://www.myob.com/
- Quick Books: http://www.quicken.com/quickbooks/

RECOMMENDED TAX SOFTWARE

For the following software, check out the company Web sites for free demos or 30-day free trials. Find the software that suits you the best before you buy.

- Turbo Tax: http://www.intuit.com/turbotax/
- Kiplinger Tax Cut: http://www.kiplinger.com/software/taxcut.htm
- For a list of other types of tax software, visit http://www.taxsites.com/software.html#prep

Zoning Laws

DO YOURSELF a big favor and check your local zoning regulations before you start your business. Call city hall and ask for the Occupational License Department. As home businesses become more and more popular, zoning laws aren't as strict as they once were. But if your neighbors start complaining about all the extra traffic you're causing, things could get ugly.

Some zoning laws will allow you only a certain number of customers per day, and sometimes it isn't even an issue. It just depends on the area where you live. If you're not properly zoned for the business you're starting, the city could shut you down. Make sure you're legal.

State/City Business Licenses

YOU WILL need some sort of license to run your home business. To see what type of licenses you will need, contact the Business License Bureau in your city or county. A good place to start is at your county clerk's office. Costs vary.

State Sales Tax/ Resale Tax Certificate

IF YOU will be selling goods, you will need a state sales tax certificate, which enables you to pay the state a little money on everything you sell.

If you plan to sell your products wholesale or plan to buy your materials wholesale, you will need a resale tax certificate. This way you won't have to pay taxes twice on the goods you buy and then sell.

Naming Your Business

WHAT'S IN a name? Everything. Once you figure out the business you're going to start, you will have to come up with a name. This is sometimes easier said than done. Don't be discouraged if someone else already has your perfect name. If you thought up one, you can think up another.

Your business name should tell the customer exactly what you do. For example, if your leaf-raking business were called Leaves of Autumn, a person walking down the street wouldn't necessarily make the connection. But if it's called We Rake So You Don't, a passerby in need of yard work will give you a call.

If you don't want to bother with a fictitious name, simply use your full legal name in the title of your business. For example, if your legal name is Liddy Moore, call your business Liddy Moore Umbrellas. However, if you name the business Umbrellas for U, then you will have to register the fictitious name with your state business office and county clerk's office. This process of registration, often called "doing business as" (DBA), is to inform the public that you are doing business under another name. You will also have to place an announcement in the paper. The county clerk will usually take care of this for you, but there is a small charge for it.

Still Need Help?

TO LEARN more about the ins and outs of starting a legal business, visit www.score.org/ and get counseling via e-mail, or call 1-800-634-0245 to find a local Service Corps of Retired Executives (SCORE) chapter in your area.

CHAPTER NINE

Marketing

✦

Wealth is the product of man's capacity to think.

—Ayn Rand

Now you know what your business is going to be. Great! How do you plan to get the word out? The first thing that comes into many people's minds is, "I've got to place an ad somewhere." If you learn just one thing from this book, learn this: Pay for an ad only as a last resort. Most home business owners spend way too much money on advertising their business. Some spend so much they no longer can afford to stay in business. You probably don't have a lot of money to put into your business, so you need to be somewhat creative. Word of mouth is your best advertisement; it's also your cheapest. The following ideas may require more of

your time, but they'll be worthwhile in the long run.

Before you start your marketing campaign, make sure you know who your target customer is. Choose the best way to reach that customer, not a random range of people who will never be interested in your product or service. You wrote much of this information in your business plan, so go back to review it before you begin.

Don't forget your most important selling tool: confidence in yourself and in your business. I don't know anyone successful who isn't filled with self-confidence. Believe in yourself and what you're selling. If you're not excited about your product or service, how can you expect your customers to be?

Practice Your Sales Pitch

GET COMFORTABLE talking about your business by role-playing your sales pitch over and over in front of a mirror, for your family, or on videotape. Get your lines down and make sure you can convey to your future customers why they need what you are selling, why they can't live without it, and why your product or service is better than what the competition provides.

Use Your Contacts

WHEN YOU first start your business, pull out your address book. Call, write, and make up postcards telling everyone you're open for business. You never know who may need what you offer. Include people in organizations you belong to, whether it's your church or your dog-training club. You will feel more comfortable doing business with people you already know.

Postcards are an inexpensive way to announce to the world that you're officially open for business. When the first edition of this book came out a few years back, I used postcards. I sent them to every single person I knew. I realize my grandparents probably aren't going to be buying my book; however, they have friends who have children who are looking for a way to work at home. What

better referral than your own relatives saying, "Well, my granddaughter has written a book that would be perfect for your daughter"?

Network

NETWORK WITH other small-business owners in noncompeting businesses and promote each other. For example, if you're a caterer you can hook up with a photographer or a florist or both. You can then refer each other for future jobs. Share the cost of a newsletter that you could put out together. Share the cost of renting a booth at bridal fairs.

Carry Business Cards

WELL-DESIGNED BUSINESS cards are a great marketing tool. Make sure your cards say exactly what you do. The next time someone asks you, "So, what do you do?" you can whip out your card, hand it to the person, and smile. Make sure you carry them at all times—you never know when you will need one. If you want to branch out, get your cards made into bookmarks or have them punched to fit a standard Rolodex. You can do this yourself with a machine called the New Merrick Punch for Business Cards, or you can have the printer do it for you.

If you have supportive friends and family, ask them to carry your business card and give it to people they think might be interested in your service or product. Stay-at-home mom and newsletter editor Trish Kasey's husband travels frequently for business. When he meets someone on the plane whom he thinks might be interested in her newsletter or organization, he gives them a brochure, business card, or even a sample of the *Mommy Times* newsletter.

Distribute Flyers

YOU CAN leave your flyers on cars in the mall parking lot or on your neighbors' doors. Some inexpensive services will do this for you. You can also leave your flyers at appropriate businesses and on bulletin boards.

Create Brochures

IF YOU'RE handy with a computer, create your own brochure. If the idea of doing something like that is beyond your know-how, have a brochure done professionally. If possible, put a picture of your product on your brochure. Make the brochure professional, informative, and attractive.

You can use your brochures in mailings or leave them in appropriate areas where your targeted market can easily find them. If you do use your brochures for mailings, be sure to follow up with a phone call. You never know who may pick up one of your brochures and use it as a public relations plug. If the brochure gets into the right hands, you could be featured in the local paper or on the evening news.

Use Direct Mail

DIRECT MAIL, also known as bulk mail, might be a possibility. You don't have to print up fancy four-color mailers—you can just use a postcard. If you send a funny or pretty card, people may put it up on their bulletin boards, spreading the word about your business even further. A 3 percent response rate is considered good in direct marketing. This can prove a bit disappointing, but it does work for some businesses. If you have 200 cards, you may be able to send them bulk-mail rate. Your postmaster will have a booklet on the how-tos of bulk mail.

The key to direct mailings is a follow-up call. If you haven't heard anything back from the recipients of your mailing within a couple of weeks, give them a call just to make sure they received your information and to see if they have any questions. If you haven't heard back from them within a month, give them another call. Persistence is the key here. Direct mailings do not work well if you don't use follow-up calls!

Write Articles

WRITE ARTICLES for your local newspapers. If you sell nationally, try trade magazines and larger newspapers. Your number one goal is to make your articles informative and interesting. Be sure you include a small biography that tells what you do and a way that interested readers (that is, prospective clients) can get in touch with you. For tips on writing for publications, read the profile on Pat Curry in part II. Also read the book *Writing for Money* (Writers Digest Books, 1995), by Loriann Hoff Oberlin. Not only can you advertise your business for free by writing an article, you could even get paid for it. What a great concept!

Write up a few sample columns in your area of expertise and see if your local paper would be interested in printing them on a regular basis. You will probably have a better chance if you don't ask for payment. Just remember, that small bio at the end of each column is a wonderful way to advertise your business. If you're an accountant, you could give tax tips. A child-care provider could give advice on kids' craft ideas. Once you get published, you become even more respected in your field.

"But I don't know how to write," you might say. Don't panic. There are people who would be happy to ghostwrite for you (for a fee, of course). Check out your local college for English or journalism students to help out.

Publish a Newsletter

A FEW of the moms profiled in this book print up a periodic newsletter for their clientele. Publishing a newsletter will establish you as an expert in your field and helps keep your name out there. Your newsletter doesn't have to be an extravagant four-color spread. A simple black-and-white

print on regular paper will suffice. Just make sure it looks professional and is fun and easy to read. Computers are great for doing this.

Don't just push your business in your newsletter. Rather, give your readers information they can really use that pertains to your business. Lisa Zaccagnini, freelance photographer, provides a great example. She publishes a newsletter about her photography business but also includes tips on how her clients can take better family pictures. Ann Masland, pet-sitter, publishes a newsletter that includes information on animal shelters and pet-care tips.

Decide how often you are going to send out your publication and stick to it. And be sure you proof it for mistakes. If possible, let someone else look it over for you. You and your business will look more professional if your marketing materials are typo-free.

Send Out Press Releases

M AKE YOURSELF newsworthy. Have you just started your business, recently received an award, or added a new product to your line? Don't be afraid to toot your own horn. If you don't, no one else will.

A good press release reads just like a news article. In fact, many of the articles you read in newspapers or neighborhood papers are really press releases. If your product or service is offered mainly in your local area, send press releases to your local newspapers and television stations. If it's national, send them out to national publications. When your article is printed, it will look like an interesting bit of news. In reality, it's an ad that would have cost you a lot of money if you had one made up that size. People are more apt to read press releases than ads in the paper. It helps give your business the credibility it deserves.

Fred E. Hahn's *Do-It-Yourself Advertising: How to Produce Great Ads, Brochures, Catalogs, Direct Mail, and Much More* (Wiley, 1993) is a good book with many great tips on writing press releases and other advertising copy. Once you do get into the paper, make copies of your "article" and send it to everyone on your mailing list. This will make you look more professional and credible and reminds your customers that you're out there working.

On the next page is an example of a press release that Trish Kasey created:

TIPS FOR A SUCCESSFUL PRESS RELEASE

- Send your press release on your personal letterhead.
- Become familiar with the publications to which you would like to send your press release.
- Use a cover letter only if you're announcing an event you want the editor to attend.
- Include an upbeat and clear photo of your product or service in use. The paper is more likely to run your story if you include a picture.
- Know the name of the editor to send the press release to and spell his or her name correctly.
- To announce the opening of your new business, send your release to the editor of the business section.
- Follow up with a phone call to the editor one week after you send the press release to make sure he or she received it and to answer any questions. This is not a time to beg and plead to have your press release printed; just offer a little reminder.
- A press release isn't a one-time thing. Any time you have something new happen in your business, let the world know.
- Get the writing and photo guidelines for each publication you want to send to.
- Your press release should have some sort of human interest aspect to it. Don't solely promote your service or product.

Moms on the Net

For Immediate Release
Contact: Trish Kasey
555-555-5555

The *Mommy Times* Presents "Moms on the Net" Workshops
to Promote Moms' Participation on the Internet

Newport Beach, CA—The *Mommy Times,* a national publication for mothers, is proud to announce its new series of workshops entitled "MOMS ON THE NET," focused on providing Internet education and training for mothers.

Based on her research while establishing the *Mommy Times*'s Web site, Trish Kasey, editor of the *Mommy Times,* found that although a large number of mothers are extremely interested in learning about the Internet, they are often intimidated by the perception that it is too technical and complex for everyday use. Furthermore, the vast majority of Internet seminars and lectures are given and attended by men, who can have difficulty relating to the female novice. Trish Kasey felt so strongly about offering other mothers the opportunity to be educated about the Internet in a manner that is relaxed, friendly, and unintimidating that she has joined forces with another mother, Debbie Simon, computer consultant and creator of Deb's Webs, to form MOMS ON THE NET workshops.

Mothers see firsthand just how much computer technology is affecting their children's lives, but often do not realize how much it will touch their own lives. In the first series of workshops entitled "What the Heck's the Net?" MOMS ON THE NET will demystify for many moms this "thing" called the Internet. In a friendly, comfortable, and feminine environment, MOMS ON THE NET will provide moms with the knowledge they need to understand just how much the Internet really will be useful in their everyday lives.

Statistics say only one-third of Internet users are women, but MOMS ON THE NET wants to increase that number substantially. Currently, the Internet provides a wealth of resources for mothers; however, Web sites are established based on participation, and the more MOMS ON THE NET can motivate mothers to actively participate on the Internet, the more sites and services will be provided for them.

HOW TO WRITE A BAD PRESS RELEASE

David Sakrison, an editorial consultant with twenty-two years of experience writing for businesses, cites ten good reasons why press releases end up in the trash:

- It's badly written.

- It sounds like advertising copy.

- The subject is not suitable for the publication.

- It doesn't contain enough information.

- It's too long.

- It's too technical for the publication and the readers.

- The writing style doesn't fit the publication.

- The information is irrelevant or uninteresting. (The story has no "local" angle.)

- The photographs or graphics are not up to the standards of the publication.

- The information is "old news" or it arrives too close to the editorial deadline.

Put Together a Press Kit

PRESS KITS are basically oversized press releases. In a professional-looking folder, send at least some of the following:

- Your latest press release on your personal letterhead

- A business card

- A 5 x 7 black-and-white publicity photo

- Your brochure

- Quotes from happy customers, especially well-known happy customers

- Your newsletter, if you publish one

- A video of short clips of your television appearances

- Your book, if you've written one

- Any articles or features that have been written about you

- A short biography of yourself

- A publicity calendar of your speaking engagements

- Anything else you feel would be significant

Don't be depressed if you don't have all these things when you first start out. Your kit will grow right along with your business.

Contact the Media

A WOMAN profiled in Cheri Fuller's *Home Business Happiness* (Alive Communications, 1996) started what she called "the five-a-week rule." Her goal was to make five new contacts each week with media professionals through phone calls and letters. Think about soliciting the community page editor at your local paper to do a profile of your business. Perhaps your business would be helped by a radio-talk-show interview (this can particularly help writers, consultants, and seminar leaders). Go to the reference section of your library and get the book *Literary Market Place* (LMP), which is published annually. In it there is a listing of radio talk shows and the subjects they discuss. Send the radio station a postcard or press release. Write something catchy and attention-grabbing. Be sure to follow up with a call a week or so after sending your materials.

Give Out Freebies

E VERYONE LIKES something for nothing. Give away your product or service at a local charity auction, or offer something for free with the purchase of one of your products. Melody Upham started by giving out samples of her homemade soap. This way her future customer was able to go home, use the product, and, of course, fall in love with it. She saw a definite rise in sales by doing this. Anna Marie Johansen got her catering business off the ground by giving away dinners at a local charity auction.

Join Business Organizations

A LMOST EVERY type of service has an affiliated organization. If your town has a women's business organization, join it and network. If a fellow member is inundated with work, she just might call you to take on some. Sound too good to be true? It happens. If you can't find a specific organization for your specific business, check out your local chamber of commerce. Don't just join and pay your dues. Go regularly to the meetings and become involved. It'll pay off.

Teach Classes and Speak to Groups

Y OU DON'T need a Ph.D. to teach a seminar or class in an area in which you are qualified. People are looking for experience and know-how. Teach a class at your local adult-learning school. If you've written a book on the subject, use it as a textbook. Arrange your own seminars, charging little or nothing (newspapers are more likely to run your announcement if the seminar is free), then sign up those who attend for a more extensive seminar.

You can also speak to organizations such

as charities, church groups, or the PTA on your area of interest. Just make sure people know what you do and how to get a hold of you afterward. Once you get your name out, people will call you for speaking engagements and may even pay you for them. If this happens, they may ask you how much you charge. Try to beat them to this and ask them first what they pay. You don't want to charge too little and not look like an expert in your field, nor do you want to charge too much and miss out on a great opportunity.

If you want to give classes or better communicate with others what your business is all about but feel uncomfortable speaking in public, I highly recommend joining Toastmasters International, a nationwide communication and leadership organization. At each meeting you are given the opportunity to practice your public-speaking skills. To find out where your local Toastmasters meet, call 1-800-993-7732.

Go Online

SEE CHAPTER 11 for more information about making money on the Web.

List Your Business in the Yellow Pages

IF YOU have a business license and a separate phone line for your business, you can get a free one-line listing in your phone book's yellow pages. If you want a bigger ad, you will pay a monthly fee. For the right business, this can be very profitable. Word processors, for example, often find ads to be very lucrative. Ask yourself what types of business you look for in the yellow pages. Does your business fit into that category?

Place an Ad

IF YOU decide to place an ad, pick a small publication that isn't going to cost you a lot but still is in your target market. If you're selling kid-related items, for example, run an ad in your local parenting magazine or newspaper. Stay away from the bigger publications like *Parents* or *American Baby* until you grow a lot bigger. Those types of ads cost a lot and your return usually isn't that great.

Ask for Referrals

DON'T BE afraid to ask your satisfied customers (including your relatives and friends) to give you names of other people who could use your service or product. Call these potential clients and tell them so-and-so referred you to them because "they thought you might be interested in my product or service." Read Bob Burg's *Endless Referrals* (McGraw-Hill, 1993) for more on this subject.

Create a Mailing List

REPEAT CUSTOMERS are your bread and butter. Every time you get a client or any inquiry, add that name to your Rolodex, database, or filing system. This list of names is worth more than gold. It is also called your mailing list. Send mailings regularly to tell customers of something new you are adding, to send them discount coupons, or to send them your newsletter.

Send Thank-You Cards

SEND YOUR new clients a thank-you card telling them you appreciate their business. Hand write and address it, and make it as personal as possible. This isn't a kiss-up card, rather it is a way to tell them how much you value them as a customer. The winter holiday season is a nice time to send all of your clients a card, but don't forget about all the many other holidays throughout the year. Your business is going to stand out even more if you send a Fourth of July greeting or St. Patrick's Day card.

One Last Bit of Advice

IN *HERS* (Allworth Press, 1991), Carol Milano explains the secret of marketing: "Creating powerful promotional material is a very particular skill. For cost-effective promotion, maximize your marketing money by getting expert help. You may think it costs more to hire an expert to help you but marketing is one area where you can throw out a lot of money very quickly if you haven't planned carefully."

Becoming a saleswoman may sound a little intimidating. This may be the last thing you ever envisioned yourself doing. But if you think about it, the experience you have had as a mom is a great background. You're always trying to sell your kids on eating their vegetables, brushing their teeth, or going to sleep. You can use that same creativity in your business.

CHAPTER TEN

Getting Online

◆

Information is power.

—Anonymous

WE HAVE SO much information at our fingertips it's scary. Accessing this information is easy for those with computer knowledge. But if you've rarely touched a computer and don't even know if you have a modem, the Internet is a bit intimidating.

Women have many excuses for not getting online, says Janet Attard, author of *The Home Office and Small Business Answer Book* (Holt, 1992). Janet runs the business strategies forum on America Online and the business know-how forum on Microsoft Network. "A lot of people are scared of the stories they hear on TV about what they're going to find if they go online. So they don't want to get hooked up." This is especially true for women with young children who keep hearing news reports of pornographic material and online stalkers. It sounds like as soon as you connect to the Internet you will have naked pictures plastered all over your screen or nasty people writing you e-mail. If this is keeping you from getting online, there are programs you can load into your computer that will keep kids from accessing questionable sites. For more information check out Surf Watch (www.surfwatch.com).

Janet Attard explains, "If you're going to go hang out in the chat rooms that have unusual sounding names, you can expect to have strange experiences, for a lack of a better word. But if you go online to get business information and you're staying in business areas, the worst that's going to happen to you is you're going to get some junk e-mail on 'great' business opportunities."

Debbie Simon is a work-at-home mom who does computer consulting, training, and programming. She has her own Web page and holds seminars called "Moms on the Web" for women who want to get on the Web but have no idea where to start. She feels that women are reluctant to get online because "It's out of their comfort zone. We've been led to believe it's a 'man's thing.'"

Both Janet and Debbie agree on another big reason women don't get online: lack of time. Janet explains, "There is a finite amount of time in the day. And if you're juggling a work schedule and family, then have to learn something new," getting online is probably the least of your concerns.

I believe going online can be a great help to the work-at-home mom. So much so, I think you should do everything in your power to get online. Debbie suggests taking a class. "Local colleges offer classes. Local computer stores offer classes. Computer repair people often know trainers they can recommend for in-home training." Take control of your life and face your computer fears.

Janet recommends just plunging in. "Get online with one of the commercial services such as America Online or CompuServe. Just look around a little and get a feel for what being online is all about. Then if you

want to look for cheaper ways to get online, consider the Internet. I'd experiment with one of the commercial online services first because they have the experience and the money behind them to make it a little less difficult and more convenient. If there is a problem, you have a little more to fall back on, someone to call."

Check the library and bookstores for books about the Internet and commercial online services. There are many books written for all levels of users, from beginners to experts.

Online Advantages

WHY WOULD you want to go online? One reason is to get and share great ideas. Janet Attard says, "A forum like mine is a way to get ideas, share them, and brainstorm solutions to problems. If you're just starting, you can find what problems to avoid and resources that can help you. Depending on what business you run, you may find a whole cluster of people in the same business all over the country who are sharing ideas on how to improve their business." For example, one of the folders in the business strategies forum is for people in the gift basket business. Every day these business owners from all over the country exchange information on buyers and on what works in baskets and what doesn't. This is invaluable information that saves business owners years of trial and error.

Debbie says, "Before you start [your business], you can check out the competition by searching for Web sites that are advertising products or services similar to yours to see what prices they are charging and what market they are attempting to penetrate. You can also check out logos and designs of other companies so you can get ideas for your own." Debbie also believes that having your own Web site for your business can definitely attract additional business.

Human contact is another reason to get on the Internet. The Net serves as a way to talk with other mothers who are in your shoes. Just knowing that you're not alone out there is very comforting. The walls of your home can be anything but friendly at times, and interacting only with children all day can make even the sanest person a little frazzled.

Need any more reasons? Remember, Janet says, "If you're going online strictly for business and that is all you use it for, your entire online bill is deductible. If you're splitting your online use between personal and business use, keep track of where you went because the business time you spent online is tax-deductible. It's a business expense, just like getting a magazine."

Debbie has the final word: "Now is the time to get comfortable with the technology. The longer you wait, the scarier it's going to get." So what are you waiting for? If you need just a little more of a push, Debra Roum and Trish Kasey, editors of *Mommy Times*, have produced a thirty-minute video called "Moms on the Net," an entertaining and educational introduction to the Internet. For more information, call 1-800-99-MOMMY.

Places to Visit on the Internet

Here's a small sample of sites on the Internet you can visit that pertain to both the mom and the businessperson in you. All of these sites offer great resources online as well as e-zines, listservs, chats, and message boards.

SPECIFIC SITES FOR THE WORK-AT-HOME MOM

- Bizy Moms: http://www.bizymoms.com

- The Home-Based Working Mom (HBWM): http:// www.hbwm.com

- Moms Network Exchange: http://www.momsnetwork.com

- Work-at-Home Moms (WAHM): http://www.wahm.com

BUSINESS HELP: WOMEN-SPECIFIC

- Cyberspace Field of Dreams: http://www.fodreams.com/home.html

- The Online Women's Business Center (co-sponsored by SBA): http://www.onlinewbc.org

- Voices of Women Online: http://www.voiceofwomen.com

- Her Planet: http://www.herplanet.com/

- Digital Women: http://www.digital-women.com/

BUSINESS HELP: GENERAL

- Business Know-How: http://www.businessknowhow.com

- Idea Cafe: http://www.ideacafe.com

- Smart Business Supersite: http://www.smartbiz.com

Online Services and E-Mail

THE MOST popular online services today are American Online, CompuServe, Microsoft Network, and Prodigy. You can also decide to go with your local Internet Service Provider (ISP). To find out who your local ISP is, talk to your friends who have Internet access for a recommendation or check out the yellow pages. All of these services will let you explore the Internet and offer you your own e-mail account. Some of you will be very content with the networking and resources available to you with Internet access and an e-mail account. Others of you may be a bit more serious about making money on the Internet and may want your own Web site to promote your service or product.

The Designer Web Page

ONCE YOU decide it's time for your own Web page (see chapter 11 for a discussion of how a Web page can complement your business), you'll need to decide if you want to hire a Web designer or create your own Web page. The latter is what I did with bizymoms.com for its first few years. I used an HTML-based software called HotDog. In 1998, my site was growing and changing with new information on a regular basis, so I decided to hand it over to a Web designer I had met online in a chat room. (You can read more about my Web designer, Jennifer Czawlytko, in the profile section of this book.) I am so fortunate to have Jennifer as my Web designer. As a work-at-home mom herself, she believes in my site and is proud to promote it. I consider Jennifer a manager as well—I'm always running new marketing ventures past her for her opinion. When you look for a designer, I hope you can be as lucky as I have been.

The following tips can help you find the best designer for your site.

- The designer believes in the philosophy and message of your Web site.

- The designer's prices are comparable with other designers. However, don't let this be your deciding factor. Remember, you get what you pay for. Consider your page as your very own cybermall store. You want a designer to create something that is informative and pleasing to the eye. When you go shopping, do you regularly patronize stores that are old and unkempt, filled with aggressive salespeople who practically beg you to buy something from them? Of course not. Make sure your Web page doesn't convey this effect either.

- You can trust your designer. This doesn't mean you have to know your designer or even have met him or her face to face. As of yet, I've never met Jennifer in person.

- Network with other WAHMs on listservs and message boards and ask them for Web designer referrals.

- Once you find a designer, ask for references. Many times designers will include on their pages links to sites that they've designed. Don't be nervous if a designer has only done a few sites. Look at the person's style, not the fact that he or she has done a hundred mediocre sites.

- Don't be rushed into finding your Web designer. Take the time to interview the designer, either on the phone, face-to-face, or in a private chat room.

- Look for a designer who will go the extra mile for you. Often designers will create your site and then disappear. Remember, your site will need maintenance. A good designer will talk about the future of your site and where you'd like to expand and change.

How to Create Your Own Web Site

IF YOU decide to create your own site, you'll have to decide what HTML editing program to use. This is a very personal decision. Some designers will rant and rave about one program, and other designers will think that same program is the worst thing they've ever used. It's a good idea to sample different programs to see which one clicks with you.

RECOMMENDED HTML EDITORS

The first part of the list below includes software you'll need to purchase. However, many of the commercial packages offer free trials, which allow you to try out the software before you buy. You can find these types of offers by doing a search on the Net for "free html editors" or "html editing software shareware."

- Claris Home Page

- Microsoft Front Page

Free HTML Editors

- AOLPress: http://www.aolpress.com
  This is available to all Internet users, not just AOL members. *PC Computing* gave this program high praises in the past, ranking it as high as some of the more expensive HTML software packages.

- Arachnophilia: http://www.arachnoid. com/arachnophilia/

- WebWerx: http://www.litewerx.dk/ programs.html

- Free-4-u: http://members.tripod.com/ asfreeware/htmleds.html

    A great site for accessing the many different free editors out there.

FINDING CLIP ART FOR YOUR SITE

This is one area where you can totally lose your mind. There is so much free clip art out there, you're liable to start to think you need all of it on your site. When deciding what clip art to use, remember—less is more. Create a theme for your site and stick to it. And, the fewer images you have on your site, the faster it will load—and the better your chances a future client will stick around for everything to download.

When searching for free clip art, please be aware of the rules of each site you access. Some do not allow you to use the graphics for a business-related site. Some request that you place somewhere on your site where you found your graphics. Be sure to read the fine print.

Here are a few sites where you can find free or inexpensive graphics for your site:

- ArtToday: http://www.arttoday.com
    You pay $30 a year to get unlimited access to 750,000 graphics, or you can opt for their free section and have access to 40,000 graphics.

- Desktop Publishing.com: http://www. desktoppublishing.com

Choosing an Internet Service Provider (ISP)

ONCE YOU get your site completed, you're going to need to figure out how and with whom you want to house your site. You can pay anything from $0 to $75+ a month for this service. Your local ISP may be a great choice for you to serve up your site.

There are many free places to house your site, but not all of them are the best way to go. I've heard many complaints from people who have gone with a free ISP that has bad customer service or that has lots of network outages. You want the best for your business Web site. Here are two free ISPs that will accommodate business Web pages that are reputable.

- HyperMart (free business hosting): http://www.hypermart.net
    It allows you 10 megabytes (MB) of Web space and will host your domain for free (Internic registration fees still apply). There are restrictions and you will be required to carry its ads on all of your pages.

- iVillage: http://auth.ivillage.com/cgi-bin/ homepages/display_homepages_login.cgi
    It will give you 5MB of Web space. However, you cannot use your own

domain name. There are drawbacks to not having your own domain name. For instance, www.bizymoms.com, my Web site, has its own domain name. Previously, I had a URL that looked like this: http://www.snowcrest.net/ folger. Now which one looks more professional and is easier to remember? These are all things to think about when creating your own site.

Overcoming the Superwoman Syndrome

WHEN WE decide to go into business for ourselves, we often feel we can "do it all." We think we can do our own accounting, desktop publishing, Web design, marketing—and yes, you might be able to. But sometimes it's a good idea to farm a few of your jobs out so you can concentrate on what you do best. If you find yourself hating the fact that you have to create your own site, yet the thought of paying someone makes you feel guilty, dump the guilt. It may be possible you can barter with another WAHM out there for what you sell or maybe in exchange for baby-sitting. Take the time to look at your options.

Keep in mind that your Web site is your own little store in this big mall we call the Internet. You want it to be inviting, informative, and nice to look at. Because the better site you have, the more money you'll make.

CHAPTER ELEVEN

How to Make Money on the Internet

✦

He who refuses to embrace a unique opportunity
loses the prize as surely as if he had failed.
—William James

HAVE YOU EVER wondered, "How in the world does a person make money on the Internet?" According to some of the advertisements out there, you may think it is pretty easy to slap together a Web site and throw it up on a server. Based on some of the information available, you may think that before you know it, droves of people will be visiting your web site on a daily basis, buying whatever it is you are selling. If only doing business on the web were that easy. If you learn anything from reading this book, let it be this: Making money is a slow process that takes time and money. The Internet world is no exception to this rule.

Do You Have to Have a Web Site?

I'D LIKE to first dispel the myth that you have to have a Web site if you are going to be in business. It's not true. Some of the moms profiled in this book do not have their own Web sites. Take for example Lisa Zaccagnini, freelance photographer: Although down the road she may decide to invest in a Web site, she doesn't have one now (she does, however, have an e-mail address and has used the Internet to buy equipment for her business). However, don't discount the power of a Web site simply because you don't know anything about it. Educate yourself. You'll be less fearful about a new venture if you know what you're getting yourself into.

Then there are those work-at-home moms such as Diana Ennen, word processor, who has a site, but admits that she doesn't get a lot of business from it. Diana says potential clients will come to her site to get a quote on a project, but that's usually as far it goes. However, she has found the Internet to be a great networking tool, both through the online chats she hosts and from the message boards where she posts. She is able to talk with other word processors about certain issues that come up in her business and get their feedback. Then there is Trish Kasey, publisher of the *Mommy Times* newsletter. Her newsletter is not even sent in the mail; it can only be read online.

The above is a broad spectrum of possibilities for using the Internet as a business tool, and although you don't have to have a Web page for your business, it can't hurt either. To many, getting their own Web page seems like a giant, uncertain step. Well, I have some great news for you. You can actually start making money online without having a Web page. The first section of this chapter tells you how to make this happen.

Signature Files

IF YOU have e-mail, you've probably started writing to everyone you know who has e-mail too. You may have visited message boards that talk about your favorite subjects. Whether you're talking to loved ones or people you've never met, it's time to start including your signature file, or "sig file," as it's commonly known. This is very easy to do and a great way to get a potential customer's attention. Some experts say, and I believe them, that if you don't have a signature file, you are getting only two-thirds the value out of your e-mails or posts to message boards.

Now, you may be asking, What is a sig file? Look at the bottom of some of the e-mails you receive—you might see the sender's name, e-mail address, name of his or her company, and/or a link to the person's Web page. That is a sig file.

When dealing with *netiquette* (that's etiquette for the Net), your sig file should be as few lines as possible. It's common practice to keep your sig file between four and six lines.

I have about five different sig files that I use in my e-mail, listservs, and message board posts. So don't think you have to stick to just one sig file. Some people change their sig files every day, some just rotate their sig files so they're a little different each time.

Here are a few examples of my sig files:

Liz Folger
Work-at-Home Mom Expert
Author, *The Stay-at-Home Mom's Guide to Making Money from Home*
Bizy Moms-http://www.bizymoms.com

———

Liz Folger
Author, *The Stay-at-Home Mom's Guide to Making Money from Home.*

Order today by visiting your favorite book-store or by calling 1-800-632-8676.
http://www.bizymoms.com
Your Complete Work-at-Home Mom Resource Center.
When you visit, don't forget to sign -up for the free Bizy Mom e-newsletter.

———

And if I'm really in a hurry . . .

Liz Folger
Author, *The Stay-at-Home Mom's Guide to Making Money from Home*
Bizy Moms, http://www.bizymoms.com

I've seen some sig files that include a quote, a funny saying, or pictures such as smiling faces, flowers, and so on, created by using ASCII (symbols and letters that are found on your keyboard).

For more information about sig files, check out www.webnovice.com/sig_files.htm.

Message Boards

WHEN YOU go online, there's a good chance there are dozens of message boards dealing with your particular business. For example, let's say you are a dog groomer and you've written a booklet on fun and easy grooming tips. You would want to look for boards that deal with dogs and pets. Although you wouldn't want to blatantly promote your booklet, you'd want to include the information in your sig file. So when you respond to grooming questions people might

have, they'll see from your sig file that you have additional information to give them.

Every message board has its own rules. Although some boards don't care if you post a blatant ad, others, such as the boards on bizymoms.com, don't allow it. It's a good idea before you post to read the rules and take the time to read the other posts to see how they are handled.

Listservs

LISTSERVS ARE very similar to the message boards. However, you sign up to receive these in your e-mail. Someone will start a subject and others will join in to discuss it. There are tons of these types of lists out there. There is a very good chance you will find a few in the area of your particular business. As with the message boards, these lists have rules too. Wait a few days and see how other people post and if you can use a sig file or not. Even if you can't use one, you can still help people out by answering their questions and slowly it will become known that you are an expert in this area. Also, you will learn a lot yourself just from just reading other posts.

Here are a few places to find listservs:

- http://www.liszt.com
- http://www.tile.net/lists
- http://www.onelist.com

The above sites are also good places to submit your list.

Listservs for Work-at-Home Moms

- http://www.wahm.com/lists/sub.html
- http://www.hbwm.com

Free Classified Postings

IF YOU'RE selling something, you'll want to tell the world about it. There are many places where you can post an ad online for free. Here's a short list of sites that let you post ads for free; however, there are numerous other sites that offer this service. To find them simply, do a search for "free classifieds," and be ready for hours of posting.

- http://www.galactic-ent.com/ classpro/newad.html
- http://www.websitings.com/classads/sites/ schwabe.htm
- http://www.WorkingOnline.com/ classifieds/
- http://www.vero.com/Classifieds/ free-ads.iaw
- http://virtual-adnet.com/cgi-bin/cl2.cgi
- http://vvalley-zine.com/classifieds.html
- http://everydaybiz.hypermart.net/ classifieds/classifieds.html

Write Articles for Publication

TO MAKE a Web page enticing enough to keep visitors coming back on a regu-

lar basis, you need to provide great information that is updated regularly. Let's say someone sells Discovery Toys on her site. To make this site even more informative, the owner might want an educational expert (this could be a preschool teacher) to write articles on how educational toys help children learn even while they are playing. You just might be that educational expert to write those articles.

Don't be afraid to find a site that is related to your business and ask if you could write a few articles for it. You probably won't get paid for this; instead, ask that in return you're given a byline that includes your name, area of expertise, name of business, e-mail address, and, if you have one, Web address (URL).

Following are four sites that archive articles. Newsletter editors and Web designers can go to these sites, download articles, and place them on their sites or e-zines. Or you can submit articles you have written to be included in the archive. The marketing-minded authors of these articles have included contact information at the end of each article for readers who want additional information.

- Archive of Valuable Business Articles: http://www.businessbookpress.com/ articles/archives.htm
- Idea Marketers: http://www.ideamarketers.com
- Biz Resource: http://www.bizresource. com/bizsheets/bizsheets.htm

- Smart Biz: http://www.smartbiz.com/ sbs/cats/home.htm

TIPS FOR GETTING YOUR ARTICLES PUBLISHED

Marnie Pehrson, owner of Ideamarketers (www.ideamarketers.com), a site that actively seeks articles for online publishers, talked to me about how to get your article published. Here's what she had to say.

- Study the e-zines for which you would like to write. What types of articles do they print? Submit accordingly.

- Don't mass broadcast the same article to a hundred e-zines. Hand-select your articles to match the e-zine. Do your research and address your article to the editor personally.

- Write about something unique. Sure, Internet marketing is popular right now—probably too popular. Unless you've got a fresh, inventive angle, your article will have too much competition to stand out from the crowd.

- Save your bio/contact area, where you "sell yourself," for the end of the piece. Don't try to include it in the body of the article.

Making Money with a Web Site

F INALLY," YOU say, "We get to the good stuff." It's almost like the Web has its own money-making mystique: You know people are making money on it, but you don't have a clue how they do it—you just figure it's only the big corporations that are raking in the dough. Think again! Even you can be making money on the Internet.

PROMOTING YOUR WEB SITE

As soon as your Web site is live (see chapter 10 for tips on creating a Web site), run, don't walk, to your nearest search engines and start submitting your URL, also known as your Web address. Search engines and directories, such as Yahoo, AltaVista, Excite, Webcrawler, to name just a few, are great places to start. You can also find a list of the major search engines by visiting www.searchengine-watch.com/facts/major.html. Once you have submitted your site to these places, you can begin to use multiple submittal sites such as Add Me (www.addme.com/) or Submit-It (www.submitit.com/) to make sure you are listed in the lesser-known search engines. Other Web sites have pages where you can submit your URL as well. Just keep your eyes open and ask your friends if they know of any sites that offer this feature.

Here's one benefit to being listed in search engines. Let's say you are a Web designer. One way future clients can find you is by going to their favorite search engine and typing in "Web designer." If you've registered your site with that search engine and followed the directions, there's a good chance your Web address will show up.

If you've done any surfing on the Net, you've probably used a search engine to find the subjects you're interested in. You know all those sites that came up for you to check out? Well, those sites wouldn't be there unless the owner had registered their site on that particular search engine.

To receive more information about search engines, check out Search Engine Watch (www.searchenginewatch.com/index. html).

WHERE DOES YOUR WEB SITE RANK?

Depending on the search engine, it can take from a few days to months before your URL shows up on searches. Some sites take longer than others. Within a month or so of submitting your site to a particular search engine, it's a good idea to see where your URL is ranking. Here are two sites where you can find this information for free.

- http://www.top-10.com/
- http://www.rankthis.com/

Making Money from Your Product or Service

To make money from your product or service, you've got to give your Web visitors a reason to come back to your site on a regular basis. Here are some basic tips to get your visitors to come back to your Web site again and again:

- Make your Web storefront appealing.

- Offer weekly drawings—post the winner on your site.

- Place polls on your site. Get your visitors to interact with your site. The more they feel a part of it, the more they'll want to come back.

- Post articles written by you or other experts that deal with the subject of your product or service. Update these stories often.

- Keep adding new products to your line.

- Have monthly sales.

- Send out a free e-zine that promotes your site and has intriguing information. Give people a good reason to open your newsletter instead of deleting it. You can send this out as often as you like—weekly, biweekly, monthly.

- On your front page, place the statement, "Be sure to bookmark this site so you can easily visit again."

One final note: Before you design your site or have someone else create it, visit a lot of other Web pages. See what you like and don't like; what attracts you to a site and what doesn't. Then design your site around these ideas. Simple is best—remember, you want your site to load quickly.

AUTOMATED REPLY RESPONDERS

"Make money in your sleep!" This comment makes me cringe when I see it headline a work-at-home ad. But for your Web site, it means something completely different. For example, I have people coming to www.bizy-moms.com day and night. By night, I mean when I'm sound asleep. However, I'm still handing out information and attracting new customers, even when I'm hours into my beauty rest. I do this is by using what are called autoresponders; a great way to keep track of who wants what info. These great little cybergadgets work hard for you any time of day. You can use autoresponders to broadcast your rates and prices or to offer information on a particular product or service you sell. People simply e-mail the address you provide and request the information they want. Within seconds, they get a response back. In the morning, or whenever you check your e-mail, you can read the letter from the person who asked for the information. You can then follow up with your potential customer. It's that easy. And, you're open for business 24 hours a day. Check to see if your Web site provider offers this service.

To find more information about autoresponders, visit www.indolinks.com/support/em-autores.htm. To get a free automated reply responder visit at www.reply.nu/.

AFFILIATE PROGRAMS

This is another feature with which you can go completely crazy. It's easy to place too many affiliate programs on your site. Before you know it, your site can look like one big, bright, flashing affiliate program junkyard.

When you decide to make a little extra money with affiliate programs, pick ones that will complement your site. Let's say you have a photography business and your specialty is taking pictures of people's pets. You might want to hook up with www.sitstay.com to sell pet crates, or maybe you'll want to become an affiliate of www.animalden.com to sell unique gift items for animal and pet lovers.

The way you make money from an affiliate can vary from program to program. Some pay you only when someone you've sent to them buys their product. Other programs will pay you if someone just clicks on a banner or a link to their site. Some pay only a few cents per "click," but others pay a bit more.

To help you determine what some of the best affiliate programs are, check out Associate Programs (www.AssociatePrograms.com) and Adbility's Web Publishers' Advertising Guide (www.wpag.com/).

Another opportunity is to start your own affiliate program. You will need to purchase your own affiliate program software, which can cost you anywhere from very little up to hundreds of dollars. Shop around to fit your budget. This is a great way to get people to promote what you're selling for basically nothing. You only pay when someone buys what you're selling.

E-newsletters/E-zines

E-newsletters and e-zines are great channels for delivering information about your business in a tidy package. In them you can include new updates made to your site and informative articles on your site's subject. You can also sell advertising in your newsletter, also known as an e-zine. I started my newsletter about four years ago. I manually entered new subscribers' e-mail addresses into my word pro-cessor, until I was spending all day adding new subscribers. I then decided to parcel this task out to OakNet Publishing, which manages subscriptions. For more information about this company, visit www.oaknetpublishing.com/services/welcome.cgi?225.

Here are a few sites that will help you create your e-newsletter:

- http://www.ideamarketers.com
- http://www.e-zinez.com
- http://Ezine-Tips.com
  This site provides daily free tips on promoting, publishing, managing, and making money with an e-mail newsletter.
- http://www.meer.net/~johnl/ e-zine-list/index

Word of Mouth

Marketing your site via "word of mouth" (the best form of advertising) has never been easier than on the Internet. Recommend-it.com (www.recommend-it.com) offers a nice way for visitors to tell their friends about your great site. By signing up with Recommend-it.com, you get a logo that you put on your site. Then all your friends do is click on the graphic to tell their friends about your site. There's even a little incentive to do so: When your friends spread the word, they have a chance to win a prize.

You can create your own word-of-mouth networking by having a page on your site where you place links to your "Recommended Sites." Ask your friends and those you network with to do the same.

Banner Ads

Banner ads come in many shapes and sizes, from the large banners you see at the top of Web pages to little button-sized banners. The goal of your banner is to get someone to click on it. It's just like creating a good heading for a newspaper ad. Make it catchy. If you're interested in working from home, and you saw a banner that said, "Make $ from home today," it would most likely get your attention, and you would most likely click on it.

Banner advertising should only be a small portion of your marketing efforts. If possible, try the free banner advertising approach with banner-exchange programs (discussed in the next section). Otherwise, you could end up spending a great deal of money on advertising that isn't all that effective.

Be aware that different Web sites only allow certain sizes of banners. Therefore, for each banner you may want to have a few different sizes de-signed. Also keep in mind that more and more statistics show that people dislike banners and prefer text links, which are story ads with a link to the product.

Banner Exchanges

Some banner-exchange programs will put together your banner for free, others may charge a small fee to post your banner. Once you have your banner ready to go, you can participate in the following programs at no cost.

- http://womensinfo.net/Exchange/

- http://www.free-banners.com

- http://f2.findlink.com/banner

- http://www.clicklink.net

Paid-for Banner Programs

Once your site begins to grow and you start getting a substantial amount of page views each day, you will begin to attract companies who will actually pay you to place their banner on your site. You can work with affiliate programs, such as Link-Share (www.linkshare.com), or you might begin to hear from advertising agencies that would like to connect you with one of their clients.

The Possibilities Are Endless

FOR THE entrepreneur, the Internet holds limitless possibilities in terms of making money. It's estimated that by 2000, more women than men will be on the Internet. Although some of the women online are just gathering information, others are finding more ways to make money from home. I hope this chapter has started you thinking and helped you explore some new money-making ideas. The technology is there for you to use—don't miss out on these new opportunities any longer.

Getting Down to Business

✦

You have to dream it before you live it.
—Rosie O'Donnell

NOW YOU'RE READY to get down to business. Home business, that is. That means doing everything for yourself, from buying office equipment and supplies to deciding whether to have clients in your home. Ready?

Your Office

YOU'LL NEED to decide whether you need a separate office. If you have an extra room, the decision is pretty easy. If you don't have a special room for your office, buy a locked filing cabinet for your important papers. This way your kids can't draw on your work when you're not looking. Although you may be impressed by your toddler's artistic ability, your client won't be. You can also buy undersized desks, files, and storage units with wheels, so you can roll them out of sight when not in use.

How to Buy Business Equipment

STARTING A business was much like school shopping for me. Do you remember those days? I loved buying my new pencils, notebook paper, and that crazy compass that I'd find in my desk only because it had speared my finger. I definitely got a little out of hand when I was starting my personalized children's books business. I bought so

83

many needless things that I am still selling them at my garage sales.

When you shop for equipment, ask yourself, "Do I really need this?" Ask that at least five times, take a deep breath, and then go home and think about it for a week. By then you will realize that you didn't need all twenty-five colored pens—three will suffice. Melody Upham says, "Don't waste your money on things you will never use. I think if I could go back and do it again, I could have started [my soapmaking] business with half the money I actually started with."

If you do need to put a lot of money into equipment, try to get the best equipment you can afford. Here are some other tips:

- **Network:** Start talking to all the people you know and see if they have the type of equipment sitting around unused that you need. If they don't, maybe they know someone else who does. If you can't find someone who is willing to give you the equipment, maybe you can offer to buy it for a low price. Or, maybe the person who has the equipment you need could use your service or product in exchange for letting you use their equipment.

- **Rent or lease:** When you lease equipment, you can get it fixed for free and you can upgrade so you aren't stuck with a dinosaur. The downside is that you usually have to sign a yearly contract. If your business takes a different direction,

you will be stuck with the monthly leasing plan. Graphic designer Julia Tavis told me, "I lease my computer system, which I wouldn't highly recommend. It does save having to put money up front, but if I had the money, I wouldn't lease. It doesn't carry the tax advantage that people think it does. I could have purchased my computer on a credit card and done much better. But now I'll finish the lease out and learn the realistic way."

- **Buy it secondhand:** Check classifieds, garage sales, estate sales, and bankruptcy auctions. Office-supply stores often sell secondhand equipment they have refurbished. Self-storage businesses often have monthly sales on abandoned possessions. Post offices often have sales on packages that no one claims.

What Type of Equipment Do You Need?

BEFORE YOU spend all your start-up money, ask yourself this important question: "What kind of equipment do I really need?"

LETTERHEAD AND BUSINESS CARDS

Business cards and your personal letterhead are essential. If you have a computer, some sort of publishing software, and a decent printer, you can easily make your own. Most office-supply stores carry good quality paper and card stock. If you're not comfortable designing or producing your own letterhead and business cards, have it done professionally. Business cards and letterhead say a lot about you and your business before anyone even meets you personally. This is one area you don't want to skimp on.

OFFICE MACHINES

With computers, scanners, copiers, and printers, at-home business owners can easily produce professional-looking products. And thanks to the communication technology of answering machines, e-mail, and faxes, no one will guess you are a one-woman operation.

I highly recommend buying a computer, even if it doesn't relate directly to your business. The online resources are invaluable, accounting software such as Quicken helps track your income and expenses, and a database is useful for keeping track of clients. If you're thinking of buying a computer but don't know much about them, take a basic computer class and start reading up on the subject. Ask around and find someone you trust who knows a lot about computers. Tell him or her exactly what you want to use your computer for and how much you can spend. Take this person with you when you purchase your computer.

Julia Tavis has a rule of thumb for purchasing a computer for business purposes. "Estimate what your needs are going to be as far as RAM, hard disk space, and all the technical aspects. Then multiply this all by two. This gives you a little growing room." A computer system can cost less if you buy it from a reputable mail-order company or purchase it at a computer store that builds your computer.

If you get your business going and you find yourself dragging the kids along to the local copy center on a regular basis, you should think about investing in a small copy machine. If you do a lot of copying, it will pay for itself. A fax machine or scanner may also prove very useful.

BUSINESS PHONE

You may want to consider installing a second phone line for your business. The advantages are many:

• You can track your business call expenses.

• You and your family always know it's a business call.

• You can always answer the phone with a business greeting.

• If you have a business license, you can have your phone number listed for free in the yellow pages.

If a second phone line is too expensive for you at first, there is another solution. Your phone company can give you a business number that rings on your regular family phone with a double ring that lets you know it is a business call. Keep all phone bills from that line, because business calls are tax-deductible.

MISCELLANEOUS

Purchase an organizer for all your business contacts, business cards, meetings, and so on—and be sure to use it! I have been known to schedule a meeting and write it down like a very organized person in my organizer, but then I didn't look at it and missed the meeting.

You may want to use a post office box for your business address, either because it looks more professional or because you don't want clients coming to your house.

Meeting Clients

JUST BECAUSE you run your business from your home doesn't mean clients have to meet you there. You have several options. You can meet with your customers over coffee or tea in a restaurant or meet at their place of business. If you feel that an office space would really suit your purposes, look for an office you can rent by the hour. Also, some clubs and community centers offer meeting rooms you can rent.

If you really don't want clients dropping over unexpectedly, don't give them the opportunity. Word processor Diana Ennen doesn't put her home address on her cards and brochures. "This helps a lot because I don't want drop-ins. This way, too, I get to screen the calls if someone doesn't feel right. I don't give my address until I feel like giving it." This way you can meet your new clients at a restaurant or another public place first before you bring them into your home.

Dress for Success

YES, PART of the fun of working for yourself is not having to wear uncomfortable clothes all day. Nonetheless, if at all possible, get dressed for work. You don't have to dress up in a wool suit, but don't wear your baggy sweats either. When quilter Tania Osborn began dressing for work, she saw a big difference. She found she wasn't so apt to do housework instead of business work, and she even lost weight. Tania swears by dressing for success: "It really makes a difference."

Keeping Friends and Business Separate

EVEN THOUGH your friends know you work at home, sometimes they can't seem to remember that you're actually working. Now and then, friends and family will drop by to visit while you're working. This potentially can become a real problem. Julia Tavis says it's important to be firm with them. "You can't be fearful when you have a business," says Julia. "You have to be bold. I know I am home, but I am running a business and it's not just a little hobby. I have to set some professional standards." Although she doesn't mind if people stop by to chat, they must understand they may not have her full attention.

Keep 'Em Coming Back

ONCE YOU get that first precious customer, do everything in your power to turn them into a repeat customer. Here are some tricks to keep them coming back for more:

HOW TO LET FRIENDS KNOW YOU'RE WORKING

- Put a sign on the door that says you're working. If you don't have clients coming over to your house, hang a "closed" sign on your door, and if someone comes over to chat unannounced, just don't answer the door. Or let them in, but tell them that work is the priority.

- As nicely as you can, explain to your friends that you are running a business. Tell them they can come over after business hours.

- Purchase a caller ID system so you can screen calls before you have to answer the phone.

- Park your car down the street. That way they won't think you're home.

- Try to keep a set time that you work each day. That way your friends and family can get into the routine of things. Friends will know you're working and that they shouldn't bother you.

- If friends keep calling during the time you're at work, talk with them for a few minutes but explain you will call them back later when you're not working. It may take a few months for this message to get through, but eventually it will.

- Don't answer the door or the home phone (if you have a separate business line).

- Always answer the phone with a business greeting during business hours.

- If a friend calls to ask a favor, tell her you have to check your appointment calendar first. She will slowly get the message that you are at work.

- Treat your business like a real business. If you don't feel like you have a real business, you will have a hard time convincing others that you're not just doing this for fun or as a hobby.

- Your number one goal should be good service and quality products. Don't cut corners here.

- Return phone calls promptly.

- When you get an order, fill it immediately.

- Keep in touch with your customers. Don't bug them, but don't let them easily forget you.

- Remember your manners. As you tell your kids, "please" and "thank you" go a long way.

- Be on time for appointments.

- Go the extra mile for your clients. Give them more than they expect.

- Believe in your product; believe in yourself.

WHAT SHOULD I DO DURING DOWNTIME?

Downtimes? Everyone has them. Instead of getting depressed and wondering if you will ever again have another customer, try to use those down times to your advantage. After a while you may notice a pattern to your business highs and lows. Here are some tips on using these times to your advantage:

- Take a vacation (this is a particular favorite of mine).

- Make calls to people you have worked for in the past. Call friends who are in the same business to let them know you're looking for more work.

- Pitch your business to other customers or send out mailings.

- Catch up on your paperwork and filing.

CHAPTER THIRTEEN

How to Manage Your House, Your Family, and Your Business

✦

Many times when the business is out of whack,
things at home aren't right either.

—Melody Upham

MOST MOMS DECIDE to work at home so they can spend more time with their family. Ironically, as your business grows, you may find yourself getting busier and busier and seeing less and less of your family. When you head into your office and your kids are hanging onto your legs like chucks of cement, screaming, "Mom, please don't go in there," then it's time to take a break and spend some time with them.

How Your Kids Benefit from Your At-Home Business

I BELIEVE THERE are some real advantages for kids whose moms work at home. Two of the big ones, especially if you have infants or toddlers, are the ability to breast-feed your child in the comfort of your own home and the end of the need for all-day day care.

We have all heard about the positive effects of breast-feeding. When you stay home, you can nurse your baby in the comfort of your own home. No more pumping breast milk at your office desk, hoping no one will walk in on you, or storing your milk for later, hoping it won't spoil. You can nurse as nature intended.

Breast-feeding makes your life so much easier. Many of the moms I spoke with highly recommended nursing for those who decide to run a home business. When you're on the phone and the baby is crying, nursing immediately calms your child. This actually happened several times as I interviewed moms profiled in this book. I would hear a very unhappy child, the mother would ask me to give her just a few seconds, and then the baby would stop crying. (If only there were such a simple solution for quieting the older kids!)

And don't feel bad that, when the afternoon comes around and you're nursing, you end up napping right alongside your baby. More than likely you will have been up late at night, and a little shut-eye will make you much more productive with your business.

For breast-feeding support in your area, visit La Leche League online (www.laleche-league.org/), or call 1-800-LALECHE.

I'm not an advocate of day care, especially for newborn babies. I believe a mother should do everything in her power to be home to raise her kids. Children need their mothers. They need that daily contact with their mom, and a mom with a business at home gives them just that. Society doesn't give mothers enough credit for the job they perform. Also, in the long run, stay-at-home moms will have healthier children. So by working at home, you're giving your child just that much more of an advantage.

As your children get older and stop drooling on everything, you might want to think about employing them. Not only is it potentially helpful to you, but when you include them in your business, they will feel as though they are contributing to the family.

Soapmaker Melody Upham explains, "My kids are learning things that most kids don't get the opportunity to learn. I think that as they grow older, they will appreciate having seen that Mom had her own business. Maybe they will also adopt the mind-set that they're not limited to working for someone else."

By working for yourself from home, you're modeling valuable entrepreneurial skills. As your kids get older and make their own career choices, they'll remember that "Mom worked for herself. I could do it, too." Also, involving your kids in your business helps them understand how a business is run.

HOW TO INVOLVE YOUR KIDS

You can include your kids in your business sooner than you think. Kids love to feel like they're helping. If you push them aside and make your business seem more important than they are, they will begin to resent your business. If you do decide to let your children help you with your business, remember to treat them as you would any employee. Don't talk down to them or yell at them for making a mistake. They're human, just like you.

One easy way to incorporate them is to give them a space in the office. Corey, Trish Kasey's daughter, has her own desk in the office. "We got that for her so she felt like she was working, too. I got her a little kid's briefcase, too." Ann Masland talks about her daughter. "She's 2½, at the age where she likes to imitate Mom. So if I give her a couple of highlighters and a pad of paper, she is working, and she thinks it's pretty cool."

Ann also has a younger son, 9 months old, who keeps her daughter entertained. "They are demanding of my time, but they are pretty good at amusing each other."

You can give the littlest ones some paper and safety scissors and explain that they could really help Mommy if they could very carefully cut each paper in half. Say, "I need you to do this for me," and make them feel needed. Or give them a real job you think they can handle. You might be surprised at what they can accomplish.

Diana Ennen has a few special projects for her kids. "For holidays, such as Easter, my kids and I will prepare Easter baskets for my clients. The kids get dressed up for Halloween and we take clients candy. Everyone looks forward to it. But I think it's really important because my children feel a part of my business."

Setting Boundaries

IF YOU place your business above your family, your family will resent your business and you will defeat the whole point of staying home. This calls for setting boundaries and enforcing them. Decide on your working hours and let everyone know what they are, including your clients. If the business phone rings when you're reading your kids a story, let the answering machine get it. Decide on one day a week that you will not work, and let the whole family know that you're free that day. This way you can plan outings that won't get canceled.

Word processor Diana Ennen explains how things got out of hand in her family. "I worked every weekend and evenings, and it took away from our family. I also had clients calling me in the evenings and on the weekends. Finally, I had to learn how to say 'no' and set my boundaries. Once I did that things went back to normal."

Hold Family Meetings

A GREAT WAY to keep your whole family happy is by holding regular family meetings. You can start these when your child is about 4 years old. At your first family meeting, decide what night you will meet on. These nights are sacred. No one is allowed to miss a meeting, especially parents. Once a parent starts missing a meeting, then kids feel they really don't need to be there, either.

Make these meetings fun to attend. Serve a special dessert at each one or have pizza—anything to get you all there. Make the meetings age-appropriate, but make sure all ages feel wanted and listened to. Whether your family consists of one child or a dozen kids, a family meeting *can* work.

Each member can bring his or her problems to discuss. For example, you may say that every time you are on the phone with a client, the kids are noisy. How can everyone solve this problem? Let the kids think of a solution, as well as a consequence if they don't follow through. If little Frankie plays his tuba when he knows Mom's on the phone, he has to do everyone's chores for that day. Your kids will be more involved if they have a say in thinking up the consequence. Beware: Kids will always think up a worse consequence than you will.

Don't forget that the kids can bring problems to the meeting, too. For example, little Betty may complain that you work all the time and you're not paying attention to her. The meeting is a good place to work on solutions. Don't get discouraged if you have to make up new solutions every week or every two weeks. It *can* work.

The family meeting doesn't have to be all about you, of course. Use it to discuss meal ideas, vacation plans, who does what chore for the week, or your upcoming week's schedule (you know you don't want to forget little Frankie's tuba recital). The sky is the limit on this, but by all means make it fun. If the kids feel that they're included, life will go much more smoothly for everyone.

One last word: Keep a journal of the subjects you cover, and let a different person each week be in charge of the book. The book is fun to look back on, and it's a good way to know if you did or didn't cover a certain subject.

Managing the Housework

KEEPING YOUR house clean is one of the hardest things to do when you run a home business. You already have two big priorities in your life, your business and your family. Some things have to take a backseat.

The one household chore that seems to permanently reside in the backseat is the laundry. It sounded like everyone I interviewed had mounds of laundry that either needed washing or folding. You, too, may soon hear, "Is this pile of clothes dirty or clean?" Don't forget that kids and husbands can do laundry, too—it isn't all up to you!

Sabrina Cuddy is a childbirth instructor. She holds her classes in her home and has found that "If I let the house turn into a disaster, I run myself ragged cleaning up for class. With two kids it can get really crazy." But try not to let the unwashed dishes in the sink keep you from your business. Rebecca Bostick, a work-at-home architect, has found that out. "I've relaxed my expectations of my housecleaning. You just can't have everything. I don't feel like I have to clean the house before I can work." If picking up as you go isn't working out, try picking up before you go to bed. If you have customers or clients coming over, at least make sure the areas they will spend time in are clean. Don't feel guilty; you are doing the best you can do.

Medical transcriptionist Luci Godwin says, "I didn't sit down at the computer last night until eleven o'clock, and nights like that can get a little frustrating. That's one of the hardest things about working from home—there is always something else. You just have to learn the dishes and the laundry can sit there and you just have to turn it all off. But you can't turn the kids off. You just have to keep the right frame of mind about the whole thing."

The following housecleaning suggestions are from Joanne Winthrop, a basket dealer and mother of six children:

- Take two minutes a day and wipe down the sink.

- Keep the kitchen counter clean, even if dishes are in the sink, so you won't be overwhelmed by the sight.

- If you can afford it, hire a housekeeper to come in once every week or two.

INVOLVE YOUR KIDS WITH THE HOUSEWORK

Enlist the help of your kids if they are old enough (any kid who can talk and walk and open a refrigerator by themselves is old enough). Just pick chores that are appropriate for your kids' ages. Have your older children take a role in keeping the house clean. Get them to do the laundry, the dishes, or even teach them how to cook.

If you decide to assign chores to your kids, make sure your kids know what you mean by "clean up the kitchen" or any other chore you give them to do. To them, cleaning may mean simply unloading the dishwasher. To you, it may be unloading and reloading the dishwasher, wiping the counters clean, and sweeping the floor.

Here's another idea for sharing the load. Have everyone draw for chores weekly so that no one is stuck doing the same chore. If Mom and Dad are assigned chores too, the kids can live with this idea a little better. "Oh, funny, Dad has to take the trash out this week."

Meal Planning

IF YOU don't keep on top of meal planning, you'll find your family eating out a lot, which will eat into your budget. Floral designer Kim Swanson-Huff suggests, "Stay organized and cook a lot of easy meals. Cook a double batch and freeze it." At your family meeting, you can discuss what you will be having that week. Schedule at least one dinner as leftovers night. Once you have the menu, you can go to the store and purchase everything you need. Now all you need is someone to cook it. . . .

Karen Potter, a child-care provider, says, "For the first year we ate out quite a bit, but my husband realized we weren't eating at six o'clock, so he started cooking." Her husband took the situation into his own hands and now prepares dinner. Thumbs up to Karen and her husband.

Before she had kids, Tania Osborn was a materials engineer. "I did a time-motion study on how much time I spent in the kitchen. I found I was spending six to eight hours a day around food, including shopping, preparing, and eating." So Tania found a company that will stock her freezer with food that she can easily prepare for her family. "Now I think I'm down to four hours." Tania also has a shelf in her refrigerator that she stocks with snacks every morning for her two kids. This way she doesn't have to hear, "Mom, I'm hungry. What can I eat?"

For more information on cutting your time in half in the kitchen, visit Deliciously Simple (www.accnorwalk.com/~heidijo/).

Child-Care Solutions

SOMETIMES, EVEN though you're at home, you will need to use child care to get your work done. You may be lucky enough to have family members who can watch your kids for a few hours, or older children who can baby-sit. If not, here are some ideas that will help.

SHARED CHILD CARE

Share sitting with another work-at-home mom on a regular basis. You're not spending any money, and you're really helping each other out. You might even find a more organized baby-sitting co-op of other WAHMs. In these groups you generally pay a small amount of money (say, $10 for a four months' supply of coupons) and receive a list of moms to call when you need a sitter. The coupons can range from a half-hour to a full hour of sitting time.

IN-HOME SITTERS

A few of the moms profiled in this book have older sitters come into their homes while they work. Diana Ennen has used this method

and gives a word of advice. "The sitter needs to be aware that she can't come to you every time the baby cries. I got in trouble with that once. Every time the baby cried, the sitter would come into the office. She has to behave like you're not even here." The following tips provide more information on finding the perfect sitter.

• Find out how much experience the sitter has.

• Ask for references, and make sure you call them.

• If the sitter claims to have taken infant/child CPR, ask to see the certificate of completion.

• Ask what ages of children the sitter has taken care of.

• Ask how long the sitter will commit to working for you. You don't want to start this process all over again in a month.

• Watch how your kids interact with the prospective sitter. If they're not happy, move on.

• Ask a lot of questions, especially questions unrelated to sitting. Ask about his or her interests or area of study, for example.

• Go with your instincts. If you don't feel right about someone and you can't explain why, don't worry about it. Continue your search.

MOTHER'S HELPER

A mother's helper is a young girl usually between the age of 10 and 12 who comes to your home and plays with your child while you get your work done. These girls don't charge much, and, unlike teenagers, they are apt to get down on the floor and actually play with your kids.

Home Schooling

MANY MOMS who work at home find home schooling an easy step to make and vice versa. From the interviews that I've conducted, each mother has a different approach to making home schooling and the home-business juggling act work.

Dayna Lawson Gilmore finds keeping to a schedule a must. She explains, "If I don't stay on any schedule, something suffers, and I feel completely out of balance." She breaks up her day into four sections: her business (DK Family Learning), family (which includes her husband, kids, and housework), the kids' home schooling, and, last but not least, her personal care. Dayna makes sure she keeps herself happy physically, mentally, and spiritually.

Although a schedule is a must for Dayna, some moms find the balancing act easier with a more laid-back approach. Mary Crenshaw has been home schooling now for four years. She explains, "I try not to stress over the schoolwork. This sounds awful, but sometimes

I have deadlines for work due"—she owns an office-support service business—"and I can't do a lot of one-on-one home schooling some weeks. I home school year round and don't define it to Monday through Friday. I think it all evens out." On heavy weeks, when Mary's business is hectic, she assigns more workbook pages. Then on lighter work weeks, she participates in more science experiments, history discussions, and field trips.

Cheryl Demas, owner of Wahm.com, home schools her oldest daughter. She explains, "Actually, in some ways it's easier [combining home schooling and a home business]. I have control over our time and our schedules."

So yes, if you've wondered if you can combine these two objectives, home schooling and a home business, it can be done. Find a schedule that works best for you and not what works best for your friends. Dawn Vaughan, owner of Vaughan's Home Design (www.vhdesign.com), has balanced her children's education and her home business by relying heavily on education software and workbooks for their curriculum. She also uses the home schooling lists on the Internet for support and information. She says, "We have an unusual household, but we enjoy our lifestyle." I hope that's your underlying goal, too.

ONLINE RESOURCE

- http://www.sagecreekproductions.com/hmbus.htm

    This newsletter/Web site is for

people who home school and run a home business.

LISTSERVS

- Homeschoolers-in-Biz
    E-mail ladysham@bellsouth.net for more information.

Balancing Kids and Work

IT MAY seem like you've given your kids attention all day long, but it probably hasn't been your undivided attention. Kids aren't stupid; they know when you're really into spending time with them and when you're not. If your kids are younger, you're going to have to face the fact that you'll be spending more time with them than your business those first few years. Toddlers tend to need that minute-to-minute care. So even if they do give you a few minutes of peace, a warning bell goes off in your head: "Oh dear, are they drinking poison, or have they walked out to the middle of the street?"

Schedule your work in short spurts so you can always spend a few minutes with your kids. Read to them or take them for a walk or a bike ride. One mom admits, "Believe it or not, those few minutes throughout the day help me be more productive than if I constantly put them off until I [am] done. I get less nagging, fewer interruptions, and they get a mom who isn't so cranky."

Accountant Victoria Philips says,

"Before a client arrives at the house, I line all the kids up and say, 'Look, I have a client coming. You have to be quiet. If you misbehave, I'll have to send you to your room.' I have a rule that they can't come into the office while clients are here, but they still do it sometimes. You just have to keep reminding them."

Anna Marie Johansen, a caterer, has found, "You have to juggle a lot. One will have swimming lessons, somebody else has science after school, and you have to make sure you get them there. You just have to work around it. Sometimes I'm up at five in the morning to cook before they are up at seven." She would also make play dates for her son. "His friends would come over here and visit with him and that was his entertainment. My other son, on the other hand, will take out his Play-Doh. Or he will fill the sink with water and put everything imaginable in the water to see if it floats."

One working mom keeps a basket full of things for her kids to play with, such as old checkbooks and checkbook registers, Post-It Notes (kids love those), and special pencils. There's also an old wallet, play money, small pads, trading cards, magnets, and paper clips. She throws new things in from time to time—stickers and stamps that come in the mail, or something she picks up at the office supply store. It gives them a focus when they do wander into the office, and it's easy to clean up when they're done. Just throw everything back into the basket.

Managing Clients and Kids

LIKE MANY work-at-home moms, photographer Lisa Zaccagnini sometimes brings her clients into her home. "Clients have to understand that my kids are home. It has nothing to do with how I do my work, but my children are here, this is my life, and they're in my home. But I will do the very best I can at this moment. I will answer every question they have for me, even if we're talking about money. They can then go home and form their own opinion based on the entire interview. If they have questions afterward, they can call me. If they need to see my work again or they want to see me again, I'll do that. And I haven't had a problem with any clients."

Explain to your clients that you do work out of your home and that there are children who live in the house. Just let them be aware that they may hear, "Mom, I have to go pee-pee," in the background, and then you won't have to explain or even lie. Always keep in the back of your mind that you have the courage to do what most people only dream of.

Keeping Appointments

JULIA TAVIS says, "When balancing home and family, everything is an appointment. It's not a good approach to tell your clients, 'I have to pick up my kids at three so I can't meet with you then.' I don't lie to them, but I do say, 'I'm sorry, I have an appointment at three.' I don't need to tell them my appointment is to pick my children up or to play Lego's with my son. I just say, 'I have an appointment and I would love to schedule you for two o'clock tomorrow,' and they never question that. But as soon as you say you have to take your daughter to the dentist that day, it makes you look unprofessional."

Dealing with Kids and Phone Calls

PHONE CALLS seem related to Pavlov's dog theory: When the phone rings, kids must behave badly. It is often the phone calls that are the biggest problem a mom sees in her home business. With children as young as 5 or 6, you can sit down with them and explain, "This is how Mommy makes money, by talking on the phone. I really need you to help me." Kids really do like to help; it makes them feel important. You may have to have this talk once a day for a while, but kids catch on. When they are quiet during phone calls, praise them like they have never been praised before. If you don't have a separate business phone, train your children to answer the phone correctly. As your kids get older and are on the phone more, you may have to install a second phone line for the business or tell them they can talk to their friends after business hours.

Julia Tavis says, "Telephone time is one of the biggest problems. My kids are 4, 7, and 9. When the phone rings, I yell very loudly, 'This is a business call, everyone be very quiet, please,' and then I answer the phone. It works. I do the same thing when I make a business call: 'I'm about to make a business call, please be very quiet.'"

Diana Ennen has found, "If kids are screaming in the background, it's best to have a portable phone. Then you can just run away from the noise. If it's too noisy, I just let the answering machine pick up. My regular clients are more understanding of the kids. But I have found that if I have a new client call and they hear kids screaming in the background, I rarely get a call back. If I'm with the kids, I just don't answer the phone. I lose track with kids pulling on me, and I miss what the client is telling me."

Here are some tips for keeping your kids quiet while you're on the phone:

- Teach your children that when you pick up the phone, they are to immediately pick up some paper and a pen and draw quietly while you're talking.

- Tell the kids every time the phone rings to pick up a book and read it quietly.

- Use a portable phone and hide from your kids in the nearest closet.

- Buy a phone with a mute button so when the other person is talking they can't hear little Betsy screaming in the background.

- Have a special toy close by that can be played with only when you're on the phone.

- Have a second phone line put in so that your whole family knows whether it's a personal or a business call.

- If your house is exploding and you do get a phone call, let the answering machine get it.

- Fill a jar with chores written on pieces of paper. If your kids bother or interrupt you, get the jar and give them a chore to do immediately.

- Forward your calls after business hours to an answering service.

- Make your phone calls during your child's nap time.

TV or Not TV?

THE TV dilemma is a tough one. If you let your kids watch it all day, you'll invariably get a lot done. However, you will feel guilty about the way your kids are spending their time. I will be the first to admit that I have used a video as a baby-sitter. When Melody Upham realized she was using the TV as a baby-sitter, she got rid of the TV. "I'm being a little more creative in how I involve my kids, which is good for all of us. It's too easy to sit them in front of the TV. One of the reasons I stayed home with my kids was so they wouldn't have that mentality."

How to Handle Summer

ONE WORD can strike fear in the heart of any mother with a home business: summer. Moms who have had their kids in school all year and have had the joy of working during normal day hours are often a little reluctant when school is out for the summer. Trying to fill long summer days with activities while continuing to work can be challenging and frustrating. You can count on your kids popping into your office on a regular basis to tell you they're bored or that they need $10 for the movies or the mall. How are you supposed to get any work done?

One solution is to get them excited about starting their own little home business. There are books out there for young people on this very subject. One of them is *Fast Cash for Kids* (Career Press, 1995), by Bonnie and Noel Drew. Maybe they'll pass on a marketing tip to you.

Here are some other ideas for keeping your kids happily occupied during the summer:

- Send your kids to a two-week summer camp.

- Sign them up for a day-camp program.

- Send the kids on a minivacation to their grandparents.

- Take a family vacation so you can all have a much-needed break from school and work.

- Set up times to do crafts. This will take some planning on your part. Check out books with crafts ideas. If your kids are old enough, they may be able to work on their own.

Marilyn Rowland, an indexer, says, "I have tried this summer to have a series of theme-related projects for them to work on. We also take field trips related to the themes. All of this organizing and supervising cuts into my work time a lot, but I hate the idea of them watching TV all summer and forgetting how to read. We also have contests in writing, art, and poetry. So far they take the contests seriously, even though everyone wins and the prize is a sharable one, like the movies or miniature golf."

Graphic designer Julia Tavis tries to schedule activities each day. "We have library days, cookie-making days, sometimes we even have laundry days or read-a-book day. It's something they look forward to. We have a calendar that we make up on the computer. This keeps their minds busy even though they have to spend a lot of time at home."

Take Time-Outs for Special Time

YOU'RE WORKING at home so you can be with your kids, but sometimes it seems like the kids are getting in the way of your work. At these times it's especially important to remember that your kids come first. Give them their special time and you won't be sorry.

One mom told me that she was busy working on a deadline when her son excitedly ran into her office to tell her that Dad had just shown him how to ride a bike without his training wheels, and could she come out and watch him. Her first thought was to say, "Great! Good job! But I have to finish this project." But then she figured, "Why not?" and went out and watched him for five minutes. That's all, just five minutes. Her son was thrilled and so proud, and she didn't have to deal with the guilt of not watching her son. And then she went back to work.

When you suddenly become aware that your kids are whining and fighting with each other, they probably really need your attention. Set down what you're doing and give them a good twenty minutes of your time. Many moms find that just twenty minutes of total attention buys them a lot more uninterrupted work time than if they had ignored their child's request.

Help Your Kids Discover Their Own Interests

IF YOU had a difficult time figuring out what type of business you wanted to start because you had no clue what you really enjoyed doing, now is the time to make sure this doesn't happen to your children. You have the opportunity to help your children discover what they truly enjoy doing.

If your child says he or she wants to be an astronaut, don't say "No, you don't. That's too dangerous," or "You have to be smart to do that." Instead get books and movies on astronauts. Because you now know how important it is to do something you love, encourage your children to explore their own interests.

Don't be frustrated when your kid says, "This week I think I want to be a veterinarian." This is their time to explore their options. It's also a good time to involve them in activities that pertain to their new interests. Who knows—maybe you can even get more work done because they are off learning about veterinarians and astronauts.

Balancing Your Job with Your Mate

WHEN YOU first tell your husband, partner, or significant other that you want to start your own business, he may be fine with the idea. When reality sets in, however, that can change. You may both feel frustrated and angry. Maybe the house that used to be spotless is now cluttered, and neither of you wants to clean it up. Dinner isn't made like it used to be, and you spend less time alone with each other. Even in the most perfect relationship, with the most supportive partner, these problems can crop up. Be prepared!

Spouses or partners are going to have their good days and bad days when it comes to supporting you and your business. Try putting yourself in your partner's shoes. What if he wanted to start his own business? What if he quit his secure job, hung up his shingle, and started drawing from your savings account for supplies and living expenses? Would you be completely supportive of him 100 percent of the time? No one is perfect. Just wait until you do start to bring in cash. Then he may have a total change of heart.

When Your Partner Resents Your Home Business

NOT ALL husbands or partners are receptive to the idea of their mates starting their own home business. Some feel threatened. Maybe he hates his own job and envies the fact that his wife has found something that she loves and can do from the comfort of home. Maybe he doesn't like the idea of his wife doing something besides raising the kids. He may feel that making money is his area. Other husbands want their wives to work at a "real" job making a steady paycheck and feel that staying home is too risky. The idea of starting a venture with no idea if you'll make the same kind of money, or any money, can be scary for both of you.

He may feel that his schedule, his ideas, and his problems are more important than yours. He may feel that you have found something else more important than him, and he doesn't like it. Things can get ugly if you and your partner don't sit down and communicate. You need to find out what he is feeling, and he needs to hear why you want to start a business so badly.

In my researching and interviewing, I have heard one phrase over and over again: "I have such a wonderful, supportive husband." Clearly, a supportive husband or partner can make your business run more smoothly. Realistically, however, not everyone is so lucky. Here's a real-life example of a husband who did not want his wife to start her own home business. We'll call her "Nancy," although that is not her real name.

My husband has tried to undermine me every step of the way in starting my word processing/transcription/desktop-publishing business. Every time I worked on an order while he was home, he would constantly walk by and say, "Turn that stupid computer off. You're wasting my electricity." If I kept working, he would sit somewhere close and sigh. And sigh. Shift positions and sigh. Then he would make disgusted sounds.

Every time I tried to talk to him about my business, he would say, "I don't want to hear about it." His attitude was really bringing me down. I've given in before and given up on my ideas, but this time I really found something I wanted to do.

Yesterday was my ribbon-cutting

*ceremony in front of the chamber of com-
merce. (We did it there because I have a home
business and can't have anyone come to the
house for business purposes.) I didn't tell my
husband where we were going, I just told
him to get dressed and get in the car. Now!*

*While we were at the chamber, my hus-
band's attitude did a complete turnaround.
Suddenly, he was proud of me and my
ambition. He smiled and shook hands with
people and bragged about how good the
quality of my work is. He even took my
portfolio and showed it to people. I kept
thinking, "This is just a front. I'll get heck
when we get home." It didn't happen,
though. He started calling me "Miss High
Society" and patting me on top of the head.
This morning when he left for work he told
me to make lots of money while he was
gone (that was his way of saying he has
confidence in me).*

*As for how things are now, well, let's
just say that it could be better. He still
doesn't want me to work when he's home. He
feels my time should be with him. I agree to
a certain extent. If I don't have something
to finish on a deadline, I don't even touch
my computer while he's home. But if I do
have something to finish, I tell him that I'll
do it as quickly as possible so that we can
spend the rest of the day together without
me worrying about deadlines.*

Another woman whose husband was
against her business explains,

*I believe that husbands who don't sup-
port their wives do so because they are
afraid of change, afraid of losing what they
have. They probably don't feel good about
themselves, are insecure, and feel that if
they can't control their wives that they will
appear weak—or if their wives are successful and they aren't, they will look especially
bad. It's very sad, but not at all unusual.*

*What I would say to someone whose
husband is a stumbling block to their goals
is, do it anyway. If you don't, no one else
will. Don't listen to his blustering. If you
have a strong marriage, he'll eventually go
along with you and will even be proud of
you. If you don't have a strong marriage, it
would have shown up sooner or later anyway. It's better to accomplish something
and have confidence in yourself before you
find yourself alone.*

MAKE A DATE

One way to get your husband's support is to
pay attention to him. Set aside time for your
husband just as you do with the kids. Take
one night a week and make it date night. No
kids allowed. Take turns deciding where you
would like to go. Pat Curry says, "You have
to plan time to do things with your spouse to
keep that relationship healthy." Often Pat's
husband will look at her and say, "We need a
date night." Your family meeting is a good
place to decide on a night for a much-needed
date. Let him know how special he really is

to you. Tell him you still desire him in your life.

COMMUNICATE YOUR FEELINGS

If your mate is not supportive of your efforts, first talk to him and tell him what kind of support you need. Be open about the responsibilities of your business and home life. If he is not going to support you, it will be difficult for you to succeed in your business, and your relationship will be adversely affected. One way to make sure your partner hears what you are saying is to write him a letter explaining your feelings. Here's an example:

Dear _____,

I have decided to take on this huge task of starting my own home business. It's all very exciting and scary for me. Exciting, because the idea sounds too good to be true. I can still work, yet be here for you and the children. Scary, because I'm putting money into something I can't guarantee will make money in return. At least not right away. I do know it takes time for a business to turn a profit. Those first few years will be lean, but I know in the long run this will be a better situation for our family.

I want you to realize that this business is very important to me. I need you to help me take things step-by-step, as I tend to look at the big picture. It can all get a bit

overwhelming. I will continually need your support.

This business is real to me; it isn't a joke or a hobby. It's a real job. Please take it seriously. I want you to be proud of me and supportive, just as I have been with you in your work. Even if you have doubts at times, I need to hear that you believe in me.

My office area is very sacred to me; please treat it with respect. If my clientele bothers you, talk to me about it, but please act respectful to them. There will be times when I just can't put my work down when you come home. But I will try to quit at a reasonable hour so I can spend time with you and the kids.

I want to make sure we have our time alone—no kids. If you see that I am close to losing it, kindly tell me to get out and do something by myself for a while. If at times you don't understand how I can get so crazy, spend a day with me.

There will be times when the house will look like it has exploded and maybe I haven't made a home-cooked meal in weeks. Just because I am working at home doesn't mean I have all the time in the world to make the house look perfect. Many times when running a home business, something has to go. I can't do it all. I'll need your help.

Love,

_____

Don't Forget Why You're Home in the First Place

J ULIA TAVIS says,

I try to always remind myself to focus on the parts of life that count. I have a sign that says "First Things First" to remind myself of these priorities. When you're dead and gone, no one will talk about how clean your house was or what a smooth-running business you owned. We leave our mark in life on the lives we touch—and especially those of our children, whose lives we mold.

When things are absolutely insane and deadlines are unreasonable, I make the effort to step away from my office and sink down on our soft, comfy couch with my three children. Often they are already vying for my attention, competing with my work on the computer. When I finally make myself break away from what seems to be very important work at the moment, I'm instantly brought back to the reality of what is really important in life.

It may not be the easiest task you've taken on, mixing a home business with your kids. You just need to realize you're not Superwoman. You will make mistakes. Just take responsibility for your mistakes and find solutions that will help. It's all worth it in the long run.

CHAPTER FOURTEEN

Staying Healthy

✦

A vigorous five-mile walk will do more good for an unhappy but otherwise healthy adult than all the medicine and psychology in the world.
—Paul Dudley White

Noble deeds and hot baths are the best cures for depression.
—Dodie Smith

AS THE OLD saying goes, "If Momma ain't happy, ain't nobody happy." When you work at home, trying to be Superwoman is a real temptation. But this is the road to burnout. And when you're burned out, nothing goes well—not your home or your business. The most important way to avoid burnout is to admit to yourself that you can't possibly do it all. You have to give up something in order to have a successful home business. There is always a trade-off. Remember, a little clutter never hurt anyone. As graphic designer Julia Tavis says, "Having realistic expectations is the real key to starting a home-based business. Your life is going to be utter chaos for an indefinite period of time." Take time for yourself, even if you feel there isn't time for it. You'll feel better about life in the long run.

Eat Right

WE ALL know that breakfast is the most important meal of the day—at least that's what we tell our kids. Unfortunately, breakfast time is also the craziest time of day. Between getting kids off to school and making sure your little ones get some of their breakfast in their mouths, you may forget to feed yourself. One solution is to make a yogurt-fruit shake. It's a quick, nutritious meal, a great source of energy, and you can sip it while you work.

And don't forget to eat lunch. Mary Kovoor, a telecommuter, suggests preparing your lunch the night before. "I make a brown-bag lunch for my husband, and I make one for me. Otherwise, I won't eat. If I do, it's something junky."

Many home businesses are run right from the dining room table, dangerously close to the refrigerator and cupboards full of food. Nonstop snacking is a real problem for women who work at home. As you're likely the one who buys the food that goes into the cupboards and refrigerator, buy healthful foods to snack on.

Get to Sleep

IF YOU'RE a mom, you're probably already sleep deprived. You're either up all night with a crying infant, or up and down soothing a sick child. Don't beat yourself up about feeling tired in the middle of the day. If you can't keep your eyes open to work, don't force it. Indulge yourself: Take a nap. (Now there's a good reason to work at home!) A 30-minute nap will leave you feeling refreshed and ready to conquer the world, and you'll do much better work.

Move Your Body

EXERCISE IS really important for work-at-home moms. It makes you look better and feel better, and—a real plus—it gives you time alone. Use that time to think about whatever you want. Make it your own selfish

time. Give yourself a reward for exercising in pouring rain or before the kids wake up. Do whatever it takes to get your blood pumping.

Tutor Daa Mahowald belongs to a gym. She goes either at 5 in the morning or 10 at night, as that is when her husband and daughter are both in bed. Mary Koover goes to the gym two to three days a week, but if the weather is bad she will work out at home. "I do sit-ups or get out for a walk." Don't want to walk alone? No problem. Many of the moms I spoke with mentioned they walk with a friend or neighbor.

Carrie Alhelm, an upholsterer, says, "What also helps me a lot is yoga. I try to do it every night, but sometimes I don't get around to it. But every Friday I hold a yoga class. The teacher comes in, and I don't have to pay anything because I contribute the space in my house. That's an hour an a half every Friday and that saves my life."

Word processor Diana Ennen says, "If I have had a really stressful day, instead of stopping and jumping right into preparing dinner, I'll take the kids for a walk or a bike ride and just unwind a little bit. This really seems to help."

Craftsmaker Amy Levitt says, "The kids have a trampoline, and I use that to exercise on. If I don't do that in the morning I do stretching and sit-ups. Now that the weather is nicer, I'll walk in the evening, and my husband will put the kids to bed."

"I try to exercise three times a week. I go to the local YWCA. I take stretch-and-tone and aerobic classes. When my husband, Roy, is home, a bunch of us get up at 6 in the morning and walk two miles. That helps a lot. My house has three stories plus a basement, so just doing the laundry keeps me in shape," says Anna Marie Johansen, a caterer.

Newsletter publisher Trish Kasey runs 40 miles a week. "I get up at 5:30 and do my run. It's a physical and mental break for me because it gives me a chance to get away. I'm not anybody's mother, I'm not anybody's wife, and I'm not anybody's boss or business partner. It's just the road and me. I can think about what's going to happen that day and get my thoughts straight."

Beware of Repetitive Stress Injuries

IF YOU work on a computer all day or perform any other tasks that are repeated over and over again, you are a target for repetitive stress injuries. Most people are familiar with carpal tunnel syndrome, which is a common occurrence for word processors and others who work on computers. The best preventative medicine is rest. Get up and take breaks on a regular basis. Diana Ennen, a word processor, has some other guidelines: "Make sure your equipment and office setup is in compliance with ergonomic guidelines. Don't type on your kitchen table. You also need to make sure your chair and your desk are at the right height. A natural keyboard is a must. Armrests or wrist rests are important, too."

Prepare to Deal with Loneliness

AS MUCH as you might like the idea of going solo, you may miss the social interaction that comes from working with other people. At first you may not feel the isolation. Between getting your business started and figuring out how to keep your house running smoothly, you're not going to have time to be lonely. But as things fall into more of a routine, you may feel your days are a little too adult-free.

Another thing that is lacking when you're working solo is teamwork. When you're at the office, you have the camaraderie of those you work with. You have the daily gossip and the times you are all on a deadline working together. Inevitably this brings you all closer.

I highly recommend getting involved with a work-at-home moms' organization (see the resources in this book). This way you don't feel like the only one out there. It's nice to know there are other moms sitting in their offices working at home just like you do. If your town doesn't have one, make up your own. Get outside, gossip, exchange battle stories, and come up with solutions for each other.

Some women, like Elaine Courtney Moskow, a professional organizer, join professional support groups of moms in the same or similar fields. Everyone has a different way of dealing with loneliness. "As far as loneliness," says Luci Godwin, a medical transcriptionist, "I have a really big phone bill."

Seamstress Barb Marshall says, "My business brings people into the home. I know I'd be a lot more lonely without it." So the degree of your loneliness depends a lot on the business you decide to start. If you know that you're the kind of person who has to have people around, keep that in mind when you choose a business.

Make Time for Yourself

WOMEN OFTEN feel the need to make everyone happy but themselves. Don't forget to invest in yourself. Take the time to quit work early and visit with your friends or just go do something for yourself.

All of the women I interviewed have special ways of taking care of themselves. Ann Masland, a pet-sitter, says, "I have always found being around horses to be relaxing even if I'm not riding. I find the actual physical labor of working with the animals is good for my mental health, too." Accountant Victoria Philips depends on her "daily devotions—reading the Bible and prayer. It helps me get through the day." Victoria also serves on several community boards. They enable her to get out of the house and interact with other people.

Setting aside time for ourselves is usually last on the list, somewhere after getting the laundry folded. Make sure you're not plac-

ing yourself too low on the totem poll. Think of your body as the phone bill. If that bill doesn't get paid, the phone gets turned off. Don't let that happen to you.

Indexer Marilyn Rowland says, "Time for yourself is essential, even if it is just time to sit and do nothing or to go for a walk or take a long bath. Lately I have taken up the piano. I find playing the piano very satisfying, a welcome break from typing, oddly enough. I find it extremely stress releasing."

Take a class you enjoy that has nothing to do with your business. That's what gives Carrie Alhelm the break she needs. "What helps me is taking that one class because it's my thing. I get to leave three times a week for an hour. I take the bus to school and I walk home and it's a really nice break. It's amazing how fast I can transition from being a mom to focusing on ancient Greek."

Melody Upham, a soapmaker, says, "I've gone to many movies by myself, or I do any number of things that are nearly impossible to do with a 3-year-old." On weekends Melody has one day to herself where she can do what she likes and her husband watches their child. Then her husband gets a day for himself the next day.

Pat Curry, a freelance writer, says, "One of the things I am doing just for me is going to a writers conference. It sounded so wonderful I signed up for it immediately. Even though it's here in town I booked a room at the hotel—and I'm staying there for the entire conference. I'm even going the night before the conference starts. I don't do this very often. It's given me something to look forward to for the last few months."

When massage therapist Teresa Jones knows she needs to have a break from it all, she does something by herself. "I don't ask, I say, 'I'm going.'" Everyone needs a break. Just don't forget to take yours.

Grow Your Self-Confidence

To have a successful business, you need to have confidence in yourself and in what you're trying to sell to your customers and clients. Your customers would much rather work with someone who is happy and outgoing than someone who is timid and uncertain. Many times, however, you may feel less than confident. When you're working for yourself, it's a little like working in a vacuum. You may consistently feel you need more praise than usual and question your own abilities as a business owner.

One solution is to talk to your peers. Hearing that someone else has been there before you can make all the difference. And if you're family is supportive, you'll be even further ahead. Melody Upham says, "It's a constant struggle with me, believing I can do this. I start thinking, oh man, what am I doing, how did I get into this, and where do I go from here? That's where my husband comes in. He's probably my biggest cheer-leader. He keeps telling me, 'Yes, you can do it, yes, you can.' After a while I start listening to him. I take a deep breath and say, 'I can do this.' If you try to look too far ahead, it's scary. If you take one step at a time, a year from now you'll look back and say, 'Well, that wasn't so hard.'"

PART TWO

Home Business Profiles

CRAFTSMAKER

Name: Lucinda Claire Macy
Location: Laramie, Wyoming
Family Facts: Single mom, three children—Noah, 25, Arindelle, 19, and Jane Lillian, 17
Business: Lucinda & Co.

Why She Started Her Business

LUCINDA LEARNED through the school of hard knocks that she needed to take charge of her own life—and that is exactly what she has done. However, it hasn't always been an easy road. As Lucinda says, "The little success that I did have has given me the courage to take that next step."

Lucinda grew up in a family that encouraged individuality. At a young age she was using her creativity, and by the time she was in her teens, she was creating backdrops for puppet theater, painting signs, and making crafts.

She attended college for a couple of years, taking classes in everything from designing house plans to making pottery. During college she got married, and seven years later gave birth to her son. After marriage, school wasn't such a big priority, and she never finished her degree.

Unfortunately, her husband realized he wasn't ready for the responsibilities of family life and left her. At the age of 11 months, her son was diagnosed with diabetes. "I actually ended up on welfare but was still making some crafts and selling them at shows," says Lucinda. She later remarried and had two more children. She went through a similar scenario with her second husband, and once more found herself alone with three children to support.

Lucinda decided to move to the country, which she felt would be a better place to raise her children. She didn't want to leave her children by taking a job outside the home, so she continued making and selling different types of crafts. She was still receiving welfare but received less and less, until eventually her craft business supported her family completely.

Her wooden silk-screened welcome signs were a big hit with customers, and she gave some to friends who were showing at a wholesale gift show. They sold like hotcakes. Lucinda says, "In just one day at the end of the show I got several thousand dollars in orders." Stunned by the response, Lucinda scrambled to start filling orders. "I had no idea that this was going to happen."

Lucinda had three months to fill orders. She and her children, then ages 1, 3, and 9, lived with her parents at that time. She ended

"In just one day at the end of the show I got several thousand dollars in orders."

up staying up late at night trying to mass produce the signs in the garage.

Marketing Her Signs

LUCINDA FOUND herself doing monthly wholesale craft shows and soon had sales reps trying to distribute her products. At one point she had three different sales reps working for her. She sold coat racks, little cabinets, towel bars, and small household items made of pine or white birch with her painted artwork on them. Lucinda supported her family for four years with these products, only periodically receiving child support from the children's fathers.

Walt Disney, Long's Drugs, and assorted catalogs wanted her products, but Lucinda didn't have enough money to go bigger. "I didn't have someone with enough experience to say, 'We'll rent a big building and fill it with tools and we'll hire people.' I just had to stop. The business was out of control," says Lucinda. At this point she was completely burned out.

Learning from Her Mistakes

IN RETROSPECT, Lucinda realized, "The product was almost too nice. It didn't look handmade." Lucinda decided to learn from

her past mistakes instead of letting them get her down. She started to look for something that required low overhead and less time to make.

Finding a New Product

WHILE LOOKING for the new product, Lucinda also looked for a regular job. Her small town didn't have much to offer in the way of jobs. For a while she had a landscaping/housekeeping business. Her friendship with one set of clients eventually led to a new career. For a Christmas present, Lucinda decided to give them a birdhouse she had made from tree trunks, branches, limbs, acorns, and moss that she had collected in the woods. They loved the gift and asked her if she would make more to put in a store they were affiliated with in San Francisco. For a year the store bought every birdhouse she made, sight unseen, and sold them all. Lucinda says, "I thought, 'My prices are too low, and if they can sell them that well, I want to try selling them myself.'" Lucinda had found her new product.

Equipment

MAKING THESE birdhouses requires no real overhead. Lucinda is always respectful of nature, and she finds most of her supplies in the forest. "I do not cut down trees, with the exception of small dead trees, but never hollow ones, or what are known as 'critter homes.' I get a lot of stuff in areas where loggers have been, where the forest has been trashed and left."

A few years back Lucinda purchased a computer that she uses for her mailing lists and invoices. Her other supplies include a compressor, air gun, and assorted shop equipment. When she first started, she worked from her kitchen table; as her business grew she moved to the garage. For the past six years she has been working from a barn.

Marketing

A T THE first craft show where Lucinda sold her birdhouses, she sold out completely. She says, "I found this to be very empowering." So she started to do more shows and quit wholesaling all together. She mainly went to juried craft shows, which "generally have a lot better reputation and higher-quality products. They don't allow mass-produced items. You can charge a better price because you get a better audience."

She attends fifteen to eighteen craft shows a year (January through March is her slow time). Lucinda recommends talking to other crafters who have been in the business for a while as the best way to find the best shows.

Lucinda now sells other items, such as gnome houses, paintings, indoor decora-

tions, and toad houses for the garden. But nothing sells nearly as well as her birdhouses. People often tell her she should stick to designing and hire people to make the products, but Lucinda wouldn't be happy not getting her hands dirty.

Today she's getting tired of traveling out of town. "I want to try to develop the wholesaling more. For a long time I didn't want to wholesale, because of the last business." But staying up late to pack the truck and leaving at four in the morning to make a show is getting old. She's also staying away from sales reps. She says, "I figure if I'm selling everything that I'm making right now, I should just rely on myself and sell them this way. It's less stressful because when you start having to fill orders it may be something you don't really like to make, plus you have to pay a commission to the sales rep and meet deadlines."

Rates

L UCINDA HAS hired two or three part-time workers to help out. She doesn't have to worry about storing her products because she can't make them fast enough. Sizes vary, and prices range from $26 to $300 per birdhouse, with the average birdhouse selling for between $37 to $50.

She has doubled her prices since she began. "I thought I was making a pretty decent wage for myself. People said, 'You've got to raise your prices if you're selling out that quickly.'" She raised the price until she didn't hear comments like that anymore, but for a while she set her prices too high. Eventually, she found her correct price through trial and error.

Biggest Challenge

DURING HER first year with the craft shows, Lucinda didn't know the ropes and had to talk her way into shows by showing the sponsors her product or asking if someone had canceled so she could take the spot. It took her about three years to get the scheduling down to apply for the shows on time.

Her greatest challenge, however, is having to apply and pay for craft shows—between $125 and $200, six to nine months in advance. "After two or three years I had a circuit of shows that were good." For many years someone who was sympathetic to her cause paid for the shows, and she later paid them back. This is the first year she has been able to pay for the shows on her own.

Rewards

"MY CHILDREN do have a sense of survival in a way they wouldn't have if I was just working for someone else,"

Lucinda says. She adds that she could never afford to stop to think how hard it really was. She admits she would have just cried. "I always looked forward and didn't spend time looking back." Lucinda has chosen to rise and meet the occasion without complaint.

Lucinda's Advice

FIND SOMETHING *that works for you. And once you make your mind up to start a business, you can do it. You don't need a $10,000 loan or a computer. Start out small; that's what I did. I started on welfare, and as I made more money my welfare check got smaller. I remember the day when I said, I don't need you guys anymore. That's not to say I wasn't afraid or doubtful. I just didn't want to be on welfare, so you need to have that motivation.*

Start with something and build on it. You can start off the kitchen table if you need to; that's the way I did it. Many times people give a lot of excuses, but it's a form of procrastination. Just do one thing, something to get your business going. Just don't think about it; do it. The last six years I worked in a barn. That's what I had, so that's what I used.

Watch other people who are successful

"My children do have a sense of survival in a way they wouldn't have if I was just working for someone else."

---

and see what they are doing. Use them as role models. You have just as much ability as anyone else. You will make mistakes; just learn from them. Don't be intimidated; just try it another way. Find the resources you need to get your business off the ground.

Recommended Resources

LUCINDA SAYS, "I try to rely on my own resourcefulness, because that's what gives the things I make their uniqueness. But I do try to keep abreast of what's current."

BOOKS AND AUDIOTAPES

- Paul Pilzer, *Unlimited Wealth*. New York: Crown, 1991.

- Clara Pinkola-Estes, Ph.D., *Women Who Run with the Wolves*. New York: Ballantine, 1992.

- Anthony Robbins, "Power Talk" (tape series), and *Awaken the Giant Within You* (book). New York: Summit Books, 1993.

- Marianne Williamson, *A Woman's Worth* (book and tape). New York: Ballantine, 1994.

CHILD-CARE PROVIDER

Name: Karen Potter
Location: Houston, Texas
Family Facts: Married, two children—
    Mike, 13, and Amy, 10
Business: Learning Train
Web Site: http://www.thepotters.com/
    ltrain.html

Why She Started Her Business

KAREN STARTED out as a geophysicist processing seismic data for petroleum companies. But in 1986 she decided she wanted to work at home so she could be with her kids. The decision to stay at home wasn't an easy financial step. "It was a major drop in pay. We lived off our savings until we got the business going."

Starting Her Business the First Time Around

KAREN ADMITS, "My first attempt at child care was a major flop." For the first year, Karen approached her business as if the parents and the children in her care were her employers. She had no written ground rules. It was as though everyone was running Karen's business but her. This led to a very bad consequence. One of the toddlers Karen cared for was using a bottle with a very old nipple. Karen mentioned this to the parents, but they paid no attention. Soon after, as the little girl was drinking from her bottle, the tip of the nipple broke off and lodged in her throat. Fortunately, Karen was right there and saw everything—but not before the child turned blue and had to be given the Heimlich maneuver for children.

Giving It a Second Try

FOR SIX months Karen quit the childcare business. She looked into working for a large day-care center, but she didn't like the idea of her children being separated in-to different age groups. She felt that sharing common experiences is part of being a family.

After careful thought, Karen decided she would give child care in her home another chance. Only this time it would be different. First, she joined her local child-care association. "I made a lot of phone calls to other day-care providers to see what they were charging, what their guidelines were, and what types of services they offered families." She took a survey of everyone's policies and adjusted them to fit her business and her family.

This time she wrote up all her policies and had each parent sign them. She had

118

medical release forms, forms required by the state, and an ID for each child. She had insurance forms, general consent forms, an outline of meals served, and her own personal child-care philosophies written out. She outlined the types of products she used, right down to diaper cream. A parent who wasn't comfortable with the product could specify something different and bring it.

Qualifications

STATE REGULATIONS differ. Some states require child-care operators to have a high school diploma. Depending on the requirements of your particular state, each year you may be expected to complete 20 hours of continuing education. This can include CPR, first-aid training, and workshops given by the child-care association. It's certainly important to have an understanding of children and child development, as well as a fair amount of patience. Karen says, "It takes self-discipline to leave the TV alone and pay attention to the kids. We are talking child care here, not baby-sitting." It's very important to have some sort of support network, particularly another day-care provider.

Equipment

SOME STATES require safety equipment. If you already have children, you may find you have already taken care of many of the requirements. All family members and pets have to have their immunizations, and family members over the age of 18 will need to undergo a criminal history background check.

Marketing

INITIALLY, KAREN put up flyers about her child-care business in grocery stores and at schools. Today, most of her business comes from referrals, and a few years ago she stopped advertising altogether. She usually has a waiting list of one to three families.

Rates

KAREN REQUIRES parents to pay for all care one week in advance. Then, if a parent stops showing up without notice, she still has that week paid for. Karen has also run into parents who stop paying. She tells them that she has a waiting list and, if they can't pay at the end of the week, they will have to give up their spot to a paying customer.

"It takes self-discipline to leave the TV alone and pay attention to the kids. We are talking child care here, not baby-sitting."

Expanding the Business

KAREN HAS gone way beyond her orig-inal business. She now offers a computer camp, teaching children basic computer pro-gramming and how to write HTML code for Web sites. She has also become a child-care consultant, teaching classes for women who want to start child-care businesses of their own. Karen also writes a quarterly newsletter for child-care providers called the *Learning Train News*. Each issue contains pertinent information that every provider can use, such as fire and bus safety and craft ideas.

Karen also teaches CPR/first-aid training classes to other day-care providers. She re-ceived her training from the American Heart Association and has been very pleased with the support they offer. To become a certified trainer, she had to have had a CPR card for two years, get her health-care provider CPR card, then take a 2 to 3 day class to become a CPR instructor.

Karen has not needed to aggressively market herself. Instead, her local child-care council has what's called a training coalition calendar. This calendar includes classes that would be helpful for any day-care provider. CPR/first-aid training is a must-have for all providers. All of Karen's classes are filled with people who call her asking for CPR and first-aid instruction. Karen receives $25 per person and averages fifteen students per class, which lasts 2 to 3 hours. She is able to hold classes when she wants, such as after school or on weekends, and averages four to five classes a month. Total investment for starting this type of business is around $2,000. You'll need to buy your own man-nequin and books and pay fees for classes. Although Karen doesn't actively advertise her classes, that doesn't mean you can't. Many teachers actively call businesses to see if they'd be interested in a CPR/first-aid class.

There are two major organizations that offer certification programs: the American Heart Association and the Red Cross. Karen recommends investigating both options and checking what fees you'll have to pay per per-son when you hold a class. Also, check if you are given free supplies such as brochures and additional information for your students.

Tips

- Karen recommends the importance of joining a day-care association. "I proba-bly wouldn't have made it without the association." If you don't have an associ-ation in your town, start one. "Even if it's three ladies who meet once a month to have coffee; that's all it takes," says Karen.

- Put your policies in writing and adjust them to fit your family's needs. For example, when Karen's husband came home from work, he wasn't able to park his car in his spot because it was usually at a busy time when parents came to pick up their kids. So Karen added in her pol-icy that no client was to park in that

When you're running a child-care business, you can't forget your own kids.

parking spot. It hasn't been a problem since. "If there is something that is bugging a family member, adjust your policy for your family. This business is so you can be home with your family. Don't make your family pay for it."

- Keep good tax records. "You can deduct a percentage of your gas, electric, water, and trash bill. Talk with your accountant about a time-space percentage."

- Every day Karen sets a goal to spend special time with each child who comes through her door. "I make it a point every day to spend quality time with every child in my care, whether that means clipping their fingernails, reading them a book, or patting them on the back when they're trying to get to sleep. Sometime during the day I have at least five minutes of one-on-one with every child."

- Each state has regulations you need to follow to run a qualified child-care center. Some states have many rules, whereas others have very few. Try to make it your goal to go above and beyond the call of duty. If your state doesn't require you to have a background check, get one anyway. State in your brochure that you have done everything possible to put the parents' minds at ease.

- Offer child care during times that other providers usually close, such as at night or on the weekends.

- Offer a program specifically for the stay-at-home mom who needs to get out a few days a week for errands or to just get some work done at home without children. Have the kids meet three times a week for a three-hour session that offers games, crafts, and interaction with other kids.

Mixing Kids and Business

WHEN YOU'RE running a child-care business, you can't forget your own kids. Most of the children Karen cares for are very close in age to her kids. Karen's rule is that all child-care children stay on the first floor of her two-story house. If Karen's children want to be alone, they can go upstairs and play. She also provides a special snack for her kids after school that they take to their bedrooms.

Rewards

KAREN SAYS, "I don't think I could ever work for someone else. It would be hard to go back to work and be a geophysicist again. [I don't miss] the politics, backstabbing, and ladder climbing. You're the boss. There's nobody higher. If a parent really gives you a problem and you can't work it out, you can give them two weeks' notice."

Karen's Advice

Look at what you like to do and what you want to do for the rest of your life. If you could do anything and money was not a concern, what would that be? Then try to find a way to turn that into a business.

Recommended Resources

KAREN PUBLISHES a newsletter for child-care providers. If you would like more information about her newsletter and the other resources she offers, send a self-addressed, stamped envelope to ABC's of Home Childcare, 15810 Crystal Grove, Houston, TX 77082.

ORGANIZATIONS

*   National Association for Family Child Care (NAFCC)
    725 15th Street, NW, Suite 505
    Washington, D.C. 20005
    1-800-359-3817

Offers accreditation, support, and a monthly newsletter for home child-care providers. This political group works to improve child care for both providers and children and covers other important children's issues.

*   National Association for the Education of Young Children (NAEYC)
    1509 16th Street, NW
    Washington, D.C. 20036-1426
    1-800-424-2460

    This organization offers a trade magazine, training, and accreditation for center-based child care.

*   CHILDHELP
    National Abuse Hotline
    1-800-4-A-CHILD

    This is a national number that you can call to report suspected child abuse.

*   The Children's Foundation
    725 15th Street, NW, Suite 505
    Washington, D.C. 20005
    1-202-347-3300

    This organization is involved in child-care studies and research. Karen recommends that a provider request a listing of child-care publications.

WEB DESIGNER

Name: Jennifer Czawlytko
Location: Baltimore, Maryland
Family Facts: Married, three children—Brandon, 13, Michael, 9, and Christopher, 7
Business: webJENerations
Web Site:
http://www.webjenerations.com

Why She Started Her Business

JENNIFER ACTUALLY started out running a desktop-publishing business from home. However, while creating a Web site for her business, she began to fall in love with Web design. This wasn't an overnight discovery, however. As Jennifer explains, "At first, I didn't even consider changing to Web design as my business because I had chosen DTP [desktop publishing] and wanted to stick with it. I didn't feel I was experienced or knowledgeable enough to be a quality Web designer." However, she soon found herself teaching other home-business owners how to create their own Web sites through chats at the iVillage forum on AOL. "After six months of teaching others, learning more about Web design, and a whole lot of urging from my friends and family, I decided to take the leap and change the focus of my business. It is a change I could not be happier with, I truly love what I am doing now," says Jennifer.

Qualifications

TO GET started you'll need a good foundation in HTML, the ability to install and edit CGI scripts (or being able to write in Perl), as well as a good knowledge of marketing on the Internet. Although you can find courses in the above subjects, you can also learn many things on the Internet for free or at a very low cost. Jennifer is entirely self-taught and believes a college degree is not necessary. Jennifer explains, "It is very important when entering this field to be sure you love to learn. A day in the life of a designer is a constant learning experience, and you need to be willing to go out there and find the information you need to stay on top of the latest Internet developments."

Start-up Costs

JENNIFER'S START-UP costs were around $500 because she already had a computer and Internet access. She has since put more money into her business as she added equipment along the way—a scanner, several Internet software programs, a graph-

123

ics program, a larger and higher-quality monitor, as well as high-speed access to the Internet. Although not all of these things are necessary, they do help in productivity and the services you can offer your clients. You may want to consider the cost of taking a few classes in Web designer (although all of Jennifer's training has come from online resources and books). If you are starting from scratch, you would be looking at about $3,000 in initial expenses, depending on the equipment you decide to use and the courses you take either online or through a local community college or adult-learning classes.

Equipment

JENNIFER RECOMMENDS a computer, a good quality monitor, a scanner, reliable Internet access, a quality graphics program, an HTML editing software package, and FTP software.

SOFTWARE AND INTERNET TIPS

• Claris Home Page, Microsoft Front Page—"I actually feel that choosing an HTML editor is really a personal choice; your decision will depend upon how much you already know about HTML, how much you are willing to learn, and how easy you want things to be for you," explains Jen. Also, most commercial packages offer free trials before you buy. This is a great way to try out either of these programs before you buy.

• Free Web site software programs include AOLPress (www.aolpress.com/), Arachnophilia (www.arachnoid.com/arachnophilia/), and WebWerx (www.litewerx.dk/programs.html). A great site for accessing the many different free editors out there is free-4-u (members.tripod.com/asfreeware/htmleds.html).

• If you're looking for graphics and icons, check out ArtToday (www.arttoday.com/). The cost is $30 for an annual subscription, but the graphics can be used for commercial purposes without any special copyrights, and the selection is amazing. Another site to check out is Desktop Publishing (www.desktoppublishing.com/).

• When searching for graphics on the Web, be sure to follow the Web site's rules on using the graphics—many people put a great deal of time into creating those graphics, and their requests for credit should be honored. Also, some free sites do not allow their graphics to be used on commercial Web sites, so be sure to read the fine print.

Rates

FIGURING OUT what to charge can always be a challenge. Jennifer first looked around on the Internet to see what other designers were charging. She saw some people charge as high as $150 an hour and as low has $20 an hour. Jennifer feels her rates

---

Some free sites do not allow their graphics to be used on commercial Web sites, so be sure to read the fine print.

---

are reasonable when compared with her competitors' rates. Because her target market is small and home-based business, she strives to make her prices affordable for her market. "It's important to avoid undervaluing your services, but at the same time you do not want to set your rates so high that you put yourself out of the grasp of your target market," says Jennifer, who charges anywhere from $45 to $65 per hour depending on the services her clients need. She explains, "Easier tasks such as HTML would be on the lower end of the range and more advanced tasks such as working with CGI programming would be on the higher end."

Marketing

MOST OF Jennifer's advertising comes from word of mouth. For some time, she held a chat on how to design a Web page, but many people found that HTML wasn't for them and asked if she would do this for them. As a result of this development, she now has one large account and a few other solid clients, which produce more than enough work and referrals for her.

Jennifer's future marketing plan does not include a sprawling office building filled with designers or a marketing department. She wants her business to continue to be something she can handle as much on her own as possible, simply because she does not want to work outside the home while her boys are young. However, if her business continues to grow at its current rate, she will eventually need to contract out some of her work.

If you have bigger plans than Jennifer has, you will need to have a strong Internet presence, solid references, a portfolio of your work both online and offline, as well as the ability to network within your local community. Jennifer says, "While that may sound expensive, it doesn't have to be. Take advantage of low-cost and free advertising such as press releases, Internet directories, affiliate and reciprocal link-type programs for your Web site, local TV and radio appearances, etc."

Mixing Kids and Business

WHEN JENNIFER started working at home, her boys were all attending school. But there are times when they are home from school or it's summer—times when she would love to have them give her a few minutes to herself. She does her best to work primarily when they are in school or in bed. "When the weather is warmer, I can also work a bit in the evenings, since they are

Make sure you have a clear contract, signed and dated, before you do any work on a project.

outside playing in the yard much of the time, but in the winter I have to cut back on that a bit. I do try to keep business contacts to the daytime while my children are in school. I design at different times of the day, depending on how busy I am and my children's activities," explains Jennifer.

Tips

CREATE A support network and meet other Web designers. The support network is vital for those days when things are not going right or [when] your family may not be the most supportive. Getting to know other Web designers can help when you run into a Web site problem that you need help with. I have been very lucky in my interactions with my fellow designers in the fact that we are not a competitive bunch. We may be looking for clients in the same markets, but we respect one another for our strengths and lean on one another in our times of weakness.

Biggest Challenge

JENNIFER HAS found client contracts, billing, and time management to be her biggest challenges. "The tedious task of billing is a particular problem I am working

on. I do not enjoy it and it is a chore for me," says Jennifer. Although she keeps impeccable records of everything she does on a Web site, it's the process of transferring all of it into her accounting program in order to produce a detailed bill that gets to her. Jennifer knows that working on her time management would help. She explains, "I need to become more schedule-oriented with the portions of the business which I do not particularly enjoy. As far as the contracts, I do well with them now, but in the beginning I was bit too naive and trusting, so I was taken for a ride a time or two." Her advice is to make sure you have a clear contract, signed and dated, before you do any work on a project.

Rewards

THE FIRST reward that came to her mind was the big boom to her self-esteem. She says, "Never in a million years would I have ever believed I could be a businesswoman. I can honestly say Web design is one of the few things I truly believe I am good at. There is nothing like that feeling of pride when you overcome a new problem with a Web site, or overhearing someone raving about a site you designed (not realizing of course that the designer is standing nearby). I have also been extremely lucky in being able to redesign and maintain the Bizy Moms Web site, watching the site grow and change, and seeing all the people who have been helped by it is just amazing to me." Every day Jennifer finds a new roadblock that she has to find a way through. However, due to her rise in self-confidence, she knows she can overcome it, which feeds her thirst to learn new things.

Jennifer's Advice

I KNOW IT *is a cliche, but "Choose something you love!" I hope as you have read this portion of Liz's book, you have picked up on the fact that I love what I do. Loving Web design is what gives me the drive to get through the most difficult of problems and gives me the biggest rewards when things are going right. You truly need to enjoy what you are doing to be willing to work hard at it when you work from home. Working at home offers you so many rewards, but it also has its distractions, and it is really easy to let your business slide. Enjoying what you are doing gives you the desire to succeed and to pick yourself up and dust yourself off if you have slipped a bit.*

Recommend Resources

ORGANIZATIONS

* The HTML Writer's Guild (www.hwg.org/) Membership is free or low-cost, depending on what level you join. The Web site also includes some great resources.

BOOKS

* Paul McFedries, *The Complete Idiot's Guide to Creating HTML 4 Web Pages.* Indianapolis, Ind.: QUE Education & Training, 1997.

* Laura LeMay, *Web Publishing with HTML 4 in a Week.* Indianapolis, Ind.: Sams, 1998.

ONLINE RESOURCES

Once you have the basics down, check out these resources on the Web:

* Webmonkey: http://www.webmonkey.com/

* Web Developers Virtual Library: http://www.stars.com/WDVL/

* Webreference.com: http://webreference.com/

* CNET Builder.com: http://www.builder.com/

* Web Pages That Suck: http://www.webpagesthatsuck.com
  The title may sound bad, but the site truly does have some fantastic design tips for making Web sites look better.

LISTSERVS

* The Web Developers Mailing List (WDVL; www.stars.com/WDVL/Forum/) is a forum for beginner to advanced Web developers to interact and learn from one another.

GRAPHIC ARTIST/DESKTOP PUBLISHER

Name: Julia Tavis
Location: La Habra, California
Family Facts: Married, three children—Miriam, 9, Marjorie, 7, and Montana, 4
Business: Got-A-Vision Graphics
Web Site: http://www.gotavision.com

Why She Started Her Business

JULIA DECIDED to quit working when her first child was born, but she found that she missed her artwork. She still wanted to be a full-time mom, but she also wanted to do some freelance work. She opened Got-A-Vision Graphics, a home-based desktop publishing business, when her daughter was 5 months old. After a couple of years, her second baby was born. Julia continued to run the business, for a total of four years, and kept very busy, but her business eventually got out of hand. "By the time my second daughter was 1½, the chaos had totally gotten to me. My business was running me, and I closed up shop, literally, overnight."

What happened? "My clients' needs were being met before my family's, and this was not my goal." Some of the pandemonium included customers coming over at 11:00 at night to drop off work. "I just didn't have the experience at that point to say, 'Listen, my hours are from this time to this time. If you need this done right away, you're going to have to wait until the morning.'"

Giving It a Second Try

WHEN HER third child was a newborn and her two older girls were in school, Julia's finances needed a boost. "I decided to give Got-A-Vision another try, but with new ground rules this time. I decided that I would run my business. It wouldn't run me again." Her children were 1, 5, and 7 years old when she started her business again.

At first, business was slow and part time. She would work during nap times and would use videos to keep her kids busy when she had to meet her deadlines. That was three years ago. "I have taken on increasingly challenging projects and have discovered, over the last year or so, that I am actually quite good at what I do. When I compare my work to the big businesses in my area, I'm right up there. It is very satisfying for me and exciting to see the progress, too. I love what I do and I know that's the key to my success." All her past experience has paid off. Julia produces anything that can be printed: newsletters, logos, graphic designs, and camera-ready artwork. And she does all of this from her dining room.

Qualifications

JULIA SAYS, "I started out learning my trade in high school. I was on the newspaper staff and began to learn typesetting and paste-up, as it was called back then." She designed ads and worked on the production art for her high school's paper. At age 16, "I landed my first job in the industry as a paste-up artist for a local classified-ads paper." Julia has worked in five different print shops over the years, where she learned valuable skills in the graphics and printing industry.

Equipment

JULIA'S EQUIPMENT for desktop publishing includes a computer, a scanner, and a fax machine with a dedicated line. Internet access is helpful, too. Julia says, "Online services have been a godsend for me. I learn something new every day." She also recommends the software QuarkXPress, PageMaker, Adobe Illustrator, and Adobe Photo Shop.

Marketing

ALTHOUGH IN the beginning Julia solicited print shops for work, she now receives most of her business through word of mouth. "I didn't market because it would have given me more work than I could handle." Occasionally she will also mail out brochures.

Rates

JULIA CHARGES $60 an hour for design and $75 an hour for writing and editing.

Tips

- Julia realized that no matter how good a graphic artist she is or how well known, "No one is going to remember that; my kids will remember whether I spent time with them or not."

- Julia has a theme that runs throughout her business: "I am committed to honesty and excellent service in all my work, and I have found that my customers appreciate that very much."

- Julia also recommends taking classes in graphic art or desktop publishing from local colleges or adult-learning schools.

"I am committed to honesty and excellent service in all my work, and I have found that my customers appreciate that very much."

- As a graphic designer just starting out, try publishing a newsletter for a church or school you or your children attend.

Julia's Advice

COMPLETE TASKS *in small chunks of time. You have to be able to shift your attention back and forth rapidly. And if you're the type of person who can't do two things at once, you're going to struggle with a home-based business. You're sitting there trying to concentrate on your work and your child comes up and begins to cry. You have to go tend to your child, then you* need to go right back and focus again on what you were doing. That is a skill that does take time.

Recommended Resources

BOOKS

- Louise Kursmark, *How to Start a Home-Based Desktop Publishing Business*. Old Saybrook, Conn.: Globe Pequot Press, 1996.

- Jan Melnik, *How to Start a Home-Based Secretarial Services Business*. Old Saybrook, Conn.: Globe Pequot Press, 1994.

CHILDBIRTH INSTRUCTOR

Name: Sabrina Cuddy
Location: Palo Alto, California
Family Facts: Married, two children—
　　Megan, 5, and Phelon, 3
Business: Bradley Childbirth Instructor
Web Site: http://www.fensende.com/
　　Users/swnymph

Why She Started Her Business

SABRINA WAS close to finishing her master's degree in public health education from the University of California, Berkeley, when she found that out she was pregnant with her first child. She didn't want to give up on her education, but she also wanted to stay home to raise her baby, so she looked for other options.

Sabrina was taking birthing classes in the Bradley method and thought she might like to become a Bradley instructor. Four months later she endured a long, hard labor that resulted in a cesarean section. The birth of her second child also required a cesarean. Still, Sabrina has been teaching the Bradley method for 2½ years and really enjoys it.

Qualifications

SABRINA SAYS, "I started the program, which consists of reading and summarizing about ten books and attending a four-day series of workshops." After each class, she would submit a report to the National Bradley Workshop program. Her final test consisted of actually teaching a class (which she was able to charge for). At the end of that class, her students evaluated her. She was then given her final written exam. After becoming fully certified, "I could then be included in the National Bradley Teachers' Directory." Depending on your personal schedule, the Bradley training program can be completed in a year. Continuing education is required annually of all affiliated Bradley childbirth educators.

Sabrina is also a doula. "Doulas are often women who have had a lousy birth and want to save others from their fate. If you have a strong mothering and protective instinct and are able to give control to the person who is laboring and be a calming influence when things don't go well, then you are ready to be a doula." Good communication skills are important, as is the ability to talk to the doctors. She has been a labor assistant at nine births so far. "That requires

"If you have a strong mothering and protective instinct and are able to give control to the person who is laboring and be a calming influence when things don't go well, then you are ready to be a doula."

a very flexible sitter, though, since you never know when you may be called for a delivery. There are many false labors and running back and forth, and then the real labor, which can last anywhere from a few hours to twenty-four hours."

Start-up Costs

IT TOOK $1,000 for Sabrina to start her business, "which is nothing compared to starting a small business that requires renting office space." Her supplies include videos and required workbooks for her students. The training program costs $695, and the books come to about $100. If money is tight you can sometimes borrow books from other Bradley instructors in your area.

Equipment

SABRINA USES half of her family room strictly for her classes. She keeps all of her teaching materials, TV, VCR, and books in that room.

Rates

THE CLASSES Sabrina teaches last from eight to twelve weeks and meet two evenings a week in her home. She averages five couples per class. Bradley instructors charge anywhere from $100 to $200 per couple, depending on the geographic location. Doulas can charge anywhere from $200 to $400 per birth, again depending on location. Sabrina charges from $300 to $400.

Scheduling

BECAUSE THESE classes are in the evening, Sabrina's husband or other family members watch the kids while she teaches. This way she doesn't have to worry about paying a baby-sitter. She says, "Remember to take into account that you make a lot less if you have to pay someone [to watch your kids]." If you do decide to become a doula, it's important to have a backup who can teach your classes, because, should you get called for doula duty, it's very hard to reschedule that missed class.

Marketing

SABRINA'S MARKETING doesn't cost her much. She belongs to a local Bradley group, which does some advertising for her. The American Academy of Husband Coached Childbirth (AAHCC) lists her with the directory of teachers, and she is listed in pamphlets sponsored and widely distributed by the Bay Area Birth Instructors. She also puts up posters and brochures at local obstetricians' offices and has her own Web page.

Sabrina finds that sometimes she has more couples than she can teach; other times she has a tough time finding enough couples to teach a class to. "You can see that this is a job that adds money to a family with a primary wage earner, not a job that can really support a family."

Mixing Kids and Business

AS CHILDBIRTH classes are all about kids, Sabrina doesn't have much of a problem with her students calling when the kids are awake. "I work on the assumption that either I am talking to a person who has kids or one who is going to. I figure it's a reality thing." She does have a portable phone and an answering machine. If she receives an urgent message, she always calls back, "regardless of the environment at my house. Otherwise I wait for nap time or a calm moment."

Sabrina's Advice

I THINK *there are a lot of home businesses that can work for a woman with children, but you need something that you can do in the odd hours, unless you have a regular sitter. I have seen moms who have tried to start a business at home, but who find the income too irregular. Somebody with more perseverance or who needs less money might do better.*

Recommended Resources

Organizations Bradley and Doula Training Workshops

- American Academy of Husband Coached Childbirth (AAHCC)
  P.O. Box 5224
  Sherman Oaks, CA 91413-5224
  1-800-4-A-BIRTH or 1-818-788-6662

- International Childbirth Education Association (ICEA)
  P.O. Box 20048
  Minneapolis, MN 55420

- Doulas of North America (DONA)
  1100-23rd Avenue, East
  Seattle, WA 98112
  1-206-324-5440

- ALACE
  P.O. Box 382724
  Cambridge, MA 02238
  1-617-441-2500

MAGAZINES

- *Mothering*, which presents a natural view on parenting.

ACCOUNTANT

Name: Victoria Phillips
Location: Loudon, New Hampshire
Family Facts: Married, three children—
    Andrew, 11, Nathan, 9, and
    Aimee, 7
Business: Victoria L. Phillips, C.P.A.

Why She Started Her Business

In HIGH school Victoria knew she wanted to be an accountant. She also knew that when she had children she wanted to be home with them. Says Victoria, "I'm a very goal-oriented person. I have these goals set in my mind and I usually go for it."

After graduating from college with a degree in accounting and a minor in computer science, Victoria took her accounting certification test and then worked for an accounting firm for two years to acquire her public accounting license. Victoria started her business very slowly. She did her first tax return in 1987, and then went a whole year with just that one client. Today, she has about sixty clients.

Qualifications

To REALLY enjoy the work of an accountant, you should enjoy and be good at math. You should also be a detail person who, at the same time, can step back to look at the whole picture. "I find a lot of accountants are perfectionists," explains Victoria, who also believes you should excel at listening to the needs of your clients. "I'll sit down and talk to my clients and sometimes I feel like a psychiatrist."

Victoria says, "The way I started out was really small, but my children were also very small. As my family grew, it gave me more free time. If someone were to start out without children, it would be a whole different ball game. So I guess from that perspective it was the best way to grow my business. I could then develop my own style and develop my own business as my children grew up. If your children are older, then you may want to jump in and do more advertising."

Start-up Costs

Because Victoria sells a service and not products, her start-up costs were small. "I basically had to buy a few office supplies, copier, and adding machine, but

To really enjoy the work of an accountant, you should enjoy and be good at math. You should also be a detail person.

with my first tax return, I didn't have any equipment at all." Her office also doubled as the family's dining room table for a while. This was difficult because at mealtimes she had to put everything away, then get everything out when she needed to work again. A few years into the business, she realized that once she got all her office supplies, her expenses would be pretty much the same every year no matter how many clients she had.

Equipment

VICTORIA'S EQUIPMENT includes a computer, a printer, a copier, a couple of calculators, letterhead, and bookshelves. Every year Victoria has to take forty hours of continuing-education classes that cost $600, and she must buy a yearly tax guidebook that costs $500.

Rates

COMPARED WITH other C.P.A.'s, Victoria considers her hourly rate low. "Because I do it here at home, there are some things my clients may not get. They don't get a secretary answering the phone; they get me or my kids." She started charging only $35

an hour, but later raised it to $40 once she got her computer.

During tax season Victoria works thirty to forty hours a week. The rest of the year she works between five and ten hours a week. How much you make depends entirely on how much you work, how you market your business, and how many clients you end up having.

Marketing

VICTORIA HAS tried several different ways to advertise her business. She runs an ad in a local business paper and lists her name in the yellow pages. This past year she sent out a direct mailing of postcards to 400 people, which cost her about $600. Her target market was small businesses. She ended up getting one client out of it. "But the one client I got, I billed more than what I spent on the whole mailing."

About four years ago, Victoria helped start a local business association. One of the things it does is publish a quarterly newsletter. Victoria has a column in the newsletter where she gives tax tips. "I think it's great promotion, and I did get new clients from it." Victoria caters mostly to small business—family businesses, sole proprietorships, and partnerships in small corporations owned by one or two people.

Working Hours

VICTORIA HAS no set business hours, especially during tax season, when it can get a little crazy. "I have such a wide range of clients that there are some who can't see me other than on an evening or on a Saturday. Whatever fits for both of us, that's what we work in." She does, however, try to keep Sundays reserved for her family.

Tips

• Victoria explains that there are times when she doesn't get paid for her services. She has even had to take someone to court or has had to deal with a client who declared bankruptcy. This is not an area she enjoys. "You don't let someone continue to use your service if they aren't paying past bills. While this seems like common sense, I am a very trusting person." She finally started to get tough with clients; she now explains that although she wants to continue to work for them, they have to pay before she will continue her service. "This seemed to be pretty effective; just be calm about it and explain you can't do any more work until you're paid. They seem to respect that."

• "Keep a good reputation. Keep your customers pleased so they'll tell other people what a good job you've done. I think that in the beginning you have to give a little more to get people interested. You almost have to have that lower rate."

• "It really makes a difference if you can have a separate work space." Now that Victoria has her own office, she finds she can leave everything as it is and go make dinner and come back and everything is how she left it. This way she isn't wasting time getting her work ready.

• If she was to do anything over again, she may have spent more time working for somebody else before starting her practice, "just because there is so much to learn in this business." This way she would have had more exposure to the different aspects of accounting and more skills going into the business.

• If number crunching is something you enjoy, but you don't have an accounting degree, don't despair. There are many people and small businesses in need of a bookkeeper.

Mixing Kids and Business

WHEN THE kids were younger and Victoria had a large job to work on, she would, on occasion, have her children cared for. She was fortunate to have a neighbor who was very flexible about watching her kids. She says, "If I had a full day's work ahead of me and I knew there was no way I could watch the kids and do that at the same time, that's when I would find someone to watch them."

Biggest Challenge

BECAUSE CLIENTS do come over to the house, things can get a little crazy with her three children. "This year has been much easier because my kids have been in school"; Victoria also tries to schedule many of her appointments while the kids are gone. But inevitably clients do stop in when the kids are around. "A lot of my clients know I work at home and know I have children. I usually tell them that right up front. If they ask me when a good time to come over is, I tell them I have children and I don't mind if they come when they're around, just be aware that they are here." The kids are usually pretty quiet, but there are times when Victoria has to get up to speak with them.

Rewards

VICTORIA BELIEVES it is important to be home for her kids. "Even though I'm busy a lot of the time, I'm still there if they need me. When they come home at three o'clock, they don't go to day care. The kids are very important; they're more important than my job." Victoria also loves the fact that her schedule is flexible. "If I want to take the day off, I can do it."

Victoria's Advice

Make sure you plan well in advance. Try to test the waters and see if you're going to like what you have chosen to do.

Recommended Resources

- Independent Preparers Service (IPS)
  P.O. Box 3069
  Chatsworth, CA 91313-3069
  1-800-442-2477
    Specialized office-supply catalog for accountants.

MEDICAL BILLER

Name: Robin Ferraro
Location: Valley Stream, New York
Family Facts: Divorced and engaged,
    with one son—Frankie, 10
Business: Platinum Billing
Web Site: http://members.aol.com/
    platbill/index.html

Why She Started Her Business

AFTER A lot of research, Robin found that medical billing was an up-and-coming field. Although she had spent twelve years in the health-care industry, she feels that having that experience wasn't all that necessary to start her own billing service, except for the medical terminology she had picked up.

Before Robin officially started her business, she took a class at a local college on how to start a physicians' billing service. Then she took a more advanced class at a different community college. Robin recommends you take as many classes as you can when you're first starting out and continue your education as you run your billing business. (An added plus: While you're learning new information, you're also making your résumé look better and better.)

Robin started out by making her own business cards, getting her "doing business as" (DBA) license, and opening a business checking account. She started her business in August 1997 and didn't get her first client until a year later. However, she was working full time while getting her business off the ground, which is something she recommends to anyone wanting to start a billing service, as it takes time to grow your own billing business. In March 1998 she quit her full-time job, in part because the high cost of day care was eating up her paycheck, but mostly because she was not spending enough time with her son. This gave her the push she needed to put her all into marketing and finding clients. Robin explains, "It took a long time to get clients, and I didn't know where to go to get them." Fortunately this didn't dampen Robin's enthusiasm: Persistence is what made her home business a reality.

Qualifications

THERE IS no certified training needed; however, this doesn't mean you won't need to educate yourself to start this type of business. As Robin explains, "I needed to be completely trained in this field, because, as I later learned, my home-care background only helped me slightly." If she could do it over again, she would have tried to find a part-time job in a doctor's office, even as a receptionist, while she was building her business, just to get the feel of the way a doctor's office works. Robin explains that even if you leave that office, the doctor may hire you down the road or provide references for you.

Robin has mixed feelings about independent study courses that can be taken from home. Be sure you research the company. Make sure it provides you with the support you'll need to ask questions as you learn. Also keep in mind that the billing laws vary from state to state. If the study course isn't in your state, it isn't going to know the rules in your area. If you're looking at a course with the price tag of $5,000, be sure you research what you're going to be getting. Often a company will include the cheapest billing software available ($99), give you old marketing materials and a small training manual, and supply you with leads that aren't really leads. This is why it's so important to talk with other billers who are experienced in the costs of starting up and what's really needed. Robin works in the medical-billing forum on AOL. Be sure to check out this resource (listed at the end of this profile).

Start-up Costs

Robin ESTIMATES she spent between $8,000 to $10,000 on her business. Not all of this was initial expense, but she has added new equipment along the way. Her expenses have included software, hardware, and various office materials.

Equipment

To RUN a billing service, you will need a computer, a stand-alone fax machine, an answering machine, an extra phone, and billing software. Some of the better-known software companies include Lytec, Medisoft, Accumedic, and Santiago, to name just a few.

Rates

ROBIN SAYS that rates vary "based on what service the doctor needs, the types of claims, whether I need to pick up the claims or mail them, the average dollar amount per claim, and what they require of me. Average would be between 4 and 8 percent of collected funds." Robin bills the doctor for payment.

Marketing

When I asked Robin how she got her first client, she immediately responded with a laugh and said, "I begged." Even though that first client didn't pan out, Robin didn't give up. In most cases, when you're starting your billing service, clients will not fall into your lap. There is a signifi-

There is a significant amount of networking involved, which is easier if you decide to specialize in a particular field.

cant amount of networking involved, which is easier if you decide to specialize in a particular field. Robin specialized in working with chiropractors. In Robin's area there was a chiropractic association that met once a month. She set up a table outside of their meeting area four different times. She gave away cookies, held drawings, and networked like crazy, all so the chiropractors would know her billing service was available. At the second meeting, they asked her to give a presentation. The result? A year later, she was still receiving calls for her service. And it was a great experience for Robin.

Although Robin has a Web site for her business (she feels it makes her look even more professional in the eyes of her clients), she realizes it doesn't bring her all that much business. She has a free one-line listing in the yellow pages, sends mailings, and attends as many conferences as she can to network with other business owners. Robin highly suggests that any biller looking to get into the business (or even billing veterans) attend as many conferences and trade shows with the theme of billing or small business as possible. "Expose yourself to everything you possibly can. Network with people in the industry," explains Robin.

Mixing Kids and Business

ROBIN DOES her very best only to work when her son is in school. The only real interference is when she teaches medical-billing classes on the weekends.

Biggest Challenge

ROBIN CLAIMS her biggest challenge has been "getting new clients, of course, and making sure to follow up on everything."

Rewards

WHEN ASKED what her biggest reward was, Robin responds, "Knowing that the money I bring in was because of my hard work."

Robin's Advice

DO IT. *I spent many years with my son in day care and after-school programs. It was hard, and I missed a lot. Now I go on school trips, help with the PTA, sell pizza lunch and ice cream at his school. I wouldn't change it for anything. Also, there is no freedom like being your own boss. But, I*

"When you own your own business, you have to be willing—not that you will—but you have to be willing to work 7 days a week, 24 hours a day, 365 days a year."

---

have always said, when you own your own business, you have to be willing—not that you will—but you have to be willing to work 7 days a week, 24 hours a day, 365 days a year (at least in the beginning!). And when starting your business, research, research, research!

Recommended Resources

ORGANIZATIONS

• American Medical Billers Association (AMBA)

    E-mail Cyndeew@brightok.net for more information.

• National Association of Female Executives (NAFE)
  1-800-634-6233
  http://www.nafe.com/
  nafe@nafe.com

• National Association of Women Business Owners (NAWBO)

1100 Wayne Avenue, Suite 830
Silver Spring, MD 20910
1-800-55-NAWBO
1-301-608-2596
http://www.nawbo.org
national@nawbo.org

MAGAZINES

• *Working Woman,* for its inspiring articles

ONLINE RESOURCES

Robin hosts a chat on America Online every Wednesday at 10 P.M. EST. Every week she deals with a new issue that pertains to billing and brings in guest speakers. Some of the subjects covered are marketing, coding presentations, and holiday ideas. "Whatever the members want to see, I provide them," says Robin. By visiting this area you will be able to hook up with a group of billers who can advise you on the scams that are out there as well. To get there, use keyword "medical billing."

MASSAGE THERAPIST

Name: Theresa Jones
Location: Fort Lauderdale, Florida
Family Facts: Partner, three children—Adria, 11, Jace, 5, and Jared, 3
Business: Licensed massage therapist (L.M.T.)

Why She Started Her Business

I WISH I would have done this earlier," says Theresa, who went back to her office job when her daughter was 5 months old. "I can't even imagine leaving my other kids like that now." Unfortunately at the time, Theresa was talked out of the idea of going to massage school to become a licensed massage therapist (L.M.T.) by her boyfriend and her boss. They told her it would be a big hassle and people would think she was a prostitute. "That taught me a lesson: not to let anybody stand in my way if I felt that strongly about wanting to do something."

After a few years, Theresa knew that becoming an L.M.T. was something she really wanted to do. She signed up for a six-month night-school program. She says, "I worked full time at my billing job from 8:30 A.M. to 5:30 P.M., and class was from 6 P.M. to 10 P.M." At the time she was a single mom with a 3-year-old daughter. "It's very hard to make it as a single parent on a single income," so to make ends meet, Theresa waitressed three nights a week in addition to her full-time job.

Qualifications

WHEN LOOKING for a massage-therapy program, Theresa did some major research. She found some schools to be very commercial, with hardly any emphasis on the healing part of therapy. She talked to graduates of different massage schools to see if they enjoyed the program. Theresa ended up attending a school she liked, even though it didn't offer financial aid. But she felt comfortable with their philosophy.

Start-up Costs

THE TRAINING program cost $3,000, which she paid for with a personal loan. The program was a general massage education course where she was able to earn her L.M.T.

"There are a lot of opportunities out there. . . . You can work in the mornings for a chiropractor three days a week or work in the afternoons for a spa."

Equipment

ONCE THERESA graduated, she purchased a top-of-the-line massage table for $700. "A lot of tables are cheaper, but I got a really good table. That way I knew it would last a long time." Her next purchase would be a pregnancy table. A hole cut out in the middle is lined with mesh webbing that supports the tummy. She also had to buy sheets and towels, massage cream, a bag to tote her supplies in, and a portable cassette player. Theresa likes to play classical music while she gives a massage.

Finding Clients

THERESA NEVER felt comfortable advertising in newspapers—"I didn't [want to] have to worry about weirdos calling up." Theresa belongs to a dog organization called the Doberman Rescue League. She has advertised in its newsletter and has put an ad on her church bulletin board. She also belongs to an organization called International Cesarean Awareness Network, for cesarean-prevention and natural-birth education. She was able to put an ad in its

newsletter as well. Now that she has regular clients, she gets a lot of referrals from her satisfied clients. As Theresa says, "It's mostly word of mouth, and that way it's people I know."

Rates

THERESA CAN work ten to eleven hours a week and make between $250 and $300 per week. In a really good week she has made $500, and in a really slow week she may only make $90. Even though she charges $50 an hour, once you figure in travel time, she averages around $30 an hour.

Her regular clients come to her either once a week or every other week, and some get a massage whenever they can afford it. She does give discounts to her church members and if a husband and wife both use her services. Theresa says, "There are a lot of opportunities out there. . . . You can work in the mornings for a chiropractor three days a week or work in the afternoons for a spa."

Tips

- Look into working for local spas and hotels. Often they hire massage therapists on an on-call basis. Or you can just leave your card with them and explain that travelers are often stressed out and sore from traveling. If their guests are ever in need of a massage, they can give you a call.

- If you want to work for a chiropractor, call to tell them that you are available for work. "I know a lot of moms who will find a chiropractor who needs someone two or three mornings a week for maybe $20 an hour, and they will make a good $200 a week for twelve hours."

- When she can, Theresa goes to the gym to work out. She has found this helps increase her strength and energy level.

Mixing Kids and Business

FINDING CHILD care has been very tricky for Theresa, "because what I do is not a consistent schedule; it's very sporadic and spur of the moment," says Theresa. When she goes out on a call, she relies on relatives and friends to watch the children. Sometimes she trades time with other parents and watches their kids, and then they do the same for her.

Biggest Challenge

THE THING about massage is that it's really hard to do long term, unless you do the lighter work." Because Theresa does the deeper massage work, she finds it's

extremely demanding. Is there a burn-out rate? "I don't think it's so much getting tired of doing massage, it's physical stress." Theresa knows of women who are in their 70s who still give massages. You don't have to just stick with massages. There are reflexology, aromatherapy, and gentler types of massage such as reiki, trager, or shiatsu. "They require less energy output, and they're not really physically demanding."

Rewards

THERESA SAYS, "People know I have kids, and when something happens, they are very understanding. Three weeks ago a dog bit my son. So I had four massages I had to cancel." It took Theresa three weeks to get back on track. Fortunately, she didn't have to worry about a boss firing her for taking the time off to be with her son.

"I've gotten to the point now where I figure the kids have to come first. After my son was bitten, I was a basket case every time I wasn't near him. I had to just cancel all those massages. Yeah, I lost out on a lot of money, but that's life!"

Theresa's Advice

THE PEOPLE *around you have to be supportive. Having moral support is really nice. Make sure you network with other people. Educate yourself to all the possibilities out there. Leave yourself open to say, "If this doesn't work, I can change*

"Be flexible about your vision. Sometimes things don't work out. But don't give up."

this." *Be flexible about your vision. Sometimes things don't work out. But don't give up. If that particular business doesn't work out, there might be something else out there for you."*

Theresa is in the process right now of furthering her education. "I tell everyone I know what I want to do when I grow up. I'm going to go back to school to become a doctor." Her goal is to become a naturopathic doctor.

Recommended Resources

ORGANIZATIONS

• American Massage Therapy Association (AMTS)
    820 Davis Street, Suite 100
    Evanston, IL 60201
    1-804-864-0123
    http://www.natural-connection.com/
        institutes/massage.html

    Through this organization you can get disability and liability insurance. It's not required, but it's nice to have. Because some massage therapists have problems with their arms and hands, it's nice to have the back-up of disability insurance. Members receive newsletters, products, and other massage publications. There is a fee for joining each association. Your state probably has its own massage therapy association.

BOOKS

• Judith McQuown, *Inc. Yourself.* New York: HarperCollins, 1993.

    If you make between $10,000 and $12,000 a year and want to incorporate, read this book.

MAGAZINES

• *Massage.* Written for masseurs and mas-seuses, this magazine is available on newsstands.

ALTERATIONS AND SEWING

Name: Barb Marshall
Location: Pickerington, Ohio
Family Facts: Married, four children—
Sarah, 21, Andy, 19, Emily, 16,
and Donnie, 8
Business: Barb's Alterations and Custom Sewing

Why She Started Her Business

WHEN HER third child was 2, Barb began to feel restless and bored. She loved mothering but felt a need to do something else. Barb had a home economics degree but didn't know how she could use it to start a home business. She says, "I was thinking crafts or something, even though I wasn't any good at them."

Barb shared her desire to start a home business with a friend, who suggested she give alterations a try. Sure, that sounded like a great idea, but Barb lived about ten miles from town. Who would travel all that way to get something altered?

However, she realized, very few people sew anymore. She decided to give it a try. Barb didn't know a whole lot about the business of alterations, "But sure enough, I started to get phone calls." One of her first customer experiences turned out to be a nightmare. One lady wanted ten pairs of pants tapered. When the customer came and picked up her pants, none of them were the way she wanted them. Barb said she would pay for new pants, but all that the lady wanted was her money back. "I think she just felt sorry for me."

At that point most people would throw in the towel and decide that this wasn't going to work out. "Something inside of me, I am sure it was God, had better plans for me." Barb knew giving up wasn't an option. She just needed to get some additional education in alterations.

A little later Barb had a chance of a lifetime. A woman who had no idea that Barb had taken up the business of sewing asked if she wanted to join a tailoring class given by a retired tailor. "It was from that point on that I started to know what I was doing." He taught her all the little tricks of tailoring and how to alter men's suits. She took her husband's clothes to class to practice on. Barb was able to study with this man for two years.

Then an interior decorator asked her to do some drapery work. Barb was a little unsure in this area, but the interior designer was very helpful and gave Barb on-the-job training for a year. By this time, Barb had 300 regular customers. Just at that point, however, she had to move to another town, because her husband was relocated.

When she left her customers, Barb says, "They all cried, because they depend on you after a while." She didn't know a soul in her new town, but she ran a $2 ad in the local paper and went to local dry cleaners to solicit work. "I'm very bold. I just walked in the cleaners and asked if they needed any help. They hired me right on the spot." She also picked up the phone book and did some telemarketing. She explained she was new in town and that she did alterations. Some kept her number and called when they needed her service. At one point she had between 500 and 600 customers.

Qualifications

TO START a business like Barb's you should know basic alterations. She recommends taking some tailoring classes and says it's helpful to know how to do drapery alterations. You may be able to find these classes at sewing machine stores. Barb recommends that you be able to sew quickly and accurately.

Start-up Costs

BECAUSE BARB already owned her sewing machine, she didn't have to worry about putting a lot of money into her business. When she did finally purchase another sewing machine two years into the business, she spent $800 on a floor model that would normally cost $1,600. If she were to start her business all over again, she would start with a better machine in the first place. Her serger cost $700. Her other supplies include zippers, buttons, and the industrial-size spools of thread that she purchases through a mail-order catalog. You will also need a vendor's license for tax purposes. Although she does have a simple sign on her property that helps customers easily find her home, she has never had any problems with zoning laws.

Equipment

BARB HAS found that if you buy a quality sewing machine you can accomplish more in a short amount of time. She started out with her basic Kenmore sewing machine. After a few years it died. "I overworked it," says Barb with a laugh. On a tip from a

---

Barb recommends that you be able to sew quickly and accurately.

---

repairman, Barb purchased a Pfaff and cut her hours from forty to thirty for the same amount of work. She also recommends having a serger to give your clothes a more manufactured look. Also, a full-length mirror comes in handy when fitting people.

Working Hours

CUSTOMERS WHO come either to pick up or drop off clothing come by appointment, but Barb is flexible with the times. Some come during the day, others on evenings and weekends. Her turnaround time is two days. Barb has no set working hours. "I'm a workaholic. If I'm not sewing I'm writing, cleaning, doing something with the kids, or involved with a project with the church."

Rates

BARB FIGURED out how to charge by calling other sewing and alteration businesses. Then she knocked a couple of dollars off what they charged. Barb charges a flat rate for alterations and $10 to $15 per hour for custom sewing. If she felt the need, she could easily expand her business and have employees work for her. She averages about $600 a month and knows she could easily make $1,000 if she was willing to work more hours. But she is very happy with her income. She has even slowed down to start working on a writing career.

Marketing

ACCORDING TO Barb, if your customers are happy with your work, they'll come back and they'll tell their friends about you. Barb hasn't needed to advertise for years now—she has plenty of work to keep her busy. She has even had people travel thirty or forty miles for her service.

Tips

- Barb guarantees all her work. "If I make any kind of mistake or they don't like it, I'll redo it for them for free. People need to be able to trust you and your work, and if you do something they don't like they should know you will fix it."

- Barb recommends a separate room for sewing, which will help with your taxes. You can write off part of your mortgage and utilities, and you can keep all your equipment and supplies out of the way.

- Make sure when you're fitting someone that you have the customer look into the mirror to decide if that is how the person really wants the end product to look. Don't make that decision for your customer. She says, "Don't ever let [customers] talk you into making any decisions for them. Just say 'No, I want to know what you want.' I learned that the hard away."

"My business doesn't run my life, my life runs my business. My kids and my family come first."

Mixing Kids and Business

BARB HAS never had to use day care while she worked. She has been lucky in that her kids have always been good at entertaining themselves while she sewed, though this situation may not work for all mothers. Luckily, she lived in the country where the kids could easily go outside and play.

Rewards

BARB SAYS, "I really didn't know what I was doing at first but it never stopped me. My business doesn't run my life, my life runs my business. My kids and my family come first."If she feels she needs to take a vacation or some time off, she takes it. She knows there are certain times of the year, especially around the holidays, when business is slow and she can relax.

Barb's Advice

FIRST YOU *need the confidence that you can do it. Don't give up; be persistent. My confidence is based on my relationship with God. If I didn't have that base, I don't think I could do it.*

Recommended Resources

CATALOGS

- Home Sew Catalogue
  P.O. Box 4099
  Bethlehem, PA 18088

- Newark Catalogue
  6473 Ruch Road
  P.O. Box 20730
  Lehigh Valley, PA 18002

Proofreader/Editor/Writer

Name: Angie Peters
Location: Benton, Arkansas
Family Facts: Married, three children—Nick, 9, Lindsey, 7, and Erin, 7 weeks
Business: Freelance Writing/Proofreading/Editing

Why She Started Her Business

ANGIE STARTED her proofreading and editing home business after quitting her job as a newspaper writer to stay home when her first child was born. It dawned on Angie that she had a very portable career. She started proofreading as part of a typing/résumé service that she started eight years ago.

"Because of the Internet and fax, I'm able to work for people from coast to coast from my home office. Who would have thought? I haven't had one day that I haven't been under some kind of project deadline for at least four years now," explains Angie.

Angie has edited or proofread more than a dozen books for publication, including *The Triumphant Return of Christ, Forewarning, When Y2K Dies, Saddam's Mystery Babylon, The Phantom's Dark Force, The Unveiling, Foreshadows of Wrath, Redemption,* and *The Rapture.* Angie explains, "As you can tell by the titles, I've worked my way into a real niche, because most of these books relate to Christianity and biblical prophecy. Some of the books have included chapters by well-known scholars such as Tim LaHaye, William T. James, and Zola Levitt. I have worked with Harvest House publishers, New Leaf Press, and the Olive Press." In addition, Angie proofreads copy for *Midnight Call,* a monthly magazine published in the United States as well as in six other countries.

Qualifications

HER BACKGROUND in the newspaper industry has helped Angie greatly, as has her degree in English (with an emphasis in writing). But don't despair if you don't

Many proofreaders and copy editors start their business simply because they were born to catch mistakes.

have past skills or education. Many proof-readers and copy editors start their business simply because they were born to catch mistakes. In everyday life, mistakes in the written word often jump out at them. If this is an area you enjoy, there is a good chance you can make this type of home business happen—with a lot of hard work.

Most publishing companies require potential editors and proofreaders to take tests to be hired. These tests, which are often demanding, are designed to weed out those who aren't up to the task. There are many technical aspects involved in editing and proofreading, such as understanding design specs, learning to typecode a manuscript, knowing how to use a pica ruler, and comprehending the entire printing process. If you're looking to be hired by a publisher, you will need a résumé that shows you have had experience in the proofing and editing business.

There are many different companies that need the services of editors and proofreaders—technical, education, and trade publishers, as well as newspapers, magazines, and online publications. All have different needs and guidelines. If the publishing business is beckoning you, it's a good idea to start to educate yourself. Begin with small jobs and work up from there.

Start-up Costs

LOOKING BACK on it now, Angie laughs at her start-up costs. "I started so small it's almost funny. In 1992, I bought a Brother Word Processor for about $300 (a real stretch, though, for a one-income family), and a file cabinet for about $40.

Equipment

ALTHOUGH ANGIE started her business with only a word processor, today she recommends a good computer, a good college dictionary, a thesaurus, and a copy of *The Chicago Manual of Style* as well as Strunk and White's *The Elements of Style*. You will also need to learn proofreaders' marks. You will need to find out from each client what reference manuals will be required for the project—for instance, most book publishers regard *The Chicago Manual of Style* as the industry bible, whereas journalistic publications tend to use *The Associated Press Stylebook*. As your range of clients becomes more varied, so too will your library of reference manuals.

Rates

I HESITATE to answer this because each job is so different," explains Angie. "For some clients whose books I edit, I get a flat fee plus a percentage of royalty. I take a look at the manuscript first to see what kind of shape it's in. If it's pretty clean, requiring nothing more than a quick polish, I won't charge as much as I would for others that might need extensive correction and revision. Others pay me by the hour for the work I do."

The key is to find an area you enjoy the most . . . , network with your target market, then don't be afraid to tell everyone you meet what it is you do.

Rates can be anywhere from $15 to $30 an hour and up. With each new prospective client, you need to consider if they are going to be a long-time client or if this will be a one-time job. It will also depend on where you live. Angie charges $20 an hour for proofreading; if she edits, it's more. She also charges for copies that need to be made and for any postage. If you don't charge for these types of things, you won't make much money.

Marketing

ANGIE FIRST started out by posting flyers for her word processing services on college campuses. She began by typing term papers and reports. However, she couldn't resist proofing/editing as she typed. She says, "At first I didn't charge extra to do that because I just 'fixed things' as I typed. My customers being impressed and grateful was enough for me! But I soon realized that I should charge for the proofing/editing as an extra service, which I did, and I found that more and more people need this type of service—and are willing to pay good money for it." She found that the real opportunities came from professors and instructors who

were writing books. According to Angie, "That kind of work [for professors] gave me some concrete experience for my portfolio. Colleges and universities are fertile ground for all kinds of creative endeavors."

In the years since, her writing/editing/proofing business has evolved to the point where she no longer has to take any typing projects at all. She now proofs and edits a variety of projects. Her main interest lies in editing and/or proofing sizable projects such as manuscripts for authors and publishers.

Because Angie is a writer, she has befriended authors and editors, and her business has grown simply through word of mouth. Authors have recommended her to their publishers, and she has written articles for magazines, which later led to proofing and editing jobs. The key is to find an area you enjoy the most (for instance, educational publishing), network with your target market, then don't be afraid to tell everyone you meet what it is you do.

Tips

SO MANY people can't communicate clearly. Writing, editing, and proofreading give those who can communicate clearly or who have been trained to do so many opportunities to make money in a wide variety of fields. Angie recommends that you think about how you can fill a specific need in a certain niche. "For example, I do lots of work in the Christian writing profession. If your background is in business, find a way to use those business skills in combination with your proofreading skills to fill a need in the business community (letters, promotional writing, advertising, etc.). If you're a crafter, try selling articles to craft magazines or proofread instructions for craft companies," says Angie. The bottom line is this: "If you have the skills and a certain interest there are so many ways you can make money. This is a very overlooked profession."

Mixing Kids and Business

A NGIE FINDS herself working when her husband is home and he is able to watch the kids. "I also have been blessed with nearby parents and parents-in-law who have always been tickled to have the kids—whether I'm working or not!" However, she admits that she has gotten pretty good about working with the kids underfoot.

Biggest Challenge

W HEN I'M *snowed under with work and someone calls me with a new project, I find it so hard to bring myself to say "no." When you're a freelancer, you* know that the client may just go to the next name on his or her list and never call you again. I can't stand the thought of a door like that closing. It's also difficult to "clock out" for vacations. I've learned that letting clients know well in advance when I'll be out allows them to send me anything urgent they have before I go. This makes them happy, and they respect the fact that I'm organized enough and professional enough to keep them posted of my accessibility.*

Although most clients understand that Angie won't be working during spring breaks, Angie has found that not everyone understands Angie's reason for working at home—to spend time with her kids. So to some clients she simple states that she will be out of the office for the week or is busy with another project.

Other challenges include what to charge for various projects. Then there is waiting for payment. Angie says, "You may bill some clients who write you a check as soon as they open their mail, but others have to pass it on to their supervisor, who has to pass it on to the business office, who has to put it in the stack of bills to be paid on x day of the month. Could be a while before you get that check!"

Rewards

A NGIE CITES her rewards as "being able to do what I love to do—write and proofread (and get paid for it!) while keeping my kids and family responsibilities at the very top of my list of priorities."

Angie's Advice

START SMALL *and build it gradually. That way you won't have such a dramatic transition to go through, your kids won't have such a dramatic transition to go through, and your wallet won't have such a dramatic transition to go through!*

Recommended Resources

BOOKS

- Joseph Gibaldi, *MLA Style Manual and Guide to Scholarly Publishing.* New York: The Modern Language Association of America, 1998.

- Thomas McCormack, *The Fiction Editor.* New York: St. Martin's Press, 1988.

- William Strunk, Jr., and E. B. White, *The Elements of Style,* 3rd edition. New York: Macmillan, 1979.

- The University of Chicago Press, *The Chicago Manual of Style,* 14th edition. Chicago: University of Chicago Press, 1993.

TUTOR

Name: Daa Mahowald
Location: Lancaster, California
Family Facts: Married, one daughter—Morgan, 7
Business: Professional tutor

Why She Started Her Business

WITH DAA'S (pronounced "Day") background as a classroom math teacher for grades 7 through 12, deciding to become a tutor was an easy step. However, Daa didn't always plan to be a tutor. During a very difficult pregnancy, her doctor explained that if she didn't quit her job, she could very well lose the baby she was carrying. As tutoring isn't an on-your-feet job, Daa was given the OK by her doctor to begin a tutoring business at home.

Qualifications

DAA SAYS, "Becoming a tutor is as simple as saying, 'I'm a tutor.'" However, it is best if you have a college degree. If you have a certain subject that you love to teach, that's great, too. Your enthusiasm is bound to rub off onto the kids you teach and hopefully give a new life to a subject they're struggling with." Daa explains that it's also very helpful if you have a knack for presenting material, so that your students can enjoy and understand what it is you're trying to teach them.

But you don't have to be a teacher to become a tutor. "If you've spent years at the kitchen table helping your kids or the neighbor's kids with their homework, you've already begun to establish yourself as a tutor." Daa has been in a teaching role most of her life—from helping her siblings when she was younger to helping classmates in high school with their homework.

Start-up Costs

DAA'S ONLY expense was printing her résumé. She simply set up a card table in her living room to teach on. She says, "Some tutors provide writing utensils and paper, but I expect my students to bring this equipment to their sessions."

Rates

WHEN DAA first started out in her tutoring business, she charged $15 an hour. This is a typical rate for someone who

"Daa has been in a teaching role most of her life—from helping her siblings when she was younger to helping classmates in high school with their homework."

is a college graduate. After a year she raised her rate to $20 and two years later raised it to $25. She says, "Currently, because I have established myself in my target area, and because I have a master's degree in educational psychology, I charge $28."

But the amount you charge has a lot to do with the area you live in. Daa explains that where she lives, $28 is about the most you can charge. But two hours away in Los Angeles, a tutor can make $50 an hour if he or she meets at the student's home. You may be able to find out what tutors get paid in your area by simply calling around and asking what tutors in your area charge. Another way to find out this information is to ask teachers what the going rate for a tutor is.

Daa recommends that your students pay for their sessions a month in advance. "I used to have parents pay me at the end of each month. I was dismayed at how many of them delayed paying for a month or two, or if they discontinued tutoring, never paid me at all." Daa goes on to explain, "If they cannot commit to a regular schedule, I let them pay me for ten hours of tutoring. I also offer a 5 percent discount to any parent who wishes to pay for twenty hours up front."

Working Hours

BECAUSE DAA'S first priority is her daughter, she arranges her working schedule around her daughter's schedule. However, the prime tutoring hours are from 2:30 P.M. until 10:00 P.M. Daa normally averages thirty hours a week, but around those last few weeks of finals, she puts in between forty and forty-five hours a week.

Marketing

WHILE DAA was still teaching school, she also sponsored and coached the school's chess team. When one of the club's founders heard Daa was pregnant and would have to quit her teaching job, she recommended to Daa she start a tutoring service. "She began referring parents to me. Soon, word of mouth from her and from other parents who were satisfied with the results of their children's tutoring caused my business to boom."

Daa also made up a résumé and used it like a brochure to promote her business. She recommends that you take your résumé to the schools in your area and talk to the school clerks or secretaries, because "parents often ask them if they know of any tutors." If the school has counselors, meet with them and tell them about your tutoring service. If there aren't any counselors, talk to the principal. Daa says, "Finally, put a résumé into each teacher's school mailbox. With permission you can also place your résumé on bulletin boards around town and at any child-oriented business."

Target Market

Many tutors find a certain age group they like to teach, but Daa tutors all ages and subjects, from kindergartners to students in junior college to people who need help qualifying for a test for a job promotion, an entrance exam for college, or for a particular training program. Daa also uses her past experience with chess to tutor children in this area. She says, "But this is not the norm. Most tutors niche themselves."

Tips

• Daa says, "A common error for many beginning tutors is assuming that they must be versatile. If you know you don't have a knack for a certain subject, don't teach it. You and your student will suffer because of it. If you feel comfortable with teaching math no higher than algebra, then don't teach trigonometry. If you enjoy working with grades one through five, then tutor just those grades. Set your guidelines in your résumé and stick with them."

• Your résumé should include who you are and how people can contact you. She says, "Your most prominent item should be your target statement: the ages or grades and the subjects you will tutor." Then you should include your experience that is relevant to being a tutor. It's best to leave out how much you charge. Wait for the parent to give you a call. "Often, during your phone conversation you will make an impression on them that will establish your value before they ask your rates. Then they are more likely to consider you worth your fees."

Mixing Kids and Business

Daa is one of those lucky moms: Her daughter slept approximately sixteen

---

"A common error for many beginning tutors is assuming that they must be versatile."

hours a day until she was 2½. When Morgan turned 3, Daa hired a high school student to come over in the afternoons to watch her once she woke from her nap, and when Daa's spouse came home at night, he would watch Morgan. Morgan also started attending a Montessori program three days a week when she was 2½. By the time she was 5, she was attending school four mornings a week.

"I have found that all my years of working with other kids have made me better able to work interactively with my own child. Through no-pressure and almost-all-fun activities, 5-year-old Morgan has learned to add and subtract, read, and print. She especially enjoys 'teaching' me, which reinforces her own learning," explains Daa.

Biggest Challenge

DAA SAYS, "If a student comes to me only because they were forced by their parents, almost no amount of jollying will lighten the mood." She finds her hardest students to tutor are high school males who do not want a tutor. She usually knows by the third session if the student is going to work with her or not. Daa will then refer the student to another tutor. "However, if a tutor can find even the slightest reason why a student wants to come, the tutor can use that reason as a hook to involve and engage a student." In these situations she will boldly ask the student, "Am I a punishment for you, or do you have your own reason for coming to

me?" Rarely does a student respond to such a daring question with absolute resentment. "They may say that they have come to me because of their grades, but with a little gentle probing, they will concede that they want the help. And once their grades start improving, they feel better about working with me."

Being a tutor is much like being a doctor—you're always on call. When Daa was having contractions and was waiting for her spouse to take her to the hospital, a parent called and asked if Daa could tutor her child for a test he would be taking the next day. Daa explained her situation, only to have the parent say, "I'll bring him right over. You can work with him between contractions until your husband gets there." It didn't end there. "Another mom brought her kid up to my hospital room the day after my cesarean. She wanted me to help her eighth-grader prepare for a next-day algebra (absolutely-critical-must-get-an-A-on-it!) quiz."

Daa's Advice

DO IT! *Plan first, of course, but don't take too long at that. Just jump in and start. Be sure, however, whatever type of business you choose, that you have a strong interest in the topic and have received feedback from others that you're good at it. If you never had someone say "Thank you for teaching me," you probably wouldn't choose a teaching type of business. Also, do everything possible to keep overhead low.*

Recommended Resources

Your local chamber of commerce: Daa attends the monthly seminars on starting/running small or home businesses held by her chamber of commerce. "They are very helpful, especially because they keep me informed about local regulations," says Daa.

WORD PROCESSOR

Name: Diana Ennen
Location: Pompano Beach, Florida
Family Facts: Married, three children—Jeremy, 13, Amanda, 5 1/2, and Amber, 1
Business: Ennen's Computer Service
Web Site: http://www.gate.net/~ gregnn/ diana.html

Why She Started Her Business

DIANA WORKED as a medical secretary for ten years before she started her own word processing business from home. After her son was born, she tried to go back to work. It took only two weeks of day care for Diana to decide, "That was enough." Diana was determined to find a way she could stay home and work. And that's exactly what she did. For ten years now, Diana has been running a successful word-processing and computer-tutoring program from her home.

Qualifications

THERE ARE many avenues you can take as a word processor. You can transcribe and type letters for professionals, type reports up for students, start a résumé service, and edit and type up manuscripts for writers.

Word processors are doing more and more transcription for their clients. Diana says, "Most of my work is transcription." Diana rented her transcriber for several months before she had the funds to buy one. "Many word processors do wait to get clients who need transcription before they purchase a transcriber, that way they know which kind to purchase. Micro and Standard are the two types used today." Diana never took a transcription class or had previous experience. "It's not too complicated once you get used to it." Diana says, "To be successful, you should type sixty-five words a minute. Remember, the faster you type, the more money you can make." Also, proofing is a must. According to Diana, "Your business is really going to grow if your work is letter-perfect." You want your clients to have the best experience possible.

Start-up Costs

IT COST Diana about $2,500 to start her business. That included her word-processing software, such as Microsoft Word and Word-Perfect, and her computer and laser printer.

Diana has turned a spare bedroom into her office. "It's nice to be able to shut the door."

She says, "Most of my clients demand the quality of a laser printer."

Diana has turned a spare bedroom into her office. "It's nice to be able to shut the door." She found it was hard to separate her work from home before she had a separate office.

Diana says, "I highly recommend your letterhead and business cards have a professional image. You can do this inexpensively on your own now with the specialized papers you can pick up at your local office supply store." However, Diana recommends two colors of ink for your business cards, which you can have professionally done. "I recommend spending a little bit more money on your business cards. Don't just go with the $9.95 special."

Rates

IT TOOK Diana about three months to see a profit in her business. She got so busy so quickly she couldn't keep up. "But that is rare. Most word processors usually take up to six to eight months to see a profit." Diana charges $30 an hour for her word processing services. But what you can charge depends on what your area will pay for your services.

Marketing

DIANA STARTED advertising by direct mail. She enjoys working for chiropractors and attorneys, "So I targeted exactly who I wanted to type for." She goes on to explain, "If you do direct mail, follow up with a phone call or the next month send another letter. It's important not to send just one letter. The key is to consistently follow up on it." She would test by sending out about thirty letters. "I usually got one or two responses from that."

Diana recommends that direct mail inform potential clients about the services you offer, such as work on an as-needed basis, fax modem capabilities, or twenty-four-hour turnaround. List years of experience and any other services you can provide for them. Always send a business card or brochure. Diana recommends not using labels on mailings, because when people see this they think "advertisement." She says she has had better results typing the address directly on the envelopes.

Although some word processors find that consistently listing a yellow pages ad supplies them with a good amount of business, Diana has found that once you establish a few clients in the word processing business, you don't really have to aggressively advertise. "Word of mouth is your best advertisement."

Hiring Help

DIANA HIRES an independent contractor for backup. "That is almost a must once you start getting established." Find an independent contractor who charges less than you do so that you will still be making money. She stresses that it is still important for you to proof their work. She says, "I'm not going to give [the finished product] to my client unless I proof it. Your client doesn't need to know that you have referred this work either, as long as you proof it and it's 100 percent accurate."

Tips

- It's a good idea to have your clients sign a simple contract. "This guarantees you're going to get paid. It also guarantees that clients know how much they are getting charged."

- When Diana first started, she offered a pickup and delivery service. However, she found herself always on the road and not getting much typing done. "I recommend the client comes to you." There are other options today, such as using a fax machine, modem, or next-day mail. It's also a good idea to have a pickup box outside your home for pickup or drop-off if you're not at home.

- Have available the name of a person who can repair your computer or printer in case it breaks down.

Mixing Kids and Business

BECAUSE DIANA needed a full-time income, she opted for a sitter to come into her home for about six hours a day. She likes this situation because if she feels like taking a break from work she can easily go and spend some time with her kids. "If you want to do this job on a part-time basis, you can do it [without a sitter]. Like getting up early and working through naps."

Diana says, "I love my business, but I'm a mom first and I always will be." If her kids are sick, Diana explains to her clients that she will have to refer their work. This is why your backup is so important. "If it's a new client I refer them to someone else. If it's a

Diana hires an independent contractor for backup. "That is almost a must once you start getting established."

regular client I find out when they need it back. If it's in a time frame I can get it back to them in, I take it. If not, I refer it out."

Diana has made the mistake of taking on too much work when her child was sick, and in the end her child was the one who suffered. "But now I let the client know what is going on. Most clients are very understanding. But for extended sicknesses like chicken pox, then it's a good idea to refer work out."

Expanding the Business

A FEW years ago, Diana also started a computer tutoring service to teach people how to use WordPerfect and other programs. Diana works with a personnel agency whose applicants sometimes fail their Word-Perfect tests, and she also advertises this service in the paper. She charges $50 for a two-hour class. "Although they won't be able to memorize the whole program in that time, they get a good understanding of how to run it." Diana finds tutoring a nice break from typing all day, too. "However, if you do incorporate the two, you really need to watch your scheduling. I learned that the hard way."

Diana has recently added bookkeeping to her word processing service as well. She explains that these businesses work well together: "This is a nice option to offer if your target market is small and home-based businesses. You can do it all for them."

Diana's Advice

I F YOU'RE *really motivated and you believe you can do it, then you absolutely can do it. There is no stopping you. Open communication with your family is very important. Let them know your needs and make sure they tell you their needs, too. Don't forget to have fun with it. Remember, this is supposed to be fun.*

Recommended Resources

BOOKS

Diana has written a book (which can be found under two titles) about her experiences at home. *Words from Home* (self-published) can be ordered by writing to P.O. Box 1773, Pompano Beach, Florida 33061. It sells for $24.95 plus $4.00 shipping and handling (Florida residents need to add $1.75 for state sales tax). You can also send her e-mail at DeeEnnen@aol.com or call 1-954-784-7416. The book is also sold at bookstores as *Success from Home: The Wordprocessing Business* (Adams Blake, 1998).

- Barbara Brabec, *Homemade Money* (along with her newsletter). Cincinnati: Betterway Publications, 1994.

- Paul and Sarah Edwards, *Working from Home*. New York: Tarcher/Putnam, 1994.

MAGAZINES

- *Home Office Computing.* This publication specializes in home-office computing needs and trends.

ORGANIZATIONS

- Association of Business Support Services International, Inc. (ABSSI) 22875 Savi Ranch Parkway, Suite H Yorba Linda, CA 92887-4619 1-800-237-1462 http://www.abssi.org

  There is a $132 annual membership fee. Benefits include standards for how long an assignment should take to finish, word processing guidelines, and a monthly newsletter.

FLORAL DESIGNER

Why She Started Her Business

WHEN J. P. was 5 weeks old, Kim had to go back to work as a teacher. Kim found a day-care provider whom she felt she could trust. "We didn't have doubts about her." Leaving her son was very hard on Kim. "I cried every day that he went to day care. I knew that it would bother me, I just didn't know how much." J. P. soon got a cold that wouldn't go away. Many times Kim would find the provider was caring for more kids than the guidelines allowed. Sometimes she would even find J. P. pushed behind some furniture in his stroller while everyone else was in another room. At this point Kim began to panic. She didn't know what to do. She had a great job, but if she took any more time off they would fire her. She talked to the provider about the problems, but only got excuses.

The last straw came when Kim went to pick up 8-month-old J. P. and she found him with a bottle propped up for him to drink from while he lay in his stroller. It was all beginning to make sense now—Kim had been wondering why J. P.'s clothes were regularly stained around the front of his shirt. Kim promptly fired the sitter. However, she didn't quit teaching right then. She was able to find a college student to watch J. P. She may have kept teaching had she been able to keep the new sitter, but the student had to return to college.

At this point Kim decided to quit teaching and work from home making floral arrangements. She had been doing this off and on since J. P. was born, and she had worked in a flower shop for five years while she was attending college for her elementary education degree. She knew she would get some business, because friends and relatives were always asking her to make something for a birthday gift or special event. Those first few months business was slow, but Kim used the time to get her business license and set up her accounts.

Qualifications

IF YOU'RE interested in floral design, Kim says it isn't that difficult to start a business of your own. To learn about basic

> *"The best ways to learn are by observing someone else and by trial and error."*

elements of design, you can find books and videos at craft and floral shops. It's also good to pay attention to other people's work and write down how they made it. If you have the opportunity to work with a florist, that can be very helpful, too. As Kim says, "The best ways to learn are by observing someone else and by trial and error."

Start-up Costs

KIM EXPLAINS that it doesn't take a lot of overhead to get started in the floral design business. She works mainly with dry and silk flowers, and when she officially started her business five years ago, she had wire cutters and a glue gun. Kim would wait for an order to come in and then go buy flowers and whatever else she needed. Kim does all her floral work in the basement of her house; she also has an office upstairs for her bookkeeping.

Now that Kim has been in business for a while, she buys as much as she can at end-of-the-season sales. She says, "Now that I'm into [the business], I can stock up. If I see holiday ribbon I grab it." Last year she was able to buy most of her holiday florals at 90 percent off. "It saves a lot of time and makes for bigger profits."

Services

KIM MAKES birthday, shower, and holiday gifts. She also gets orders for housewarming gifts for doors, walls, or kitchens.

Every Christmas season Kim and other crafters hold a holiday open house for two days. They decorate the space (usually the basement of one of the participants) with the wares that will be sold. In the morning they offer baked goods and cider; in the evening, wine and cheese. They send out between 150 and 200 invitations. At the last event Kim made about $350 in eight hours.

One of the big moneymakers for Kim is weddings. Wedding assignments are nice because they are usually arranged several months in advance, and Kim has plenty of time to order and make up her arrangements. She also sets up and takes down the flowers after the wedding and will even move them to the reception if the bride desires. Kim has done this so many times now she can do it easily by herself, or her sister will come along and help her out. "The brides don't expect me to do so much work," says Kim, but they are very grateful that she is there.

Kim finds that the cost of working outside of the home was almost equal to what she does now, because she no longer has the costs of day care and eating out.

Marketing

IT TOOK Kim a good six to eight months to get the word out about her business. Although she never actively solicited any, she soon had plenty of business to keep her going. Other happy customers refer most of her customers to her. She has a brochure for weddings, but other than that she hasn't had to spend a dime on advertising.

Kim happened by accident on a wonderful marketing tool. Her sister-in-law had a friend who worked at a local television station, and this woman invited Kim to do some five-minute segments demonstrating different techniques of floral design.

Mixing Kids and Business

KIM MEETS with clients in her dining room. She tries her best to arrange these meetings around her son's schedule—J. P. goes to a pre-preschool once a week for five hours (some weeks it's two days).

Because J. P. has grown up with his mom's flowers, he knows he isn't supposed to touch her work. He does have his own room that is made up especially for him to play in during the day when Kim needs to work. If she needs to, she will work while he is napping or at night. However, Kim tries to involve J. P. in the business as much as possible. If she is working on an arrangement, she will give J. P. some flowers and he will make his own arrangements. Kim has found that "If I spend some good quality time with him, that will go a long, long way."

Biggest Challenge

KIM ADMITS that everything isn't perfect. She says that it is hard to keep up with the housework, and it can get tight as far as money goes. However, she finds that the cost of working outside of the home was almost equal to what she does now, because she no longer has the costs of day care and eating out.

Kim's Advice

CHOOSE SOMETHING *you really like. Look at your hobbies. Do you have enough money to invest in this business? Can you easily run this business out of your home?*

Recommended Resources

BOOKS

- *1001 Floral Tips for the Floral Industry,* compiled by the top florist companies.

    You can't buy this book in stores. For more information, write to *Florist Review* (see below).

MAGAZINES

- *Florist Review*
  Department S
  P.O. Box 4368
  Topeka, KS 66604-9933
  Subscription: $36/year

    Included in the magazine are articles on marketing, trends, and design ideas, along with new product ideas and free sample products. Also provided are sources for supplies such as containers, balloons, ribbon, and more.

- *Professional Floral Design*
  3737 NW 34th
  P.O. Box 12309
  Oklahoma City, OK 73157
  Subscription: $66/year; single issue, $14

    This magazine is much like a catalog, heavy and glossy. It gives you ideas for the higher-priced occasions—will often profile weddings with an $80,000 floral bill. This is for readers with experience in the floral industry.

TRAVEL AGENT

Name: Jennifer Dugan
Location: Los Alamos, New Mexico
Family Facts: Married, two sons—Dil-
    lon, 2^1/$_2$, and Travis, 6 months
Business: Dugan's Travels
Web Site: http://www.onlineagency.
    com/duganstravels

Why She Started Her Business

WORKING AT home as a travel agent was not Jennifer's first thought when she attended travel school in January of 1994, nor when she started work—outside the home—in March of that same year as a leisure travel agent. However, her plans changed when her son was born in 1997. Jennifer says, "I attempted to return to work part time when my son was 2 months old, but realized it was not going to work out. Between his getting sick, doctors' appointments, paying a sitter, and all of the other hassles, it was not worth the small paycheck I would get every two weeks."

Fortunately Jennifer was able to start working part time, from home, for an agency she had already been working for. She was paid a commission for each trip she booked and soon had a regular clientele. However, she began to realize how small those commission checks were compared to all the work she was doing, so she decided to start working with another certified travel agency that is also referred to as a "host agency." She worked without having to pay any fees; rather, the agency just took a small amount of commissions when she used its accounts (accounts include cruise lines and tour companies that book trips). Because Jennifer has slowly begun getting her own accounts and gets commissions paid directly through her, she considers her business self-sufficient. She explains, "I have my own business license. I pay for all my expenses and taxes. I am in charge of getting all of my own business and keeping clients happy."

Qualifications

JENNIFER'S TRAVEL agent experience was very helpful in starting her business. If you don't have this experience, you can take travel agent classes. However, a good knowledge of travel may be all you need.

Some tours and cruises are select and will only sign up large agencies that have their ARC # (an ARC # enables you to print out tickets), so Jennifer still needs the host

Believe it or not, a travel agency in your local area may let you work under them.

agency to run her tickets—only agencies with ARC #'s can run tickets. To get your ARC # you need to have a bank account with $250,000 in it at all times. Many starting their own home-based travel agency won't have that kind of money and will most likely need to find a host agency to work under.

When searching for a host agency, you may come across the words, *card mills.* Card mills will give you what's called an IATAN card—a card that gives travel agents discounts on plane tickets and hotel rooms—for approximately $490. Don't think this will make you a travel agent. To get one of these cards as a legitimate agent, you will need to make $5,000 in commission sales a year if you're an outside agent, or you can get one if you're a full-time agent working in an agency.

Believe it or not, a travel agency in your local area may let you work under them. The travel agency may set you up or it will let you fax ticket info to them. Many of these agencies have computer programs that are user friendly and easy to use from home; in exchange, they may charge you a monthly rate or take a percentage of your commission. Some agencies may loan you the soft-

ware, whereas others might require $100 or more.

Start-up Costs

JENNIFER SPENT $390 for six-month computer access, and continues to pay $65 per month. Her initial investment in equipment included $150 for a fax machine, approximately $200 for travel agent books and guides, $15 for business cards, and $250 to establish her Web site. In addition, she pays $164 for her liability insurance.

Equipment

ALL JENNIFER has needed for her agency has been a computer, a fax machine, books on travel, brochures (which are free from suppliers), Internet access, and business cards.

Rates

JENNIFER DOESN'T charge her customers any kind of fees. She gets paid strictly from the commissions that the airlines, cruise lines, hotels, rental cars, and tour companies give her. The service she provides is to simply look at all the prices at once, as opposed to the average person who has to make many phone calls or visit many sites to get the best possible prices. Due to her contacts, she has the heads-up on specials, as well as the knowledge to help someone plan the best trip possible.

Marketing

JENNIFER RECENTLY had an article in the local paper written about her, which has increased her business tremendously. Although she has a Web site, she hasn't gotten much business from it, but feels it shows people what she does and what she has to offer. She says, "It seems like a requirement now to be on the Web. I do most of my business locally, although I do write articles for a few Web sites in order to increase my traffic."

Her Web site offers many services for her customers. Royal Caribbean cruise lines automatically posts its latest specials on her site. People can also buy books on travel or luggage on her site. She regularly updates her Web site with specials on many destinations. She says of her site, "It's a site dedicated to helping people obtain information on vacations and being notified of specials." Jennifer also offers a guest book for people to sign so they can receive regular e-mail regarding specials the cruise lines and tour companies are offering.

Jennifer explains, "I wanted to show customers that I am up-to-date on technology. Many people are using the Internet for their travel plans but do not get personal attention. In addition, many big travel sites claim they will get you the best price, but I believe it still takes a travel agent to do that for you. I have tried some of the big sites and compared the prices to what I have gotten and I am either the same or lower. I have also had people who have called me after having booked their trips online with problems when canceling their trips. They do not know what to do and, unfortunately, there is nothing I can do because I did not book the trip." She sees the Internet as offering a wide range of information, but still also sees the importance of personal service.

Jennifer says that her main advertising has been through publicity in her local paper, articles she has written, and word of mouth. She says, "A happy customer is the best advertising I can get. That customer will tell all his or her friends and family and then they will call me for their next trip."

Services

SOME COMPANIES offer training specific to their tours. For example, Jennifer became a Disney specialist by taking a course offered by the Walt Disney Travel Company via the Disney College of Knowledge. She is also a specialist in Premier Cruise Lines, Princess Cruise Lines, Outrigger Resorts, and Mirage Resorts. She has received training

---

Your best bet as an agent is to find a niche.

---

from Florida's Visitor Bureau and is a certified Small Ship Partner with Cruise West. She also loves to plan honeymoons and romantic getaways for couples.

Tips

- Beware of all the disreputable companies out there. There are many, and you'll need to research each company thoroughly before you invest any money. You don't need to pay outrageous fees to become an agent, like some companies ask you to do.

- Compare different companies' rates, and don't be scammed by the big companies, which can end up costing you more than you need to be paying to get your agency started.

Mixing Kids and Business

JENNIFER'S OFFICE hours are seven days a week, with no certain hours. Customers can leave voice mail if she is not available or send e-mail any time they wish. People can thus make their travel arrangements when it is convenient for them; this schedule also lets Jennifer spend most of her day with her two young ones. She can do much of her Internet research in the evening when the boys are asleep. She leaves her most important phone calls for the day times.

Biggest Challenge

THANKS TO a number of big sites on the Internet, people now have more access to make their own travel reservations. Jennifer says, "It's definitely taking away business from agents." And now that the airlines have cut commissions, agents now have to charge fees. Your best bet as an agent is to find a niche—Jennifer specializes in family travel, for instance. Although customers may come to you just for their family trips at first, down the road they may make all their travel arrangements through you.

Rewards

HER BIGGEST reward is that she can be home with her children, which is the best thing she can ask for. She explains, "I am my own boss and don't have someone looking over my shoulder telling me what to do. If I have a terrible customer, I can just tell him or her I am too booked to get to his or her travel and refer them to another agency. I love what I do and I enjoy it."

Jennifer's Advice

L OOK AT *all your options, and don't get yourself in over your head. Don't spend a lot of money on you starting up. First make sure you're going to love it and have what it takes to make that business run. Travel business or any business, keep those costs low and if you do well, you can invest in your business down the road.*

Recommended Resources

ORGANIZATIONS

- Outside Sales Support Network (OSSN)
  1340 U.S. Highway One, Suite 102
  Jupiter, FL 33469
  1-561-743-1900
  ossn@ossn.com
  http://www.ossn.com

  This organization will help you determine how good a particular travel agency is to work for.

- The National Association of Commissioned Travel Agents (NACTA)
  P.O. Box 2398
  Valley Center, CA 92082-2398
  1-760-751-1197
  nacta@aol.com
  http://www.nacta.com

  This organization's mission is to create recognition for, and offer support to, professional independent travel agents.

This will be obtained by effective representation within the travel industry through education, training, and increased exposure of this growing segment of travel professionals within the travel industry at large. Its site also lists host agencies that are looking to hire travel agents.

BOOKS

- Kelly Monaghan, *Home Based Travel Agent.* New York: Intrepid Travel, 1999.

- *How to Start a Home Based Travel Agency*

  This book can be purchased via the www.nacta.com Web site.

MAGAZINES

- *Travel Agent Magazine* (To subscribe, call 1-888-527-7008.)

  This publication offers educational programs via mail for different tours and cruises. If you're a certified travel agent, these courses are free.

TELECOMMUTER

Name: Mary Kovoor
Location: Forest Hills, New York
Family Facts: Married, one child—
   Nicholas, 3
Business: Telecommuter for Air
   France

Why She Started to Telecommute

DURING THE 1980s, many women were making their way into the corporate world. Mary Kovoor was no exception. After receiving an M.B.A., she dove right into the workforce as a systems coordinator for Air France's computer department. She knew someday she would have children, but figured like many women she worked with, that she would put her kids in day care.

But Mary's '80s philosophy was put to the test by the news that she was expecting her firstborn in the '90s. The thought of having to leave her baby on a daily basis didn't seem like such a good idea anymore. Mary decided to approach her boss about the idea of doing her work at home once the baby was born. Fortunately, her boss was a forward thinker and thought the idea sounded great.

Mary started working almost immediately from home once her son, Nicholas, was born. However, she now wishes that she had more time getting to know the baby instead of rushing right into the job.

Equipment and Start-up Costs

AIR FRANCE supplied all of Mary's equipment: computer, modem, fax, and dedicated line. She had no start-up costs.

Working Hours

MARY SET up her schedule so that she works from 10 A.M. to 2 P.M. during the week. Her office is in the family's second bedroom, and she has sectioned off a spot so her son can play while she is working. Nicholas's play area consists of colorful mats and toys.

Mixing Kids and Business

FOR THE first year, Mary was a computer-help person. If someone at the main office was having any type of computer problem, she would help to find a solution. Sometimes Nicholas needed her help, and Mary would have to simply state that she would call back as soon as she could.

175

Usually everyone was very accommodating and was happy that she was able to stay home with her child.

When Air France decided that it needed someone to do the computer help line on a full-time basis, Mary realized her job was in jeopardy. "I was worried, but luckily they found other work for me to do at home." She now dials into the system and checks out the promotional offers of other airlines. She tells Air France's marketing department what the offers are, and then they decide if they are going to match the other airlines' prices or not. This job is even better because she doesn't have to answer phone calls, and she does it early in the morning before Nicholas gets up.

Mary is considered an independent contractor for Air France and gets no benefits. To continue this contract she may have to go to the office and fill in during a busy time during the summer. The thought of leaving her son really bothers Mary, and she hopes that she won't have to. "But if it means another contract from them, then maybe two months would be worth it."

Rewards

M ARY HAS found, "Nothing replaces you as the mother of your child. If this means working nights and losing sleep, at least you can get up in the morning and smile at your baby, knowing you're doing the hardest but most rewarding job in the world."

If She Could Do It All Over Again

M ARY NOW wishes she had received her French translation certificate. "It would have been a lot cheaper than the M.B.A. and I could have been doing [translation] now [from home]." Mary still may do translation. As for the M.B.A., she says, "It's really for someone who wants to stay in the corporate environment."

Mary's Advice

A PPROACH YOUR *employers [about telecommuting]. I think the more women who do this, the sooner companies will understand that it has to be done for all women who plan on having children.*

Recommended Resources

BOOKS

• Dr. William Sears and Martha Sears, R.N., *The Baby Book*. New York: Little, Brown & Co., 1993.

"Nothing replaces you as the mother of your child."

- Dr. William Sears, *Creative Parenting: The Complete Guide to Child Care.* New York: Everest House, 1992.
- Dr. William Sears, *Nighttime Parenting.* Franklin Park, Ill.: La Leche League International, 1995.

Mary explains, "These books don't directly have anything to do with working, but they helped me feel more competent as a mother because they support the 'trust-your-instincts theory.' Once I was able to do that, I was able to work better."

MAGAZINES

- *Working Mother.* "While it's really geared to the mother who has gone back to work, it's [written with] the same kind of mind-set and [discusses] the same kind of problems you might have."
- *Business Start-Ups.* Gives business ideas, tips, and resources for entrepreneurs.

HERB GARDENER

Name: Carol Dowling
Location: Tiverton, Rhode Island
Family Facts: Married, two children—
    Hallie, 8, and Elias, 3 months
Business: Gray Cottage Herb Farm

Why She Started Her Business

CAROL STARTED out teaching elementary-age children general music, but her heart was in gardening. She quit her teaching job and found work as an assistant manager at Washington's National Cathedral Greenhouse and then later worked at the American Horticultural Society, but this still wasn't quite enough for Carol. She wanted to run her own business. "I really liked the idea of being my own boss."

So Carol and her family left Washington, D.C., and headed for greener pastures in Rhode Island, where Carol worked for a nearby herb farm. "That really gave me a good idea of what the retail herb business was all about," she said. For her own herb and flower farm, she needed to find a place that was zoned for the type of business she wanted to start. "That's an important thing when people want to start something like this. You really need to check into it, because

if you buy [land] and you later find out you can't have a business on your property, what are you going to do?"

Start-up Costs

CAROL STARTED her business with money from the family's savings and a loan from her parents. Her costs began with the land being cleared, which ran about $2,500. Her 50-foot greenhouse (or hoop house), covered with plastic on the inside and the outside in order to insulate the air in the middle, cost about $700. Wood to make the doors of the greenhouse ran $200. The heater used to keep the hoop house and its herbs warm cost $1,600. Carol likes to keep her plants off the ground. "It's easy to step on the plants, hoses can knock them over, and there are more bug problems." So Carol made approximately eight waist-high tables that cost a total of $250. Carol also ended up buying a used truck for $3,000 to deliver her herbs in.

Learning from Her Mistakes

CAROL CONSIDERS her first year in business a trial year. She made a few mistakes that slowed her down. One of those mistakes was thinking there was a big mar-

178

> *The first year, of course, is the most difficult. "The second year you have somewhat of an idea, but even then . . ."*

ket out there for antique or heirloom annuals, such as the fragrant mignonettes or the single-flower hollyhocks. "I didn't really make any money and I thought, 'I really want to be an herb farmer, why am I doing all these annuals?'"

How Her Business Works

CAROL STARTS planting about the first week of March. She writes down what she plants and the dates in a journal and on the seed packets. Once she starts planting, she does successive sowings about every three weeks.

She plants all her seeds in seed trays that are placed on heating pads. "It's very important to have bottom heat." She also has the furnace going at about 45 degrees Fahrenheit at night. Once the seedlings are transplanted into their very own pots, the temperature is kept at 50 degrees Fahrenheit.

To decide how many of each plant she needs, she looks at what was used and ordered from the year before. The first year, of course, is the most difficult. "The second year you have somewhat of an idea, but even then . . ." says Carol with a laugh. Don't despair; even people who have been in the business for years still have a difficult time

with this one. "From year to year I try to remember what sold well and what I should have planted more of later or earlier."

Rates

AS WITH any business, what you can charge varies in every town and state. Carol has two different prices for her plants: wholesale and retail. Carol admits that she charged a little bit less in the beginning, when people weren't familiar with her business.

Carol charges by pot size. Her retail price for a square 3½-inch pot is $1.75. A round 4-inch pot is $2.25. She also has some annual flowers she sells in six packs for $1.75. Wholesale price for a 3½-inch pot is $1.00. The six packs are sold by the flat for $10.00, and there are eight packs per flat.

If you don't have a clue as to what you should charge for your products, check out your competition. Carol says, "It's very important with this business or any business to see what your competitors or other greenhouses are charging for things."

Marketing

IT'S REALLY important to market yourself and to be diligent about it," says

"Sending out press releases has been an excellent way for me to advertise without having to pay any money."

Carol. Don't worry that your future customer is going to say no. It will happen at times but don't give up. Carol found that she had a better response when she called her customers every week to see if they needed a resupply of herbs. At first she felt she was bugging them all the time, but nursery owners are usually so busy around springtime that they don't have time to think about what they need to order.

In January, Carol sends all the nurseries a price list of her flowers and herbs and when they will be available. Then in March she gives them all a call again to make sure they received the price list and to see if they have any questions. At the end of April she will call them again to see if they want to place an order. "Usually, at that point people will say, especially if they are new clients, 'No, but we'll call you when we want to place an order.'" So she will leave it at that. If they don't call by May, they usually aren't interested.

By the end of the season, if Carol has leftover plants, she holds a sale at her house. "It's either a buy one, get one free, or 50 percent off," explains Carol.

Carol also sends out press releases, describing the herb and gardening classes she

offers in May and June, to about seven newspapers every year. The papers will publish the whole list when she first sends it to them, and then every week her classes are printed in the calendar sections. "This has been an excellent way for me to advertise without having to pay any money." Carol is also going to start paying for an ad in one of the papers to increase customer turnout.

Expanding the Business

BECAUSE THE growing and selling season for herbs is rather short, Carol expanded her business a bit so she can work until December. She sells herbal vinegars, hot pepper oil, catnip pillows, eye pillows (small rectangular pillows made from silky fabric filled with flax seed and a blend of herbs that help you to relax), dream pillows, natural car air-fresheners, all-natural face cream, salve for gardener's hands and cuts and rashes, rose balls, and dried flowers.

In the fall she teaches two classes a month—on making face creams, vinegars, and salve—from September to December. She charges between $12 and $15 a class. She usually gives a lecture; with some classes, students take home one of the products discussed. Carol holds these classes in her home.

Mixing Kids and Business

LAST SPRING was very interesting because I had just had my son in March. It was rough." At that point all her herbs were in their seed trays, and the plants needed to be transplanted. "So he was right out there with me, in the Snugly."

Carol also had a teenager baby-sit a couple of days a week, and the sitter even helped her out in the greenhouse when there was a lot of work to be done. At the time, Carol's daughter was in pre-kindergarten three days a week. During the summer Carol was able to send her daughter to a couple of weeklong day camps, and that helped her out a bit.

Carol does her best to involve her kids in her business. "Hallie will come out and plant some things with me, and after she is done with that I'll set up a little table for her and she will draw. That occupies her for a long time." Carol also plays stories on tape. Although Carol isn't a big fan of television, she does let her daughter watch public television. But other than that, she tries to keep her children's time occupied with other things.

Biggest Challenge

As FAR as the herb business goes, Carol is finished by the middle of July. "It's a very short season and that's difficult, because if you don't make your money in the spring, you don't make your money." Carol does earn some money with the crafts and classes in the fall, but not a lot.

Farming isn't an easy industry to get into or stay in. There are many factors that need to be taken into consideration, including weather and when to plant.

Rewards

CAROL SAYS, "It's really nice to be able to stay on my property, enjoying the gardens and meeting a lot of really neat people."

Carol's Advice

A HOME *business shouldn't be [overly] idealized. . . . You can do it, but it takes a lot of maneuvering. It takes a different mind-set. If you're used to working outside of the home and concentrating on your work all day and then you start to work at home, you're going to find you have a half-hour to do one thing and then you have to deal with [the kids], then you'll have another half-hour free. You just need to get used to that.*

Working at home can be very joyful, and when you finally find [a job] that you love, things just start clicking. It may take a while and a lot of planning, but I think if you find the right occupation for you, it will work out really well.

Recommended Resources

ORGANIZATIONS

*   Herb Growing and Marketing Network
    1-717-393-3295
    www.herbnet.com

    The $60 annual membership includes a quarterly magazine and free advertising.

BOOKS

*   Betty E. M. Jacobs, *Profitable Herb Growing at Home*. Charlotte, Vt.: Garden Way Publishing, 1976.

    Talks about culinary products to make with your herbs, basic herbs to grow, and ways to market them.

*   Lee Sturdivant, *Herbs for Sale: Growing and Marketing Herbs, Herbal Products, and Herbal Know-How*. Friday Harbor, Wash.: San Juan Naturals, 1994.

    Profiles six different herb farms and tells what they sell and how they do it.

MAGAZINES

*   *Herb Companion*. There's not much in this magazine about starting an herb business, but it has some great creative ideas.

FREELANCE PHOTOGRAPHER

Name: Lisa Zaccagnini
Location: Beacon Falls, Connecticut
Family Facts: Married, three children—Jessica, 7, Matthew, 4, and Brian, 2
Business: Beacon Hill Photography

Why She Started Her Business

LISA GREW up in a traditional family—her father worked and her mother stayed home and raised Lisa and her brother and sister. Although her mother enjoyed being a mom, Lisa explains that once she and her siblings had grown up, her mom realized she didn't have much substance to her life. "I remember as I got older her regretting that she didn't have anything of herself to offer to anyone. She didn't know who she was except that she was supposed to be there for her husband and her kids. I didn't want to wake up one day and wonder, 'Who am I?' and not have anything to call my own."

Lisa's career started when she was asked to be a model for a local photographer. After a couple of sessions she got her nerve up to ask if she could apprentice with him. Lisa had always enjoyed taking pictures as a hobby, but this was her first step toward becoming a professional.

Qualifications

AFTER STUDYING with the photographer, Lisa realized that she needed more training and wanted to go to school. After a few years of school and more training with a photographer, she felt more confident and found a partner and started working with him in a home-based setting.

Lisa eventually wants to get her B.A. in photography. So far she has gotten through two years. Once her children are older she plans to finish her degree, but she has found, "Every time I think I can get back to school, I get pregnant. So I have had to put it off for a while. But I am going to finish my degree in photography. It is one of my goals."

Start-up Costs

WHEN LISA first started her business with her partner, they both went into the business 50/50. It cost about $5,000 for them to buy the equipment they needed, including lighting, backdrops, cameras, props, and posing tables. Lisa felt they had a great

By the year 2000 Lisa knows she will be using more digital technology in her photography business, which will undoubtedly involve new equipment.

setup. Their main selling point was that they could provide a client with double coverage at all times. She says, "Since my partner was a man and I was a woman, it worked out superbly. The bride felt comfortable, the groom felt comfortable. It worked out great."

But in 1995 her business partner felt he needed to move on. Lisa was hesitant about going on alone but decided to give it her best shot. She was able to buy him out and keep the business. She still is able to offer the double coverage by hiring another freelancer who happens to be a mom with two older children. She explains how she does this. "Since she has two older children, she has more flexible time than somebody in my situation with young children." Lisa usually uses her when she has to do an eight-hour wedding. By the year 2000 Lisa knows she will be using more digital technology in her photography business, which will undoubtedly involve new equipment.

Whether you decide to freelance for other photographers or choose to start your own business, Lisa recommends you make sure you have good equipment—"More than just a 35mm camera." Lisa uses a Bronica camera, but there are many different cameras

available. "I just happened to train with this camera, and I felt very comfortable with it. I felt like, 'Yeah, this could be a part of me.' That's something very important. If you don't feel comfortable using the equipment, you're not going to do a very good job."

Services

ALTHOUGH WEDDINGS are the bread and butter of Lisa's business, she also does bar/bat mitzvahs, birthday parties, newspaper work, family portraits, school pictures, pet pictures, greeting cards, and engagement sittings. Lisa has found that school pictures are a great way to reach out to a lot of families in a short amount of time.

Rates

LISA HAS two pricing plans for weddings: an eight- or four-hour day. For four-hour coverage she charges $450. This includes 75 to 100 photos in an album the client gets to keep. The eight-hour day costs $1,500 and includes 150 to 200 pictures and an engagement sitting along with a 12-sided bridal album. "I try to offer a price that's fair. I pretty much let them decide how they want to break up the time. They can take a four-hour day and add two hours to it. Or take a four-hour day and take two hours from it." It usually comes down to what the client can afford, but Lisa tries her best to accommodate clients.

Marketing

LISA BEGAN by getting referrals from a catering hall. This is a great way to begin, as most people who are planning a wedding usually try to find a caterer first. Her main mode of advertising is through word of mouth and the newsletter she puts out called *Picture This*. It's four to sixteen pages long and is sent out twice a year. Along with the different services she offers, it offers tips for amateur photographers on how to take better pictures.

Lisa's mailing list consists of her client base of about 200 people. She also leaves the newsletters at flower shops, hair salons, and "Whoever is willing to let me put them out."

In a few years Lisa may be moving to another state. If so, she plans to start out first by getting contracts through schools to take school pictures. She'll work on getting together a mailing list of families and will send them her newsletter, explaining that she is new to the area, and she'll also hand out business cards and go to bridal shops.

Hiring Help

SOMETIMES A person needs a photographer and Lisa isn't able to cover it. This is when she calls her freelancer to cover the job. It's still very necessary for her freelancer to meet with the client. "They need to see her, they need to speak with her, and they need to feel comfortable with her."

Tips

• Lisa knows how important it is to create your own special niche when starting a small business. Although most people have to leave their home to find an appropriate photographer, Beacon Hill Photography comes to the customer. "I don't ever want to get so big that the customer has to come to me." To give a quote on a project, Lisa will go over to the client's house. Depending on what kind of work she will be doing, she brings all her sample books with her. "It empowers them more for me to come out to them. [It gives] them a sense of interviewing me. They are more relaxed and ask more questions. I don't think that will ever change if I do have a studio outside the house. I'll always try to offer a quoting process in their homes."

• Lisa does not advertise her phone number. "I want to grow the business slowly. I'm afraid people will call for quotes at a rate that I wouldn't be able to handle, because it's very enticing to take almost every job that is offered to me. But I don't have time to do every job." Lisa admits, "I know myself, and I would say yes to just about everything that came through. I don't want to do that. I want to grow slowly so I have control over my time and my children's time."

• Talk to other photographers about what photo lab they use and recommend. Once you locate a lab, explain to them that you will be giving them all your business. Lisa advises, "Establish some sort of rapport with them so they know they will be seeing you a lot." They probably will give you some sort of discount. Lisa doesn't trust sending her film in the mail and drives forty-five minutes to get to her lab. "If I wasn't happy with them, I would travel farther."

Mixing Kids and Business

MOST OF Lisa's clients have no idea her office is in the basement of her townhouse. She does some studio work, and that is all done in her home. She has set up a play area in her studio for her children as well; so if she needs to get some work done, the kids can be with her and play with their toys.

Currently Lisa's husband works from home too, so he is able to watch their children when she goes out on assignments.

Most of her jobs are in the evenings or weekends. But if for some reason her husband or parents can't watch the kids, she won't take the job. "I'll just say, 'I'm booked that night.' The client doesn't need to know that I can't see them because my husband won't be home." Lisa just explains what times she has open and works from there. "I do try to leave some days open so we can have family time. I could fill up every night and every weekend."

Biggest Challenge

LISA ISN'T a big fan of bookkeeping, so she hires an accountant. "Just let me go and let me take my pictures, and leave me alone about the money."

Rewards

LISA SAYS, "I am helping someone create memories for the rest of their life, and I'm helping myself because I'm out there; I'm living a life away from the children for a little while. I need that mental break. I can let another side come out. I can be creative by saying I produced this many children and look, they're doing this, this, and this, but my photography is me."

Lisa's Advice

DO YOU *think you can do it? Do you have enough confidence in yourself that you can meet the challenge? My feelings were, "I can do this, I can take these pictures, I have something of myself that I can offer." If it's going to make you feel guilty because you are taking too much time away from A or B, because you have had to ask for these favors from C, then don't, because guilt will override the passion of doing something on your own.*

Recommended Resources

BOOKS

- Michael Willins, *Photographer's Market.* Cincinnati: Writer's Digest Books, 1996. Provides an extensive list of markets in which you can sell your work.

GIFT BASKETS

Name: Kathy Lindberg
Location: Wooster, Ohio
Family Facts: Married, two children—
    Erik, 6, and Alexis, 3
Business: Gift Basket Gallery
Web Site:
    http://www.giftbasketgallery.com

Why She Started Her Business

KATHY WORKED for herself and considered her business, working for eight years as a music therapist, to be home-based. After her second child was born, she wanted to find a way to stay-at-home a bit more and still work. "I always wanted to be home with my kids. Working as a music therapist was taking me more and more out of the house," explains Kathy. One day as Kathy was visiting her local Borders bookstore, she found herself in the business section, where books on starting your own gift basket business almost jumped off the shelf at her. Kathy says, "I have been doing this now for a little over two years." It's been a perfect match for Kathy, who was looking for a business where she could use her cre-

ativity and design skills. Kathy offers gift and bath baskets to businesses, new moms, and kids.

Qualifications

KATHY SAYS, "My experience has been, if you have any kind of business background, it is beneficial [when starting your own business]. . . . However, you can always take classes and read books [to educate] yourself on the business aspects." Kathy sees a lot of people starting a gift basket business because they like the creative side—"At least I did." But she goes on to say, "I went into it without thinking about the marketing or the business part of it."

Those who start this type of business should have good design skills. You can also brush up on design by taking classes on making gift baskets. Kathy did this and found it very helpful.

Start-up Costs

TO START her business, Kathy spent between $3,500 and $5,000. "Start-up costs will vary greatly, depending upon the location of your business and how you purchase your inventory, etc." Kathy has

The business classes she took and the networking with other people in the gift basket industry helped Kathy with her pricing.

heard of people who have started their business with as little as $100 or as much as $50,000.

Equipment

YOU WILL need a worktable, baskets/ containers, filler, wrap, and a basic inventory of the types of baskets you will want to create, such as baby items, gourmet foods, bath products, and so on.

Rates

HER BASKETS range from $25 to $100+. The business classes she took and the networking with other people in the gift basket industry helped her with her pricing, as there is a standard formula for figuring out basket prices.

Marketing

MARKETING IS the hardest part for Kathy. Although she can come up with very creative marketing ideas, she struggles with implementing them. Kathy has tried a variety of marketing ideas. The ones that brought her the least amount of business were ads in a local college paper and placing a radio ad.

She has found that word of mouth from happy clients and networking are her best forms of advertising. She is able to network with her local chamber of commerce and has joined a local women-in-business organization. Kathy is also able to do a lot of networking online: She is a member of Moms Network Exchange, Digital Women, and several women-in-business listservs.

Direct mailing is another form of marketing Kathy uses. She gets addresses of businesses in the area from her chamber of commerce (Kathy's target market is business), or she finds companies in the yellow pages. She never sends out a mailing without first calling those on her list and letting them know about her products. Making those phone calls is not easy for Kathy. She admits, "I was petrified to pick up that phone." She has found it helpful to write a script so she knows what she's trying to convey. Even though she may not follow it word-for-word, it's helpful for her to look at it as she talks. When she first started making these phone calls, she felt she needed to make a sell. "I've changed that thought. Now I'm looking for businesses that are interested in what I have to offer." She finds this to be a great way for companies to become aware that her service is available. Once she sends out a mailing, she always follow ups with a phone call to see if there are any questions or if someone is interested in purchasing baskets for clients.

Kathy also sends out a monthly newsletter to those who purchase her baskets. Her target is businesses, so she includes articles on the benefits of gift giving and how to use gifts in your business. She also highlights the basket of the month. As more people continue buying her products, she will include articles of interest to particular companies. She has also placed an ad in the yellow pages and has found her Web site to be helpful in obtaining new clients.

Tips

RESEARCH, RESEARCH, research. Network with others in the gift basket industry, and if you can find classes on starting or running this type of business (either in your local area or on the Internet), take them.

Mixing Kids and Business

KATHY FINDS herself juggling her kids and her home business on a daily basis. Kathy explains, "I work when the kids don't have an immediate need. [I make] sales calls in the morning while the kids are playing.

My son is in school during the afternoons till dinnertime, so I can get work done here and there while my daughter plays in my office. I also take her when I need to pick up [a] product or to shop for inventory. I try not to take her when I make deliveries. At those times I either use a sitter, my husband, or my mom to help watch the kids." Sometimes she hires a sitter to watch her kids while she works at home. She also works late at night when the kids have gone to bed.

Although Kathy tries to stick to certain business hours, she says, "I eat, live, and breathe gift baskets seven days a week, ten to twelve hours a day."

Biggest Challenge

THE TWO areas that have been the most difficult for Kathy have been juggling the family needs with the business needs and marketing her business. Working while the kids are sleeping or away at school or camp has worked well for her. Her other obstacle has been marketing her business. And even though this isn't her favorite area, she has figured out the best ways that work for her.

Rewards

HER BIGGEST reward? "Being able to be home with my kids while building a business that is all my own, and watching my business slowly grow," she says.

Kathy's Advice

GO FOR *it! Don't let fear stand in your way. If you want it badly enough you can find a way to make it work.*

Recommended Resources

BOOKS

- Shirley Frazier, *How to Start a Home-Based Gift Basket Business.* Old Saybrook, Conn.: The Globe Pequot Press, 1998.

ONLINE RESOURCES

- Baskets, Balloons & Blooms Free Newsletter: http://www.fantastic-baskets.com

- By Design discussion board TOC: http://www.bydesignmagazine.com/board/

- Gift Basket Exchange Message Board: http://autumnwinds.com/mssgbrd/board.html

- Gift Basket Service Toolkit: http://www.entrepreneurmag.com/resource/toolkit/giftbas.hts

- Gift Baskets 101—How-to manuals and supplies: http://www.giftbaskets101.com

- Start Your Own Gift Basket Business: http://www.basketbusiness.com

- America Online has a gift basket forum—you can find it by going to keyword "gift basket pro."

NEWSLETTER

You can subscribe to Kathy's newsletter *It's a Wrap* by visiting her Web site (www.giftbasketgallery.com).

INDEXER

Name: Marilyn Rowland
Location: East Falmouth, Massachu-
    setts
Family Facts: Married, two children—
    Nathaniel, 12, and Gabriela, 9
Business: Indexer
Web Site: http://www.marisol.com/

Why She Started Her Business

MARILYN ROWLAND has been indexing books and periodicals for twenty-five years. "My father was an indexer and he got me started," says Marilyn, who now resides in Cape Cod, Massachusetts, where she indexes full time from her home.

Qualifications

MARILYN SAYS, "Indexing is a hard business to break into without a concerted effort. You should be intelligent and like detailed, analytical work. Similar to a computer programmer, you have to see the whole picture and also be able to work with the nitty-gritty details. You need to be able to organize information so that it makes sense to others." If you love to read and enjoy re-

search and puzzles, then indexing may just be for you.

There is a lot more work to indexing than people realize. Most indexers actually index part time, in addition to writing and editing. It takes a good amount of effort to get started in the indexing business. Marilyn recommends taking an indexing course (your local adult-education program may offer classes), reading books on indexing, and attending indexing conferences. From there you will need to do marketing and networking. Once you do get work, you will have to deal with deadlines.

Equipment

WHEN MARILYN first started indexing, her equipment consisted of a box of index cards. She now uses a computer, indexing and word processing software, a laser printer, a second phone line, a fax machine, and a modem for Internet access.

Rates

EXPERIENCED INDEXERS can usually index five to ten pages per hour. You can make anywhere from $2.50 to $10 per book page, or $15 to $60 per hour. However, rates vary based on publisher, how technical the

> *Depending on the individual, it takes a good six months to get started in indexing and a good year to receive steady work.*

book is, the region of the country, and your experience. Depending on the individual, it takes a good six months to get started in indexing and a good year to receive steady work.

A full-time indexer can make between $40,000 and $50,000+ a year. A part-time indexer can make about half that. You can work with as few as one or two publishers. Marilyn works with between twelve and sixteen different publishers in any one year.

Marilyn has found networking with other indexers to be very helpful. "I was an indexer for years and years before I ever encountered any other indexers." She finds it very useful to ask around and see what other indexers are charging. "That's the burning question everyone seems to have: How much do I charge?"

Marketing

MARILYN EXPLAINS that it's very important to pick your niche. "Any woman who has kids has some field of expertise. Whether it's parenting books or something else, they should seek out that niche. Eventually, something will come through. When it does, you do the best possible job on that index. Spend twice as much time on it.

Make sure you have all their guidelines. Seek all the help you can through the American Society of Indexers and INDEX-L." (You can learn more about these two organizations in the resources at the end of this profile.)

Marilyn says, "If you have experience or interest in a particular field, you can use that knowledge to find clients. I had a particular interest in scientific and technical topics, so I called technical publishers. Someone else might try publishers specializing in medical, gardening, or computer books." Marilyn goes on to explain her approach: "Call the publisher and ask to speak to the person who hires freelancers. Ask if the publisher has a need for freelance indexers. Tell why you are interested and offer to send a résumé and sample indexes. Then follow up with a phone call. You will have to do this numerous times to establish a client base, but keep at it."

Once you have been in the indexing business for some time, you will have to do very little marketing. Marilyn now relies on repeat business and referrals from satisfied customers and other indexers. But when you first start out, "You will need to call publishers, authors, and other indexers to ask for work. Sometimes you can find an indexer who needs help and is willing to train you in exchange for some assistance. Find names of publishers in *The Literary Market Place* and other publishing-industry publications available at your library. Clients do not have to be in your geographic area, but it may help to start with local publishers."

Marilyn explains, "If you can create good quality indexes that meet clients' needs, you have a much better chance of being called again and building up a list of clients [and referrals]." Marilyn discovered that once she found one publisher to take her on, her good work spoke for her. She was highly recommended by the first publishing firm she started with.

Tips

- Marilyn would recommend that someone with older children become an indexer. "I think it really helps to have the kids in school while you are working. It does take some concentration. It can be done at night, after the kids are in bed, but by that time most people are exhausted. If you have younger kids, you can hire baby-sitters or work with a partner."

- It also helps to do some volunteer work. Index the school cookbook or the town history book. This way you can gain experience, have a sample or two to show clients, and perhaps some paying jobs will result.

- If you think you're interested in becoming an indexer, practice indexing a book that's already indexed, then compare the indexes. Was this experience fun or pure torture?

Mixing Kids and Business

WHEN MARILYN started her indexing business from home, her children were 1 and 3 years old. She chose to go with a day-care provider part time. Now that her kids are older and in school, she doesn't need sitters or day care.

Biggest Challenge

MARILYN SAYS, "I am always working." She admits that from time to time her house isn't as clean as she would like, but she has no regrets. "On the whole I love working at home. And I love having

"On the whole I love working at home. And I love having the kids around me, too."

the kids around me, too. Indexing can be very stressful with its short turnaround time, so you are always faced with looming deadlines. There are lulls and then there are periods of too much work and lots of juggling."

Rewards

A S STRESSFUL as her work can be, Marilyn says, "I think I am less stressed than my friends who work outside the home. They have less flexibility and tend to have to deal with difficult people (bosses, clients, co-workers) on a daily basis." Although indexing does require a certain amount of concentration, it doesn't require a lot of time on the phone or running off to meetings.

Marilyn enjoys the fact that she works from home. "I love the freedom and flexibility of working according to my own schedule and being able to volunteer at school, take the kids places, and be there when they get home from school. And, since being an indexer is such a portable job, picking where you want to live is your choice."

Expanding the Business

M ARILYN HAS also started working with Web page design. She sees this as an excellent business that moms can do at home. As the Internet grows, there will be a bigger need for people who know HTML authoring.

Marilyn's Advice

P ICK A *home business that fits your talents and meets your needs as much as possible. For instance, if your primary reason to work at home is to spend more time with the kids, don't pick a high-pressure, high-concentration job that requires you to meet rigorous deadlines or have to work specific hours. Find something that allows you to work at a slower pace, at night, or during nap times or preschool time. In other words, analyze your needs and know what you want and what each type of business requires. Don't pick indexing [for the money], pick it because you have an understanding of what it involves and you think you have the talents, interests, and work environment that would make indexing work for you.*

Recommended Resources

ORGANIZATIONS

*   American Society of Indexers
    P.O. Box 48267
    Seattle, WA 98148-0267
    1-206-241-9196
    http://www.asindexing.org

    The $120 membership includes a subscription to the newsletter *The Indexer*, listings in the annual Register of Indexers, membership in local chapters, and reduced rates on society publications.

There are national and local chapter meetings that you can attend.

Marilyn is active in many support groups and recommends them for anyone wanting to become an indexer. One of them is the American Society of Indexers. Marilyn says, "I started the Massachusetts chapter and am now president and serve on the national board."

BOOKS

- University of Chicago Press, *The Chicago Manual of Style,* 14th ed. Chicago: University of Chicago Press, 1993.

- Hans H. Wellisch, *Indexing from A to Z.* Bronx, N.Y.: H./W. Wilson, 1996.

- Nancy Mulvany, *Indexing Books.* Chicago: University of Chicago Press, 1994.

ONLINE RESOURCES

To talk with other indexers on the Internet you can join a listserv group. To join INDEX-L, send e-mail to listserv@bing vmb.cc.binghamton. In the body of your letter, write "Subscribe INDEX-L." Then type your first and last name.

CATERER

Why She Started Her Business

WHILE MOST of us agonize over what to make for dinner, Anna Marie has made preparing the perfect meal her business. For six years, Anna Marie and her partner have been catering meals for every social event there is. "We will do anything. And if we don't know how to do it, we will learn." Learn they have. They've done bridal teas, funerals, fund-raisers for political candidates, weddings, library functions, Christmas parties, or just a meal for a simple family dinner.

Before Anna Marie began the business with her partner, she worked as a personnel manager. She says, "We were both stay-at-home moms coming from other careers." They both felt they needed to do something where they could make some money but still keep their kids at home. "We were both really good cooks, so we said, 'Let's try it.'"

Qualifications

TO GET started in the catering business, you should first really like cooking. "Because you may be doing a lot of it at one time," says Anna Marie with a laugh. You need to be very organized and have good communication skills. "You should be somewhat creative in your presentation, because a lot of it is in the way it looks, such as the garnish or what platters you use."

Equipment

ANNA MARIE says, "I started by using everything in the house." They also rented equipment until they saved enough money to buy what they needed. Even when they hired a lawyer to incorporate their busi-

To get started in the catering business, you should first really like cooking.

197

ness, they traded services such as child care and catering with the lawyer to pay for their incorporation fee.

After six years, their equipment includes steam trays, coffeemakers, giant bowls, serving dishes, serving spoons, stockpots, good knives, cutting boards, cleaners, and aprons. They have a supply of china and glassware that they make available to smaller parties. If they need servers for an event, they try to hire at-home women who are interested in making some money. Says Anna Marie, "We recommend them, and they are paid directly by our clients."

Anna Marie has most of their menus on the computer. However, "We don't have set menus; our name is *Catering to Your Taste*." She sits down with her clients and figures out what they need, then she comes up with an individualized menu.

Rates

IN THE beginning, most of the profits went into buying equipment. Although initially their prices were a little low, they never lost money. In fact, when they started they saw a profit almost immediately.

To figure out what to charge, Anna Marie and her partner read books on catering and talked with other caterers. The standard procedure is this: Start by figuring out your menu and how much food you need per person. Once you figure your cost, triple it. "That takes in the resources that we have and our time. That is actually a standard for-

mula for caterers," explains Anna Marie. She charges between $45 and $60 per person for a buffet and $12 to $15 per person for a luncheon.

They usually pay themselves once or twice a month. To do this, they figure out all their expenses, including future insurance costs and sales tax. They figure out what's left and split it down the middle. "We have to do that because we are a chapter S corporation." This means that the company cannot make any money because of tax reasons, and the profit has to be split between the shareholders of the corporation. At the end of the year there can be no money in the bank—if there is, they get taxed on it. "We have to split the profits so it becomes individual tax and not corporate tax."

Last year Anna Marie made between $12,000 and $14,000. Although this is much less than what she was used to making, she feels it's fine. "I don't have commuting costs, and I don't need a great wardrobe or have to pay child-care costs."

Marketing

ANNA MARIE and her partner started their business (Mattson and Massaro) in a unique way. They didn't put an ad in the paper or pass out flyers. They simply started by donating their time and talents to charitable events such as auctions for the Red Cross, AIDS associations, and Friends of the Library.

The first job they catered was a fundraiser for the local symphony. "I volunteered to do the food for that. It was very elaborate, and people were impressed. Of course people wondered who had made such wonderful food and wanted to use us at their next gathering." The organization paid for the raw ingredients, so it didn't cost them anything but their time.

They sometimes auction off a meal at a charity event, offering to donate a dinner for two or four. "So people get to know us that way." Then, if these people are ever in need of a caterer, they know who to call. Most of their business has grown by word of mouth.

Business can be sporadic at times. Some months are slower than others. "Because we have children, sometimes having time off is good. It's wonderful being home with them, but it's very difficult saying, 'Mommy has to cook right now. Can you go play a little while longer?'"

Tips

- If you decide to become a caterer, you might want to seriously consider incorporating your business. Anna Marie explains why: "Because of the nature of the catering business, it's safer. If somebody, God forbid, got sick eating our food, they could sue our corporation." They also carry a liability policy.

- "Make yourself known as quickly as possible—volunteering is the way to do it."

- Personal chefs are becoming a hot business; some cook pre-made meals for couples who work and don't have time to make home-cooked meals.

- Start a lunch delivery service for office workers who are tired of the fast-food menus.

Mixing Kids and Business

ANNA MARIE has seen her children become very interested in her business. Her oldest son has begun to ask if he can work with her. "And I let him, and he's good. It would be my dream to open a business with him, actually." Anna Marie is finding that sometimes the best way to keep her kids entertained while she works is to let them help her.

Her youngest son, Conrad, has just started nursery school, so he is gone three mornings a week. "I have also learned to work very fast. It's either get up very early in the morning . . . or work very quickly when they're at school. But I still have time for school events."

Rewards

ANNA MARIE knows she is doing a good job. One day she received a card in the mail from a client. The card read, "I hope someday you have the opportunity to sit back and really enjoy a party. But then again you'd have to find an Anna Marie

Johansen, and that's really hard." Anna Marie says, "It makes me feel good that people appreciate what I do."

Expanding the Business

MATTSON AND Massaro have started to get into whole-party planning now. "I bring in a florist, deal with all the rentals, and create this whole look for them." Anna Marie still does events with her partner, but she has started to do some events herself.

Anna Marie's Advice

HAVE A *solid relationship with your family before you start something like this. I think that is very important.*

Recommended Resources

MAGAZINES

- *Bon Appetit.* Includes recipes from restaurants from around the world.

- *Food and Wine.* Provides menus along with its recipes.

- *Gourmet.* Keeps you abreast of what's happening in the food industry.

COOKBOOKS

- Sarah Lee Chase, *Cold-Weather Cooking.* New York: Workman Publishing, 1990.

- Sarah Lee Chase, *Nantucket Open-House Cookbook.* New York: Workman Publishing, 1987.

- Julee Rosso, Sheila Lukins, and Sarah Lee Chase. *The Silver Palate Good Times Cookbook.* New York: Workman Publishing, 1985.

ARCHITECT

Name: Rebecca Bostick
Location: Alexandria, Virginia
Family Facts: Married, two children—
    Taylor, 10, and Patrick, 7
Business: Architect

Why She Started Her Business

REBECCA WORKED for an architecture firm for six years before she started to work from home seven years ago. After four months at home with her baby, she felt she was ready to go back to work. "But as soon as I went back to work I thought, 'Why am I here? I should be home with my son.'" She went through this for two months. She was constantly wondering what her son was doing and how he was getting along.

The firm she was working for at the time was getting ready to relocate, and Rebecca wasn't looking forward to an hour-long commute. "All of a sudden I thought, 'I can't be that far away from my baby.'" Rebecca had been doing a few architectural jobs at night in addition to her day job, and around this time a couple of home-addition jobs came her way. Rebecca felt sure she could leave her job and turn these moonlighting jobs into a home career. "I took these house additions and jumped in with both feet." Everything went great, until those two jobs were finished. Then Rebecca had to figure out how to start getting regular business.

Services

AT FIRST, most of Rebecca's work consisted of drawing up plans for house additions and renovations. A few years into her business, she started to get county contracts for schools. Rebecca rarely has to worry about clients coming over to her house. She usually meets with them at their home or place of business.

Start-up Costs

REBECCA ALREADY had all the equipment she needed to get her business off the ground. The one thing she did do was build an office for herself.

Marketing

MOST OF Rebecca's advertising is through word of mouth. "Every time I did an addition, I'd think, 'How did I get that so I can do that again?'" Rebecca says, "You have to network and join organizations. You

"You have to network and join organizations. You have to meet people."

have to meet people." Rebecca found this out her second year of working from home. Business wasn't just going to come to her without some concerted effort. "That was the hard part, learning how to network and talk to people."

After working at home for three years, Rebecca was hired by the county for a school project. "Every two years they award projects, and I'm now on my third school project." The county was already familiar with her work through her old job. "That got me in the door. The interview went okay, and I proved myself. They may have given me a chance on the first project because they knew me." However, she did such a great job on the first project that they have given her consecutive jobs.

Rebecca explains how one of her interviews went for one of the school projects. "All I had was my briefcase and a tray of slides to put on their projector. Another company had all the fancy, cutting-edge computer technology to use for their interview. [I met with] three men all in business suits, and they walked out and looked at me and said, 'Oh, you're doing this all by yourself? Where is all your stuff?' I answered, 'Here is my tray of slides.' They laughed and

said, 'Good luck.' I said, 'Thanks, I don't think I'll need your luck.' I was so amused that I was put down by this large firm because I didn't have all these bells and whistles."

Rebecca thought she would use slides of her home additions instead of the school additions she had done. She knew they were going to see a lot of school shots. She wanted to show them something they'd remember. "Everyone lives in a house, and everyone likes to see what other people do to their houses. So that was the approach I took," explains Rebecca. "The interview committee told me they remembered my name the most because they got so sick of seeing faraway shots of school buildings, but they remembered my home additions. Sometimes you don't have to be big and flashy, you just have to figure out a way to relate to people. That is what I feel is my key to success."

Hiring Help

REBECCA COULD definitely use the help, but doesn't like the idea of someone she doesn't really know working in her home. That would feel like "an invasion of my family's privacy, so I just work a lot of nights."

Rebecca has found that if she involves her kids, they will cooperate better.

Mixing Kids and Business

WHEN HER kids were small, Rebecca used a sitter from 8:30 A.M. to 4:30 P.M., which sometimes varied. Some days she would pick them up earlier just so they could go do something together. Some mornings, if everyone was having a tough time getting ready, Rebecca found it nice that they could take their time and get to day care late. Now her son is in second grade, and she works while he is in school.

Rebecca stresses the importance of having your own office if you want to be an architect at home. "My kids love to come into my office and play with my things and I find [my equipment] all over the place. Or I'll leave my drawings out, and as far as my kids are concerned, they're drawings: 'Let's color them in.'"

Rebecca has found that if she involves her kids, they will cooperate better. "So I tend to save some of my blueprints, and if it's one of those afternoons and I have sick kids, I take out a blueprint and ask them to color it for me. They will sit by my desk and work and work and work. Sometimes I can get something accomplished."

Biggest Challenge

REBECCA FOUND her first school project a challenge. "I had done the work several times before, but I always had someone looking over my shoulder checking my work, and it was always their responsibility. On that first project, I knew what I was doing, but I had never been through the whole process of meeting with the client, getting the job, signing the contract, and lining up the engineers."

Another challenge Rebecca has found is learning not to work nine to five. "Maybe I work a little in the afternoons and a little at night. I get more accomplished in the late evenings. I don't have people calling me on the phone, and I don't have to worry about where the kids are because they are asleep. I'm breaking out of the idea that business hours are nine to five."

Rebecca's Advice

RESEARCH. MAKE *sure you know what you're getting into. Make sure you're the kind of person who can do it, because I don't think everyone can [work from home]. I think you have to be self-motivating, and you have to be enthusiastic about what you're doing. Work hard, and you can make it work.*

I find in my MATCH (Mothers Access to Careers at Home) group that we have women coming in who are looking to start a business. You need to be realistic. These women come in and think they'll do this career and make all this money, but they find they have only ten hours a week and they're trying to do a full-time business during their children's nap time. It's great if you have a kid who sleeps twice a day for an hour and a half. But kids are going to grow up, and next year they will be sleeping only an hour once a day. Then how do you handle your business?

Recommended Resources

ORGANIZATIONS

- Mothers Access to Careers at Home (MATCH)
  P.O. Box 123
  Annandale, VA 22003
  1-703-205-9664

- American Institute of Architects (AIA)
  1735 New York Avenue, NW
  Washington, D.C. 20006
  1-202-626-7300
  http://www.aia.org

  The $175 annual fee includes a monthly newsletter, member discounts, and professional seminars.

BOOKS

- Sarah Breathnach, *Simple Abundance: A Day Book of Comfort and Joy*. New York: Warner Books, 1995.

- Stephen Covey, *The Seven Habits of Highly Effective People*. New York: Simon & Schuster, 1989.

Wedding Planner

Why She Started Her Business

WHEN SHE worked in a bridal registry department, Packy fell in love with the idea of organizing weddings and working with soon-to-be-married couples. There was only one problem: Packy didn't enjoy the forty-hour week. She explains, "Life became more about work and less about family, which was not what I had in mind."

She liked the fact that wedding consulting allowed her to use her organizational skills, be creative, and use her clerical skills to create the various documents necessary for running the business.

Qualifications

ALTHOUGH SOME associations offer certification, it's not necessary for wedding planners. Instead you're going to need to have strong organizational skills, creativity, and a good knowledge of the wedding industry. Packy explains, "I also have clerical skills and have created a database of vendors." Letter writing is a useful skill to have as well, as this profession is big on people skills. You will need the ability to work not only with the client but also with vendors, extended family, and anyone else associated with the wedding. "It's important to be able to do a presentation of what your business is all about so that the client understands the complexity of planning a wedding," says Packy. It's also important to present a professional, reputable, thorough, and organized

It's important to present a professional, reputable, thorough, and organized service that follows the rules of etiquette and of business.

service that follows the rules of etiquette and of business.

Packy recommends wedding consulting courses, which you can find through various organizations (see the resources listed at the end of this profile). In the future she plans to incorporate her business.

Services

As a wedding consultant, Packy acts as liaison between the bride/wedding party and the vendors, such as the florist, disc jockey, and so forth. She goes to all meetings, helps with the rehearsal, and is there for the entire wedding. Her number one goal is to make sure everything runs smoothly and that the wedding is the best experience for the newlyweds. She is accomplishing just that. In March 1999, the organization June Wedding, Inc. named Packy the wedding consultant of the year at a conference in Dallas, Texas.

Equipment

Packy started out without much equipment, but she recommends that as your business grows you should work toward acquiring a computer, a fax, and a cell phone. She has created a wedding day schedule for vendors—if they don't show up at the proper time, she immediately gets on her cell phone to track them down to see if there are any problems. Packy also plans to purchase a two-way radio. While Packy is with the bride and bridesmaids, someone from her staff is always with the groomsmen; having radio contact will help ensure that everyone is ready at the same time.

Packy also has what she calls "the kit" and takes it to every one of her weddings. Everything she needs, from emergency phone numbers for the wedding party's doctors and phone numbers for plumbers to super glue, a sewing kit, extra stockings, a bee sting kit, and more, all fits nicely in a suitcase. Packy is always prepared for an emergency.

Rates

Packy's rates range from $150 for a single consultation to $1,500 to $6,000 for full-service consulting. Packy charges her clients a flat rate, which she calculates from taking all the wedding information, including the number of people they plan on inviting and how much planning they have done to date. She explains, "I need to know the date of the wedding and a general idea of what will be happening and the sequence. I take a lot of factors into consideration and arrive at a flat rate. I have to evaluate the responsibilities of the project."

Marketing

Networking with vendors and other consultants has become Packy's best method of advertising. She has learned that reception site managers are the most beneficial, as the reception site is one of the first places a bride visits. She also has a listing in the yellow pages and belongs to a wedding professionals association that sends her referrals.

Packy has also found the Internet to be an invaluable tool for her. It has helped her find unusual wedding items, such as the pillow for the rings and various sources for favors. She freelances for the Cleveland Live newspaper Web site, were her forum is called The Wedding Planner. She also hosts a chat on America Online, which helps her tap into trends across the country. "Knowing consultants across the country gives me a valuable resource when I am looking for a particular item for a wedding. It is almost like a professional association on the Web. I've even gotten referrals from other wedding Web site hosts," explains Packy, who has had brides who live in other cities plan their weddings in Cleveland.

Packy has received a lot of her recognition due to networking with individuals through the Internet. She says, "I take advantage of all the free listings on wedding Web sites. I write to magazines and authors of books whenever I find an e-mail address. Many writers of books and newspapers have found me in the AOL directory. Writing for Web sites such as the Bizy Moms site has increased the traffic to my message board. Hosting chats has also been beneficial to my business. I have had many wedding profes-

sionals, as well as editors of major magazines (such as *Special Events Magazine*) and online editors of wedding Web sites (such as USAbride), as guests at my online chats." Packy has also contributed articles to *The Wall Street Journal* articles as well as to wedding publications. "I know this is a direct result of the Internet," says Packy.

Tips

PACKY SAYS, "Read as much about the industry as you can and be sure that you enjoy the tasks that you will be called on to perform. I also recommend taking a course in wedding consulting to learn not only about the industry, how to do a wedding, but also how to operate your business in an ethical and professional manner."

Mixing Kids and Business

PACKY'S YOUNGEST child was 16 when she first started her business, so day care was never an issue. However, that didn't mean that juggling family responsibilities and business activities was not necessary. Packy's family also cares for her husband's mother, which requires Packy to work around her mother-in-law's schedule. "I have worked out a system of prioritizing important business activities and upon completion tackle home activities that are top priority, and then return to finish the rest of my business activities in the afternoon," she explains.

"Start out small and add to your business as you become more comfortable with it."

Biggest Challenge

WORKING TOO many hours, especially when she first started her business, was Packy's biggest challenge.

Rewards

PACKY'S REWARD comes from "running a well-organized, coordinated, orchestrated, and perfectly timed wedding, resulting in a happy bride. Helping others is a major reward. I have the opportunity to help the couple, and vendors are grateful for the business I send them."

Packy's Advice

IF YOU *really want to work in the wedding industry but aren't sure if you can handle it with young children, I recommend doing it part time, such as specializing in finding reception sites for couples. I get a lot of calls from brides who want only this service. You could sell wedding invitations and/or favors or promote yourself as a decorator coordinating the flowers, favors, and place cards and formatting the reception site. Start out small and add to your business as you become more comfortable with it.*

Recommended Resources

PROFESSIONAL ASSOCIATIONS

*   June Wedding, Inc.
    1331 Burnham Avenue
    Las Vegas, Nevada 89104-3658
    1-702-474-9558
    robbi@junewedding.com
    http://www.junewedding.com

    This is an association for wedding and event professionals. It offers a correspondence course in wedding consulting, which includes three one-on-one phone classes.

*   Wedding Careers Worldwide
    1-877-933-9244
    http://www.weddingcareers.com

    This relatively new association offers courses in becoming a certified wedding consultant.

BOOKS

*   Madeline Barillo, *The Wedding Sourcebook Planner.* Los Angeles: Lowell House, 1997.

*   Robbi Ernst III, *Great Wedding Tips from the Experts.* Los Angeles: Lowell House, 1999.

- Alan and Denise Fields, *Bridal Bargains*, 4th edition. Boulder, Col.: Windsor Peak Press, 1998.

- Alan and Denise Fields, *Bridal Gown Guide*, 3rd edition, revised. Boulder, Col.: Windsor Peak Press, 1999.

- Carley Roney, *The Knot's Complete Guide to Weddings in the Real World.* New York: Broadway Books, 1998.

MAGAZINES

- *Special Events Magazine*

- *Vows*

- *Modern Bride*

There may also be small regional magazines you need to check out in your area.

ONLINE RESOURCES

- Cleveland Live: http://www.cleveland.com/weddings

  Packy writes articles about wedding topics and wedding vendors for this site. You will also find a message board for brides to ask questions on etiquette or wedding planning. This site has attracted brides from all over the world.

  Packy also hosts a wedding-consultant chat on American Online every Tuesday at 9:00 P.M. EST. To get there, use keyword "iVillage," then click on "careers."

BASKET DEALER

Name: Joanne Winthrop
Location: Oregon City, Oregon
Family Facts: Married, six children—
    Sheridan, 29, Trey, 27, Jordan,
    21, Brittan, 17, Canaan, 14, and
    Eastan, 11
Business: The Basket Connection

Why She Started Her Business

THE SIGN on Joanne Winthrop's desk reads, "Generation Technician." Her husband had given it to her to help bolster her self-image. Even though Joanne had made a conscious effort to raise her children herself, being "just a mom" was tough at times. She never attended college and knew nothing about business. Then Joanne's family encountered a crisis. Her husband became ill and was unable to work at his job as an independent basket salesman. Joanne says, "He was not eligible for unemployment benefits. We had no savings and lots of bills."

With no marketable skills, Joanne knew minimum wage wasn't going to support her family. Her brain went into overdrive. She knew how well Tupperware and Mary Kay sold at home parties and figured she could use that same method to sell something she loved—baskets.

Start-up Costs

JOANNE WENT to a few different home parties to see how they worked. Then she purchased $200 worth of baskets on credit from a buyer her husband knew. She first started advertising her parties by placing a $20 ad in a free local paper.

Rates

WHEN JOANNE first started, she sold her baskets at keystone price, which is double the wholesale price. But now she triples the price, and her products are still selling very well. Her baskets now sell from $5 to $45. The average price for one of Joanne's dealerships is $2,995. How did she come up with this price? "I just made it up. I figured out what I thought people could afford." Joanne sells her dealerships at franchise shows, where she charges a little more because of the cost involved in setting up a booth. She also sells her dealerships through mail order.

Marketing

JOANNE'S VERY first party consisted of three neighbors and her mother. Her sales came to only $50, but everyone agreed to host another one of Joanne's basket parties. From one of those parties, Joanne was able to take home $580. At that point Joanne realized that she could support her family with this business.

Although Joanne started out marketing her business with a $20 ad, she now travels and does franchise shows and runs ads in major magazines. She also has a public relations person who gets her into magazines. Her business has been profiled in six magazines, and she has appeared on *Oprah*.

How Her Business Works

BY THE end of Joanne's second year, she had fifty independent contractors and was grossing $250,000. Not bad for someone with no marketable skills. Then Joanne decided to change her business a little. Instead of using independent contractors, she decided to sell dealerships. "Instead of women working for me, I decided to create an opportunity for them to start their own

basket business. This way they could pick their own business name and have the satisfaction of owning their own home-based business."

Each dealer receives a 140-page manual that Joanne has written and a video on how to create a productive basket party. Dealers also receive training and consulting services and $1,500 worth of baskets.

Tips

• Joanne created her own niche by selling unique baskets and exotic styles that were not readily found in stores. She sold one-of-a-kind tribal African wares and popular Victorian and country styles.

• Another great advantage of Joanne's basket parties is that customers can take the baskets home immediately. They don't have to wait for their order to come in.

• You can sell many types of products using the home party idea. Find something that you love, like Joanne did. It can be something you produce or something someone else makes. One lady I know paints whimsical designs on women and children's clothing and sells them at parties.

Instead of using independent contractors, Joanne decided to sell dealerships.

Each year Joanne has seen a 45-percent growth rate.

Mixing Kids and Business

WHEN JOANNE started her business in 1978, she had three children, ages 1, 5, and 7. But as her business grew, so did her family. She still runs her business from home. Now all six children help out with the business in some way. Out of her nine full-time employees, three of them are her children. Her older children do most of the accounting.

Joanne feels her children have benefited greatly from her home business. She says, "I have had the opportunity to teach them valuable entrepreneurial skills." Joanne likes the fact that she was always available for her children. "If they are excited about something at that moment, I can celebrate with them. If they are down, I can comfort them."

But raising children and running a home business can be tough, especially with six children. "Sometimes my kids are crying or fighting in the background when I am on the phone. I try to explain to them that this is the way I make my money—by using the phone. I sometimes reward them with a special outing or ice cream. But sometimes I do feel guilty about being on the phone so much."

Joanne believes, "It's important for moms to stay home with their kids no mat-ter your income. Children need their mom to raise them. It's important to the child to have their mom available to them on a regular basis."

Rewards

THIS YEAR Joanne has sold $1 million in baskets and next year plans to sell $2 million. Each year she has seen a 45-percent growth rate. Just in the past two years, Joanne has purchased two vacation homes and plans to buy a horse ranch. However, this is not an overnight success story. It has taken her seventeen long years to get where she is today. Joanne attributes her success to being driven: "Wanting results and doing what it takes to get those results. No matter if I feel like it or not."

Joanne's Advice

JOANNE TRULY believes any mom could start a business like hers. She had no business experience or computer skills. "Find something you like, believe in it, and do it. Find out how to market it. You can have the best product in the world, but if you don't know how to market, you won't sell a thing. Another important piece of advice is, Don't grow too fast. It costs money to grow. My business grew so fast I couldn't keep control of it."

Recommended Resources

IF YOU would like more information on Joanne's dealership package and a free video, call 1-503-631-7288.

ORGANIZATIONS

* Mothers Home Business Network
P.O. Box 423
East Meadow, NY 11554
1-516-997-7394

BOOKS

* Barbara Brabec, *Homemade Money.* Cincinnati: Betterway Publications, 1994.

MAGAZINES

* *Entrepreneur.* A resource guide for starting and growing a small business.

* *Inc.* A resource guide for those who own their own business.

* *Small Business Start-Ups.* Geared for those starting and growing a small/home business.

PET-SITTER

Name: Ann Masland
Location: Carlisle, Pennsylvania
Family Facts: Married, two toddlers
Business: Horse & Hound

Why She Started Her Business

ANN HAS always enjoyed riding horses. When she was younger, she would take care of other people's horses to earn the right to ride, "which is one of my favorite things to do," says Ann. Even though she has her own horses now, she has turned the idea of taking care of other people's pets into a business.

At first Ann thought about buying a pet-sitting franchise. But after researching the idea, she found that she would be putting the same amount of money and time into the business, but the franchise would be making money off her ideas. As she already had contacts with horse owners in the area, she didn't want to build a market niche and give all the profits to someone else. So in April 1994, Ann set up her own personal pet-sitting business.

Ann's main reason for starting the business at home was because she and her husband were starting to raise a family. Ann's husband is a farmer and works unusual hours. If Ann were to get a nine-to-five job, she knew they wouldn't be able to see much of each other. And she knew if she worked at home, he would be able to see the kids more. Ann says, "If they were at a day care all day long while I was working at an office somewhere, we would almost never see each other or our kids."

Qualifications

TO BECOME a pet-sitter, you don't need to be a veterinarian or even a vet tech. You just need to love and know how to care for animals. Ann has degrees in political science and English, and she is close to finishing a graduate degree in public administration. She has worked for a couple of temp agencies as a secretary. She also worked as a graduate assistant doing research for one of her professors.

In addition to loving animals and being organized, Ann says you need to be professional. "People leave their keys, their alarm codes, their home, and their property with us. You have to go beyond their expectations, and most people's expectations are fairly high."

To become a pet-sitter, you don't need to be a veterinarian or even a vet tech. You just need to love and know how to care for animals.

Services

ALTHOUGH ANN'S specialty is horse care, she also sits dogs, cats, birds, and rabbits when their owners decide to go on vacation. She feeds, exercises, walks, and plays with the animals and gives them medicine. She will also pick up mail, water gardens and houseplants, rotate lights and shades—and, of course, "We give the house a once-over to make sure the plumbing hasn't exploded or nobody has tried to break in."

Start-up Costs

ANN STARTED her business with about $6,000. "I have twice gone back to the bank for loans." In June 1995, Ann opened a second office five miles from her home that another person operates. So far she has put about $18,000 into the business, "and a whole lot of sweat," says Ann with a laugh.

While some pet-sitters don't get the licensing and insurance they need, Ann doesn't recommend starting out this way. Ann is bonded, insured for liability, insured for care custody and control, and carries worker's compensation.

Equipment

HER EQUIPMENT includes a portable phone and a computer. Ann was in business for a year when she bought a truck, which she needed for dealing with horses. Her office is in a separate building next to the house, where she has a crib set up for her littlest one and an old-fashioned school desk for her older daughter to use. When the weather is nice, the kids are able to play outside, and it's easy to keep an eye on them from the office.

Rates

FOR DOMESTIC pets, Ann charges $10 a visit for one animal and $1 to $2 for additional pets. Horses are $25 a day (this includes two visits) and $6 for each additional horse. For regular customers that she sees eight or nine times a month, she charges $9 to $11 an hour.

Hiring Help

HIRING HELP is almost a must for this particular business. At the time we talked, Ann had nine employees. At one point she was up to sixteen. Her help mainly works with the horses. Most of their work involves acting as temporary employees for horse owners in need of emergency help.

Marketing

ANN HAS found word of mouth is her most effective way to advertise, as horse people are a close-knit group. As Ann says, "If you get one or two people who really like you, they almost become sponsors. I have had calls from people saying, 'So-and-so used your service, and they can't stop talking about you.'"

She places brochures at vet offices, coffee shops, and anywhere else she is allowed. She also has a yellow pages ad and attends equestrian trade fairs. These fairs include all types of arts, crafts, and equipment for horses and horse farms. Ann was always the only one there who offered the horse care service. Ann says, "That was two years ago, and I still get calls."

Ann also publishes a newsletter she sends out to her clients. She does the layout, and the printer takes care of everything else. The total cost is between $500 and $600, and it goes out to about 1,300 people. The newsletter is turning out to be more effective than her yellow pages ad. "The name of the game is to just keep my name in front of them." She tries to keep her newsletter informative with lots of information on taking care of pets. She also includes articles on local pet shelters.

Ann has recently become very active in her local chamber of commerce. She takes part in some of its marketing seminars and networking groups. This has also supplied her with many clients.

Tips

- Ann recommends that once you do decide to become a pet-sitter, take a good six to nine months to organize, research, and start your business. During this time, you should also join a pet-sitting association.

- If you decide to become a pet-sitter, you need to remember that when everyone is off on vacation or enjoying holidays, you're working. Ann tries to take off one major holiday a year.

- In addition to using her computer to maintain her client list, she uses it to access the Internet, which has been an amazing help. She visits the vet news groups to get ideas for her newsletters, and she also reads the business sites. "It's a nice contact. Working for yourself, you don't get the same type of networking or support that you would in an office or a professional environment, and the Internet has pretty much compensated for that."

Mixing Kids and Business

WITH PERMISSION from her clients, Ann sometimes takes her kids with

---

Ann spread herself out too thin and didn't know how to say no to a client.

---

her on her visits. When this isn't possible, she has a good friend who runs a day-care center from her home. "We can use her because we don't have a set amount we have to pay every week. She is very flexible; if we need her forty hours in one week it's fine, and if we need her for two hours the next week that's fine. It's really the only reason we can do day care."

Biggest Challenge

JUGGLING HER time is Ann's biggest challenge. "Every once in a while I have to stop, or my husband has to stop me and remind me, You started this to be with the kids. Being with the kids doesn't mean just physically being in the room with them. It means paying attention to them. If you really need to get stuff done, wait till they are in bed."

Another challenge for Ann was her success. "I started off much too fast. My first nine months in business I made over $6,000 in profit and that was after paying myself a salary." Ann spread herself out too thin and didn't know how to say no to a client. "I worked way too many hours. If I had it to do all over again, I would cut my expenses way back, and I would grow much slower. I had

an 8-month-old infant when I started the business, and it was really insane for a while. Things took off so fast, and everything went haywire. I would drive 170 miles in one day, retracing to get to other clients. I should have spent more time planning."

Rewards

ANN SAYS her reward is "being able to spend time with my kids more than I would if I worked a normal job. Despite the stress of all the clients, I am the boss. I decide [when enough] is enough, because I don't have to worry about a boss firing me. I can block off time to see the kids and my husband more. I have flexibility."

Ann's Advice

YOU CAN'T *do everything. Hire things out that you're not an expert at. In the long run it will be less expensive and less frustrating. If you're not real great on the computer or desktop-publishing software, sketch out what you want and bring it to a reputable printer and pay them to do the layout. It will look more professional, and you won't be banging your head against the wall. Try to get a good relationship with other pet-sitters (this could work for any business). Let them know you're not going to be infringing on their territory, but ask them for help in your area. Every area is different. What works in mine as far as marketing wouldn't work twenty miles from here.*

Recommended Resources

ORGANIZATIONS

• Pet Sitters International (PSI)
  418 East King Street
  King, N.C. 27021
  1-910-983-9222
  petsitin@ols.net

  The $79 annual membership includes a pet-sitting magazine, information about conventions, and insurance benefits.

• National Association of Professional Pet Sitters (NAPP)
  1200 G Street, NW, Suite 760
  Washington, D.C. 20005
  1-202-393-3317

  The $130 annual membership includes liability and bonding protection, a bimonthly newsletter, information about conferences, an 800-number referral service, and more.

• Your local chamber of commerce is a great networking resource.

• Business Women's Expo. A branch of the chamber of commerce.

• Small Business Administration and SCORE. Ann says, "They were probably the most beneficial. Their publications really targeted my problems in the areas I didn't have a background in and put me on track."

BOOKS

• Patti Moran, *Pet Sitting for Profit*. Pinnacle, N.C.: New Beginnings, 1992.

  Many pet-sitters consider this book their bible. For information about this book, call Pet Sitters International or order it from your local bookstore.

MAGAZINES

• *Business Start-Up*. Offers resources for starting a small/home business.

• *Entrepreneur.* Resources for starting a small/home business.

• *Home Office Computing.* Profiles the latest computer technology for home offices.

ONLINE RESOURCES

To find the different pet-sitting forums on the Internet, go to your favorite search engine and conduct a search.

A chat group for pet-sitters meets on America Online every Thursday at 10 P.M. EST. Keyword: "sitters"

GREETING CARD WRITER

Name: Sandra Louden
Location: Pittsburgh, Pennsylvania
Family Facts: Married, two children—
    Logan, 17, and Alexis, 15
Business: Jottings

Why She Started Her Business

I LOVE MONDAY mornings. Then the house is mine and I can get back to work." With a comment like that, you may wonder what Sandra does for a living. It could only be a devoted work-at-home mom who writes humorous captions for a living.

Before Sandra started her new life as a caption writer for greeting cards, she worked as a secretary and receptionist. She left the workforce when her son was born. Although her colleagues thought she would be back, Sandra hoped she had enough means to come up with something she could do in her home.

Sandra has always wanted to write—she graduated from college with a degree in English. Sandra says, "I think all English majors dream of becoming writers." Deciding to stay home with her kids helped her to start a career she loved, one that might never have happened if she had stayed at her nine-to-five job.

Sandra started her business when her kids were 1 and 2½. She explains, "Writing for greeting card companies is a great job if you have younger children. You can easily write while the children play, because writing captions requires only little blocks of time. Then, when the kids are sleeping, you can write or type out your ideas."

Qualifications

IF YOU think humorous caption writing might be something for you, here are a few things to keep in mind: You should have a love for the written word, a natural wit, and a love for puns.

Start-up Costs

YOU DON'T have to fork out a bunch of money to start this kind of business. Sandra says, "That's a great thing about greeting cards; the overhead is really low." You can start the business you desire for around $50.

Equipment

YOU'LL NEED stamps, envelopes, unlined 3 x 5 cards, a notebook, a pen to jot down ideas—and patience. For research,

Current magazines will keep you up-to-date on trends and will get your creative juices flowing.

you may want reference books (dictionary, thesaurus, current almanac) and current magazines, which will keep you up-to-date on trends and will get your creative juices flowing. A lot of your supplies may already be sitting on your bookshelf or in your magazine bin right now. Eventually, you may want to get a typewriter. But most editors have no problem with work submitted handwritten in black ink.

Just remember, first impressions do count. If you don't have great penmanship, a secondhand typewriter might be a good idea. But even when you do type your ideas on a 3 x 5 card, make sure you've checked your grammar and spelling, because those two things done incorrectly can turn off an editor very quickly.

Because a lot of cards today are geared to Generation X, Sandra has to keep up with what's hip. "I'm in my 40s and I have to know pop stars like Hootie and the Blowfish and Alanis Morissette." Current magazines like *Entertainment Weekly* or *Wired* help her. Other helpful magazines include *Family Circle* and *Good Housekeeping*. Some of the talk shows can also help you find out what's popular.

If you have a computer, you can keep track of your submissions that way. Sandra codes her own cards to help her keep track of where she has sent each idea. Sandra also uses a master sheet to keep track of submissions.

Rates

SANDRA CAN make anywhere from $25 to $150 a caption. For as few as ten words, you can make a good amount of money.

Marketing

IN FEBRUARY 1986, Sandra sent out her first batch of ideas, and by May she sold her first caption. She sold one more caption that year. As with any business, it takes time to get established. Her second year she sold eight captions, and every year after that she has sold more and more.

For the first few years it can get very depressing. "Most people quit before they sell anything, but some of us keep plodding." Sandra teaches a class on how to write for greeting card companies. She explains to her students that every year they will do a little better. "No matter what, you just have to keep on going. Because if you don't have confidence in yourself, nobody else will."

It took four years for companies to start

calling Sandra to give her assignments. She made a lot of mistakes in those years. Sandra tries to help save her students from her mistakes. "Not that they weren't valuable; I'm glad I went through them. I just try to help my students leapfrog over those first four years and start right in selling."

Tips

- Sandra recommends starting with the small companies. Stay away from Hallmark, American Greetings, and Gibson. Sandra has never sold to Hallmark, only one caption to American Greetings, and twenty-five captions to Gibson. "I've sold hundreds and hundreds of captions; I don't keep count anymore, and I've made my mark in the smaller to midsize companies. You can make good money without all the competition of the bigger companies."

- Sandra warns that some smaller greeting card companies aren't very organized, especially those that have been established for less than a year. Sometimes these companies will hold your work from six months to a year. Sandra says, "I would sit back and be passive and wouldn't follow through." She advises that if you don't receive a response within twelve weeks of submitting your work, you should write them a nudge letter. The inquiry letter should contain the code numbers of the ideas sent. If you still don't hear from them? "I recommend another letter saying you are withdrawing your work from consideration and would appreciate its immediate return in the SASE you originally provided."

- Another mistake: "I would send out a batch of material and sit back and think, OK, I'm done with my work, then wait for it to come back." Sometimes that wait would be four to six weeks. "That's not the way you sell. You forget what you sent out and begin to work on your next ideas." Sandra usually has between thirteen to sixteen batches with eleven captions in each batch.

- If you do get a rejection, don't throw that idea out. It has taken Sandra up to nine tries to sell a caption, and sometimes she's made more money from that idea than she expected. If a caption comes back rejected, Sandra always types up another card so it looks nice and fresh and sends it out again. First impressions are very important.

- If writing humorous prose tickles your funny bone, comedians, morning radio shows, and public speakers are always looking for sidesplitting material. Some magazines want anything from your one-liners to full-length articles. And the pay isn't too bad, either.

Mixing Kids and Business

IDEAS FOR captions come to Sandra in many different ways—while sitting in the

Ideas for captions come to Sandra in many different ways—while sitting in the park flipping through magazines, or watching Sesame Street *with the kids.*

park flipping through magazines, or watching *Sesame Street* with the kids. Even her kids give her ideas. Because of this, Sandra has made a deal with them. "When they do give me an idea and it does sell, I split the profit with them." For example, one day when Logan was 4 years old he asked, "What would happen if I put ketchup on my yogurt?" Sandra says, "All kinds of bells went off in my head. That's a good calendar caption, I thought." She ended up using it by showing a woman who is having trouble with her diet, saying, "I'm still not used to dieting. I keep putting ketchup on my yogurt."

Rewards

SANDRA'S CAPTIONS not only appear on cards, but on posters, mugs, magnets, beverage napkins, and more. In 1991 Sandra won the coveted Louie Award (the top award for writers in the greeting card industry) for the best humorous friendship caption in a card under $2.

Sandra has now expanded her writing. She has written a children's suspense thriller and book reviews. She has also written a book on how to write greeting cards that is in the process of being sold to a publisher.

You can honestly tell Sandra loves what she does. "It's just a fun job. It's a fun way to look at life, and I'm still having fun after ten years."

Sandra's Advice

DON'T SIT *there and say, "What can I get into?" Look around and see what you're good at and what you've been doing for years. What do people compliment you on? Maybe you make the best cookies or you have the best recipe for quiche. So that is where you start. Everyone has some sort of unique talent, and if you can find out what that is, there is probably going to be a market for it.*

Recommended Resources

- Sandra Louden
  P.O. Box 9701
  Pittsburgh, PA 15229-0701

  For tip sheets and current addresses of companies who hire freelancers, send a SASE for more information.

BOOKS

- Sandra Louden. *Write Well and Sell; Greeting Card Writing*

     To order, contact Sandra via e-mail FelshamLdy@aol.com or at her mailing address above.

- Mark Garvey, *The Writer's Market.* Cincinnati: Writer's Digest Books, 1997. Includes a greeting card section.

ONLINE RESOURCES

- On America Online, Sandra runs a greeting card forum. To get there, use keyword "writers," click on "message boards," click on "club news and updates," then click on "greeting cards."

- Sandra also teaches a six-week course on greeting card writing at www.writersclub.com. This is an independent study class. You learn at your own pace and download the class at your convenience.

NANNY-FINDING SERVICE

Name: Suzette Trimmer
Location: Philadelphia, Pennsylvania
Family Facts: Married, one son—
    Pierce
Business Name: Your Other Hands

Why She Started Her Business

SUZETTE TRIMMER had been trying to get pregnant for four years before she finally gave birth to her son, Pierce. She says, "After taking so long to have him, I just couldn't give him back to someone else. I tried!"

Before the birth of her son, Suzette worked for a large corporation. Even though she didn't want to go back to work, she had to for three months to pay back her maternity leave. Fortunately, she was able to find a great nanny for her son. She says, "I had other people asking me how I did it. They wanted to know how I interviewed and found such a great nanny. All my corporate friends were asking me to help them find nannies. One day my friend Debbie and I looked at each other and said, 'Hey, we can make a business out of this.'"

Suzette started by looking closely at her competition to see how they ran their child-care businesses. Not only did she check with local day cares, she also checked out the day cares in New Jersey, New York, and Boston.

Suzette's husband was very supportive of her for the first few months. But around the ninth month, he began to have doubts because, as Suzette says, "I had no business experience and had no idea of what I was doing. It was pretty shaky there for a while. But how could I fail? My family, friends, and relatives all knew I had this business. I couldn't let myself fail."

Start-up Costs

SUZETTE AND Debbie, who also had no prior business experience, started Your Other Hands by contributing $750 each. With that, they hired an accountant and a lawyer and paid to become incorporated. This way their personal assets will not be touched if legal issues involving the business arise.

Equipment

SUZETTE HAS a computer, fax machine, portable phone, and a cellular phone. She also has an answering service so she is always accessible.

Hiring Help

THE BUSINESS started with three employees: Suzette, Debbie, and Suzette's nanny. They began by watching each other's kids while they went on a job. Now the business has anywhere from 90 to 150 employees. Neither Suzette nor Debbie have to go out on job assignments anymore. Previous work experience and how long she has worked with the company determine the nanny's pay.

Rates

THIS BUSINESS is very helpful to parents, whether they are professionals who need full-time help or just a mom and dad who need a night on the town alone. Clients receive a price list of the different hourly charges. There is a yearly fee of $100, and every year that you register, it is lowered in increments of $25. Once you have been with the service for five years, you no longer have to pay this fee. The charge for an emergency sitter is $9.50 an hour. Someone who needs care from one to eight hours a week will pay $8.50 an hour, and it goes down to $7.75 an hour for thirty to thirty-nine hours per week.

For forty hours or more, there is a flat rate of $300.

Marketing

FOR THE first year, they ran an ad in a local free paper for $30 a week, but their best advertisement comes in the form of parents who are extremely satisfied with the service they receive.

Tips

- It takes a while for her prospective nannies to fill out the applications. Suzette's son is usually right there. If she notices the applicant doesn't pay attention to her son, she knows that person doesn't really like kids. She says, "Sometimes I just have a bad feeling about someone. I can't put my finger on it, but I will not hire them."

- "Always keep your priorities in mind, rely on an answering service, stay up late returning calls if need be." Suzette reminds moms that even though you have a home business, you may still feel guilty that you're not spending enough time

This business is very helpful to parents, whether they are professionals who need full-time help or just a mom and dad who need a night on the town alone.

with your kids. "But get rid of it." Just remember to make time for your kids. As Suzette says, "They are probably the reason you have a home business in the first place."

Biggest Challenge

THINGS CAN get hectic. "A lady will come for an interview and at that moment the puppy acts up, my son spills his juice, the smoke alarm is going off, my coffee spills, I am talking on the phone, and the UPS man is knocking at the door. Sometimes I want to put my head in the freezer and scream," says Suzette with a laugh.

Suzette's Advice

IF YOU *have that entrepreneurial spirit, if you have the drive and the ambition, you can do it. Just don't let your business run*

you. You need to be in control. Don't let yourself be driven by guilt. If my son is feeling sick or I just need to spend some time with him, I let my answering service get my phone. My son is my biggest priority. If it's important to you, you can do it.

Recommended Resources
BOOKS

• Jay Conrad Levinson, *Guerrilla Marketing Excellence.* Boston: Houghton Mifflin, 1993.

MAGAZINES

Suzette tries to get her hands on every parents' or women's magazine and watches anything on television that has to do with day care and nannies. "I read everything I can, especially in the area of day care," says Suzette.

INFORMATION BROKER

Name: Phyllis Smith
Location: Georgetown, Ontario, Canada
Family Facts: Married, two sons– Erik,
    6, and Graham, 3
Business: In the Know
Web Site: http://www.in-the-know.
    com

Why She Started Her Business

PHYLLIS STARTED her own information and resource service, also known as information brokering, by using her past skills to make money at home. Her education and work experience was in library science. She had worked as a reference librarian in a government department before her husband accepted a transfer to a new city. After the transfer she thought about where she would work next. Phyllis explains, "Rather than try and get into a new 'rat race' finding a job, we decided that I would try and work from home."

You may be asking yourself, What do information brokers do? Phyllis explains, "Qualified professionals have an intimate understanding of information and how it is organized. They maintain their skills and stay up-to-date in the latest innovations in search tools. They are more than just 'finders'; they navigate the swells of information and help clients make more productive, more profitable use of their time." If you think all an information broker does is find current, relevant data by plugging a word or two into a search engine, obtain the needed information, and give it to their client, you are sadly mistaken. Phyllis will be the first to admit there are many brokers out there. She suggests that someone looking into this business should "seriously examine their skills and look for ways of developing their credentials to differentiate themselves. I believe that the information professional who has the training and experience will stand out in this crowd."

Instead of being a traditional information broker, which would require Phyllis to be available at a moment's notice with little control over when she would work, Phyllis was able to work out an arrangement with her former employer to retain her services. They have had a contractual arrangement ever since. Along the way she has picked up other clients.

Qualifications

QUALIFICATIONS AS an information professional vary," Phyllis says. "A

227

"Specialized education or training can be very valuable to an IP who wants to market to a niche clientele."

---

library degree is nice to have but not essential. Specialized education or training can be very valuable to an IP who wants to market to a niche clientele." In the case of Phyllis, who works mainly for government agency information centers, having the library degree is preferred.

Phyllis has extensive experience and training in a variety of commercial information systems, such as Dialog and Lexis-Nexis, which is important. She explains, "Being handy at searching the Internet is nice, but doesn't give you an edge in the IP business."

Start-up Costs

PHYLLIS HAS found start-up costs to be minimal. She started out by working with the computer and equipment she already had and then added on new equipment as she needed it.

Equipment

YOU WILL need a computer, a printer, and a separate phone line for the computer. A fax machine or program is desirable, along with an Internet connection with unlimited hours. Phyllis added com-

mercial database subscriptions as her business grew.

Rates

DEPENDING ON the job, rates can range from $40 to around $100 an hour. She also charges any online usage fees she incurs to fulfill the service needed. Fees will depend on what subject you are dealing with and your niche, or the specialized area you are working on.

Marketing

CURRENTLY PHYLLIS is writing articles for professional publications and participating in conferences, which helps to get her name out in the library field—a potential source of clients.

She participates on some business lists on the Internet and generally tries to make herself known whenever possible. She has received some free publicity from times she was quoted in newspaper articles.

Mixing Kids and Business

WHILE WORKING part time Phyllis uses day care for the days she works.

"Working from home can be a great experience, but it is far from the perfect setup for everyone."

She explains, "I give the kids my time when I am not working, and my clients get my undivided attention when I am working. For the type of work I am doing, I think this works best for my family."

This particular business requires more than just sitting at the computer, surfing the Net. There are other parts of the business, such as marketing and billing, that need to get done. There are networking meetings to attend and prospective clients to phone. Then there are the conferences/training work-shops you may need to attend. Although you don't always need to meet your clients face-to-face, they may want you to participate in on-site activities or need you to provide some of your services on-site. Phyllis explains, "These activities are made more stressful when you have to juggle the care of children as well. I won't say it can't be done, but you need a system in place that you can depend on."

Can you successfully become an information professional working from home with kids around? Phyllis believes you can, but she suggests partaking in a healthy dose of reality. In this type of business some areas may not be as ideal for WAHMs as others. Phyllis explains, "Some clients commonly have urgent requests that you may have difficulty managing when you have the unpredictable

nature of small children to deal with. Some clients may be less understanding of the noise of kids during a conference call."

You may find yourself searching one of the many fee-based services that are very expensive and that charge for each minute you are online. If you are interrupted a lot due to your children these searches will become expensive and your clients may not like the charges that can incur. Phyllis recommends careful consideration when targeting clients, offering services, and planning your work hours.

Biggest Challenge

ISOLATION AND marketing have been Phyllis's biggest challenges. She is used to working in a team environment with colleagues to throw ideas at and to work with as partners. She explains, "It can be tough to motivate oneself sitting alone in the office. I get really excited now when I get an opportunity to collaborate with someone on a project."

When marketing, Phyllis has to be careful not to take on more than she can handle. Anyone with a home business finds it hard to turn down work, and Phyllis is no exception. Taking on more than she can handle is not conducive to her home-based situation.

Getting out to network is the most difficult thing for Phyllis to work into her schedule. Attending 6–7 P.M. meetings is a trial when she has to make baby-sitting ar-rangements or coordinate schedules with her husband.

"Working from home can be a great experience, but it is far from the perfect setup for everyone. It can be isolating [and] stressful as you try to be all things to all people, and difficult to maintain. I highly recommend everyone, moms included, to think carefully about what they want from their home-based business before hanging out their shingle," says Phyllis.

Rewards

PHYLLIS SEES an opportunity to do things as a professional that she couldn't do before because she was so busy working. Phyllis explains,

I have a couple of articles in professional publications, I've participated in a conference as a speaker, and I have some similar opportunities opening up for the future.

I also feel that I really do get to have it all. I contribute to the family finances, I have more time to devote to home and family, I can retain and develop my professional skills, and I can stay connected to my professional network. I don't see myself as having sacrificed it all for the good of my kids, but I am not stressed to a breaking point trying to balance work and family.

Tips

- "Research your ideas for a home business carefully. Read profiles, articles, books. If you are very serious, join relevant associations even before you start up. Contact people already in that business and ask them specific questions to help you understand the pros and cons. (Be more specific than, 'What do I need to do to start this business?')"

- "Define your strengths and weaknesses with honesty. Don't choose a business that involves a lot of selling, if you hate selling with a passion. Consider alliances or partnerships to compensate for areas you are weak in. Make the most of your strengths."

- "Try to develop a business around something you enjoy doing or for which you have special skills. You will be doing it every day, so you need to sustain your enthusiasm."

- "Be realistic about your schedule and time commitments. A business with clients who are most likely available in the evenings won't succeed if you are available during the day and are committed to family in the evenings. Don't take on what could amount to full-time hours if you don't have the hours available."

- "Think of ways to work into a business gradually. No one says you have to invest a lot of money to get started—use your profits to finance new equipment or supplies. No one says you have to work 40 hours per week right away. Find ways to work part time to start."

• "Be flexible and experiment. There are no failures, only ideas that didn't pan out the way you thought they might. If a service you offered wasn't popular, dump it and find out what clients might really want. If working with kids at home is proving too stressful, don't assume using day care is a sign of total failure. Make up your own rules."

Recommended Resources

ORGANIZATIONS

• Association of Independent Information Professionals (AIIP)
10290 Monroe, Suite 208
Dallas, TX 75229-5718
1-609-730-8759
aiipinfo@aiip.org
http://www.aiip.org

This is a must-join. Phyllis is an associate member and this is her primary professional network. Its private listserv is a vital source of information and ideas. The association holds an annual conference that is considered very informative

• Special Libraries Association (SLA)
1700 Eighteenth Street, NW
Washington, D.C. 20009-2514

1-202-234-4700
1-202-265-9317 (fax)
sla@sla.org
http://www.sla.org

As a librarian, Phyllis finds SLA valuable. A number of consultants are members. An SLA membership includes a subscription to the newsletter *Information Outlook.*

BOOKS

• Sue Rugge, *Information Broker's Handbook.* New York: McGraw-Hill, 1997.
This is considered a bible of sorts.

• Deborah Sawyer, *Sawyer's Survival Guide for Information Brokers.*

• Deborah Sawyer, *Sawyer's Success Tactics for Information Businesses.*

MAGAZINES

• *Online Magazine* and *Database* are both online.

• *Inc.* and *Worth* magazines are also helpful.

ONLINE RESOURCES

• CyberSkeptic's Guide to Internet Research and Information Broker: http://www.biblodata.com
Phyllis has created a series of pages devoted to the subject of information services. You can find it at http://www.in-the-know.com/wip/wip1.html.

NEWSLETTER PUBLISHER

Name: Trish Kasey
Location: Newport Beach, California
Family Facts: Married, one daughter—
    Corey, 7
Business: *Mommy Times*
Web Site: http://www.mommytimes.
    com/

How She Started Her Business

THE IDEA for the *Mommy Times* newsletter was first conceived in January 1992. The first issue rolled off the press the following November. Trish wrote and designed it just as she does now—from her own computer and printer.

This wasn't Trish's first home business. She first sold personalized children's books. She says, "I did this before I even had a child, because I knew I wanted to get some experience running a business." After a while Trish came to the conclusion that she wanted to start her own business where she was in total control. But she never regrets starting that first business. "It was a very good experience for me, because I still had to go through the motions of getting a business license and coming up with a name for my business and

checking account, everything you have to do to run a business."

Trish's inspiration for her newsletter came from her daughter. No matter how much she had read before she had Corey, she found that her best advice came from other mothers. Trish was familiar with other newsletters, such as *The Tightwad Gazette*. She wondered if maybe she could produce something like that. Although the topic of *The Tightwad Gazette* wasn't her forte, neither was mothering. As Trish says, "I was looking for help myself, but I thought what a neat idea to publish a newsletter that would have advice from other moms."

Trish first started her business on the East Coast. She really wanted her newsletter to become a national publication instead of regional right from the start, a mistake that she wouldn't make again. "If I had to do it all over again, I would start locally and branch out from there."

About the Newsletter

THE CONCEPT of mothers helping and supporting other moms is the focus of the *Mommy Times*. The newsletter mainly focuses on moms-to-be and motherhood. *Mommy Times* is an electronic newsletter, which means you can read the publication

The concept of mothers helping and supporting other moms is the focus of the Mommy Times.

online or print it and read it that way. The publication comes out on a quarterly basis with a special Mother's Day edition. Trish uses volunteer writers who are moms themselves, so it's always moms writing for moms. It has a down-to-earth, folksy approach with practical advice that's complete and concise.

Equipment and Start-up Costs

TRISH USES a computer, a printer, a fax, and the Microsoft Word software program. She also has four different phone lines. Another expense was her business license, which cost $100. Trish also puts together press kits and press releases, which are a great way for her to advertise and which have helped her get on talk shows, local and regional news, radio, as well as in parenting magazines and other forms of media.

Rates

AT FIRST, Trish tried to keep advertising out of the newsletter. "But then I realized [that] to make money in publications, you've got to have advertising in there. If you just want to break even, that's one thing. If you want to make some money, you have to have advertising." Besides the advertising, she charges a subscription rate of $12 a year.

Marketing

WHEN TRISH first advertised her business, she bought 5,000 names and addresses from a birth-announcement company for $200. From 5,000 names she received 100 subscribers. The postage cost her $900. Although her results weren't too bad, she doesn't know if she would recommend the idea to others.

Advertising in big magazines was another costly mistake. "You've really got to sit down and figure out what things are going to cost before you start putting prices on your product." Trish used family funds to start up her business, something she doesn't know if she would do again. "If that works for you, fine. But I would say go into the business with the idea we will lend this business some money but give it a cutoff, say $5,000. After that we look for funding, sponsorships, or business partners."

When Trish first started using press kits, all she included was her newsletter and a letter explaining her business. Then she got a letter from Maria Shriver saying what a great newsletter Mommy Times was, so that went into the press kit. She now has letters and recommendations from other famous moms, such as Jane Pauley, Leeza Gibbons, and editors of parenting magazines. Trish writes to famous moms asking for a tip to put in her newsletter, but she doesn't bug them or ask for money. She also includes a videotape of small clipped segments of the different shows she has appeared on.

Trish says, "I send my press kits to producers of TV shows. I call and find out the appropriate producer for what I'm doing and send out a kit. It just so happened that one of the producers of *Caryl and Marilyn* saw an article in the *Los Angeles Times* about the newsletter and called me. Crazier things have happened."

You may have seen Trish on any number of television shows—*Mike and Matty,* The Family Channel's *Home and Family*—and on several local television stations. "My biggest break ever was when I was on KNBC, a local NBC affiliate." It did a small piece on the news about the publication and what Trish was doing. They gave out her 800 number and her phone line exploded, because at that point she wasn't hooked up to an answering service. According to Trish,

I got a call from someone in North Carolina. She said she was in charge of all the affiliates in the country, and they were going to release this story across the country. About three in the morning the phone started ringing because we're Pacific time.

I got a thousand calls at least that day. That's all we have a record of. We know the phone company said the phones lines were jammed.

My point to all this is, you've got to publicize yourself. Be your own publicity person. Just put a packet together. I'm big on press kits. Put a tape together of everything you've done and make sure your tapes are no longer than five minutes long. You may not have all that when you first start, so just send your product and a letter telling about yourself. . . . From the very beginning when you start your business, there is always an opportunity to write a press release. Always.

Trish's publicity has definitely helped. *Mommy Times* has approximately 2,500 subscribers nationwide. As Trish says, "No one else is going to toot your horn; you've got to do it. Don't feel weird or embarrassed. Because if you don't believe in what you're doing, no one else is going to. This is not the time to be shy."

Mixing Kids and Business

TRISH RECOMMENDS having your own workspace for your business. Her office is in a spare bedroom. She does have a child's desk set up for her daughter to play or work at while she works. On occasion, when Trish needs to get some work done, she sends her daughter to a children's center. "I get most of my work done when she's in

"I think the best thing you can do for yourself is to find a mentor."

school, and a lot of times at night when everyone's gone to bed."

Trish's Advice

I THINK *the best thing you can do for yourself is to find a mentor. Find a person or an organization with other moms who have done something similar to what you're going to do. Really be a sponge. Make sure it's okay with them and don't bug them. But really absorb as much knowledge as you can.*

My second piece of advice is to really do your research on what it is you want to do. Determining what you want to do is sometimes the hardest part. Look back on your background, see what you really enjoyed doing. Because you know you'll never have to work another day in your life if you enjoy what you do.

Recommended Resources

If you are interested in the *Mommy Times* newsletter, you can find it online at www. mommytimes.com/ or call 1-800-99-MOMMY.

ORGANIZATIONS

*   MOMS Club
    c/o 25371 Rye Canyon
    Valencia, CA 91355
    momsclub@aol.com
        For more information on this national organization, send $2 to cover postage to the address above.

*   Moms At Home Entrepreneurially Minded (MAHEM)
    P.O. Box 886
    Newport, CA 92661
        Trish Kasey is the founder and president of this organization.

*   Also check out your local chamber of commerce, an organization for business owners.

BOOKS

*   Judy Ryder, *Turning Your Great Idea into a Great Success.* Princeton, N.J.: Peterson's/Pacesetter Books, 1995.

MAGAZINES

*   *Entrepreneur.* A resource guide for those starting a small business.

*   *Parents, Family Circle,* and *Women's Day.* Trish says, "I try to read as many family and parenting magazines as I can."

PROFESSIONAL ORGANIZER

Name: Elaine Courtney Moskow
Location: Austin, Texas
Family Facts: Married, two children—
daughter, 4, and son, 3
Business: All In Order

Why She Started Her Business

IN THE early '80s, when Elaine was working as an occupational therapist, she picked up Marsha Sinetar's *Do What You Love and the Money Will Follow* (Dell, 1989). "It got me thinking," says Elaine, who considers herself very independent and doesn't like to take orders from other people. She decided to start her own business doing something she really enjoyed doing, and that was organizing. Elaine has been a professional organizer now for seven years.

Elaine points out that being an occupational therapist is much like being a professional organizer. "We were trained as therapists to find the most efficient way of doing something. We had to help disabled homemakers redesign their kitchens so everything was more accessible."

Qualifications

ELAINE SAYS, "You need to be able to put things into categories and organize your thoughts. I compare it to map reading—that cognitive ability to look at things and put them into categories and organize things."

Start-up Costs

ELAINE DIDN'T need a lot of money to get started, just the cost of business cards and clothes so she could be well dressed for networking at chamber of commerce meetings. Over the past seven years, she has accumulated a combination step stool/toolbox, in which she carries a drill; a hammer; an extension cord; a flashlight; screwdrivers; picture hangers; nails; graph paper for planning things out; and one of her most important pieces of equipment, her measuring tape.

Elaine gets some of her organizing equipment from local thrift shops, and she buys products on sale and stocks up. She is always looking for anything that could help a person get organized, including drawer dividers, scarf organizers, boxes, cup holders, lazy Susans, and more.

Elaine has a second phone line for her

In parts of California and New York, organizers can get paid between $75 and $100 an hour.

business calls that costs her $35 a month. She also uses a truck or a van so that she can easily haul away unwanted items from a client's house.

Rates

WHEN ELAINE first started out, she charged $15 an hour. She knew she was underpriced but felt a real need to help people get their houses organized. Over the years she has raised her rates to between $20 and $25 an hour. If she is working for a senior citizen on a fixed income or someone who just doesn't have the money, she will lower her hourly rate. Elaine asks her customers to pay on the spot, as soon as the project is finished.

What you charge, of course, depends on what the market will hold in your area. In parts of California and New York, for example, organizers can get paid between $75 and $100 an hour. (Now that made your ears perk up, didn't it?)

Marketing

ELAINE HAS used many different ways to get the word out about her business.

In just the past year she had a one-line yellow pages ad and received several calls a week from it. Before that she would network with other organizers, and they would refer business to her. One of her friends, also an organizer, enjoyed working for corporations, whereas Elaine enjoyed organizing kitchens and other parts of people's houses. So if her friend was offered a house-organizing job, she would refer it to Elaine.

All In Order has also been written up in several local publications. It didn't bring her a lot of business, but it helped to get her name out there. One of her biggest marketing windfalls was when she was mentioned in a local daily advice column called Ask Ellie. Two years later she still gets calls from people saying they cut her number out of the paper.

Elaine says, "Once you start telling people what you do, everyone freaks out. 'Oh, I could really use you.' So don't be shy about talking to everyone you come in contact with about your business."

Services

CALLS FROM clients usually sound like this: "I'm overwhelmed; I can't stand it anymore; I can't do this by myself; I don't have the time to do it by myself." Her clients need organizational help *now.* Many of her clients include working mothers, retired people, and others who are too busy or just don't have the skills. Elaine likes to offer a free thirty-minute consultation in the client's home. Having that face-to-face contact is very reassuring. "You can then present to them ideas about what you can do. It gives them a little more confidence."

Elaine asks her clients such questions as, "What is your biggest priority right now? Where are you having the most difficulty in the house? What do you want to accomplish?" Then she figures out the most efficient way to organize the space that needs attention.

She will also recommend organizing products and purchase them, or she may already have them on hand if she uses the particular piece a lot. She will then install the equipment for her client. Time spent on each job can vary greatly, depending on the amount of clutter, but the average kitchen usually runs about four hours.

You can take several different avenues as a professional organizer: residential, corporate, financial management, and even computers.

Expanding the Business

ELAINE HAS started another service for her clients: "It's basically recycling their belongings." She drops the less valuable items at thrift shops and places more valuable items at consignment shops, and the client receives the money or tax deduction. "They are quite thrilled with that," says Elaine.

Tips

- As part of your equipment, Elaine suggests buying a Polaroid camera. "I take before and after pictures and put them into an album." This is a great way to show your clients what you can do. She also includes letters of recommendation that people have written to her on what a wonderful job she did for them.

- Elaine taught a class on kitchen organizing through the University of Texas's informal classes. "That's where anybody who wants to teach anything, can." She contacted the school and they set everything up for her. She was paid a little for teaching the class, and she also got business from it. Elaine has also given talks at rotary clubs and different organizations. Although you don't get paid for these talks, you still may get business from an interested listener.

Mixing Kids and Business

ELAINE RAN her business from home for more than five years before she had

---

Elaine recommends setting aside a certain time every day to go into your office and work.

---

children. Now she hires a nanny to come in part time during the day. Even if she doesn't have a client's house to go to, she tries to spend some time in her office working on marketing her business and calling clients.

Biggest Challenge

ELAINE FINDS her challenge with marketing. "When you're on a job and you're out there visiting with a client, you still need to keep marketing to keep getting clients. You have to be juggling both things at once, or you will end up with a month with no clients." Elaine goes on to explain, "I think part of it is having the discipline to go to my office and sit down and work. It's so easy to get distracted when you're home." Elaine recommends setting aside a certain time every day to go into your office and work. Whether it's calling back clients, marketing, or filing, just do something.

Rewards

ELAINE FINDS her reward comes with the end of an organizing project, "the

satisfaction I get from people saying things like, 'You don't know how much this helped me' or 'You don't know how much better I feel.'"

Elaine's Advice

HAVE A *separate place for your office so people don't hear your screaming child on the phone. Have a definite business plan. Stay in contact with other people in similar businesses so you can keep motivated and get validation for what you're doing.*

Recommended Resources

ORGANIZATIONS

• National Association of Professional Organizers (NAPO)
1033 LaPosada Drive, Suite 220
Austin, TX 78752
1-512-454-8626

The $120 annual membership fee includes a quarterly newsletter. This group acts as a referral service and offers conferences throughout the states.

Books

- Stephanie Culp, *How to Conquer Clutter*. Cincinnati: Writer's Digest Books, 1989.

- Stephanie Culp, *How to Get Organized When You Don't Have the Time*. Cincin- nati: Writer's Digest Books, 1986.

- Stephanie Culp, *Organize Closets and Storage*. Cincinnati: Writer's Digest Books, 1990.

- Deniece Schofield, *Escape from the Kitchen*. Cincinnati: Writer's Digest Books, 1986.

Freelance Writer and Editor

Name: Pat Curry
Location: Fort Lauderdale, Florida
Family Facts: Married, two girls—ages
   11 and 9
Business: Words and Pictures Com-
   munications Inc.

How She Started Her Business

PAT HAD worked for daily newspapers in some capacity since she was 17. As soon as she found out she was pregnant, she decided to go freelance. "I knew what the schedule was like. It is very unpredictable. We decided I would stay home for a year because it was important to us. If it worked, fine, and if not, that was okay, too. After a year I discovered I could do just as well working from home and decided to stay." She started her business three months after her daughter was born, and then wrote a story a month. "I started to do more regular work when she hit about six months."

After Pat had worked at home for more than eight years running a successful writing and editing business, she got an offer to work for a multibillion dollar company as a corporate writer. "I really debated long and hard over whether I wanted to do this. I had spent years building up a business that was really successful. Did I want to give up all this to go work for someone else?" She couldn't refuse. Not only did it pay well, but there were a lot of great perks—corporate yachts and jets, workout rooms on-site with a trainer, and on and on.

But after seven months, Pat decided to go back home and resume her business. "It took me four months to figure out that I had become a spectator parent." Yes, her kids were older, but they still needed her. Pat is still in the process of getting started from home again. Fortunately, she says, "I wasn't really out of everyone's frame of reference for very long. It just took a few phone calls to a few people letting them know that I was available."

Pat has written for many different publications, from the local dailies to the National Enquirer.

Her Work

PAT HAS written for many different publications, from the local dailies to the *National Enquirer,* which "loves freelancers. The kinds of articles I did for them were the kinds of stories that run in any daily newspaper. They were weird, offbeat features." Pat also does technical writing and newsletters for a variety of organizations.

Qualifications

TO BECOME a freelance writer, Pat says, "You don't need a degree in journalism or a background in the newspapers." You do need good communication and writing skills and a good command of the English language. Because you're probably going to interview people, it's good to have "reporting skills and an outgoing personality."

Equipment

A FREELANCE WRITER needs a computer, a printer, and lots of stamps for self-addressed stamped envelopes. It's also nice to be able to quickly fax your work if your editor needs it right away. Pat also recommends a dedicated phone line for your fax line. Another helpful piece of equipment is an operator's headset. "The best investment I ever made was spending $75 and buying a telephone operator's headset because I spend so much time on the phone all day. I've worn out three of them."

Pat also uses a pager. "The whole idea behind me working from home was so I could spend time with my kids. They would want to go to the park or the library after school and I'd be saying, 'I can't because I'm waiting on this phone call.'" Eventually she also purchased a cell phone.

Rates

MOST NEWSPAPERS pay anywhere from $50 up to $200 for a feature article. A Sunday magazine piece may pay between $750 and $1,000. Magazines can pay anywhere from a penny to $1 or more per word. Pat charges $75 an hour for short-term projects and $150 a page for newsletters where she is the editor and writer.

Marketing

PAT REALLY doesn't need to advertise. She says that the best way to advertise your freelance business is by networking. "It's crucial. I really do no formal advertising, but I network. I have a professional association I belong to called Women in Communications. It's a national organization, and there are chapters all over the country."

Finding a Mentor

AS WITH any business, it's always nice to ask those who have gone before for advice. Pat believes strongly in mentorship. When she was just starting out, she was able

Pat says that the best way to advertise your freelance business is by networking.

to call another writer and ask her questions. "She was very gracious in providing me with that kind of help when I was getting started." Pat has extended that same help to three or four other people. She asks two things from whomever she helps. The first is that they do the same for someone else. And two, if they are ever at a point where they have an assignment they are unable to take, they refer it to Pat.

The best way to find a mentor is to read the local papers and see who the freelancers are. You can usually tell a freelancer by their byline, which will say "special to this publication" or "correspondent." "You look for the people who are doing it regularly and are showing up in the regional magazines. Give them a call."

Tips

• The best way to start writing for magazines is to start with the ones you already read, because you know what type of story the publication is looking for. When you do send a query, "Give them good story ideas. Most editors are looking for people who can generate good story ideas." Write them a query letter that includes a good story idea, present the outline and the idea, explain why it fits their readership, and say why you're the best person to write this story. Once you've proven yourself, you'll establish some relationships and eventually they will assign you pieces.

• Pat says, "For a freelance writer, about the only thing you have to offer is your credibility. There is nothing in the rule books that says they have to use you again. If they are going to get complaints from sources you have interviewed that you haven't actually talked to or you misquoted, then you have blown that relationship and they're not going to use you anymore."

• Never send a letter that says "Dear Editor." Use the editor's name and make sure you spell it right. "If you want to get your stuff thrown away without it being looked at, misspell their name in the cover letter. The hallmark of a good reporter is accuracy, and if you can't even get the name of the editor right, what is that saying about the rest of your work?"

• If you're interested in freelancing for a newspaper, "Put together a list of between three and five good story ideas and target it to a specific editor." Editors are extremely busy people. "Follow up within a week after sending your material out to a daily newspaper. The phone call should be to the point. State your name and explain that you sent them some story ideas. Ask if they received them and if they have any questions."

- Remember what type of publications are more in need of story ideas. A publication that comes out once a day, like a newspaper, needs more stories than a magazine that comes out only once a month.

- "I highly recommend finding a good writing class. But it's very important to research the teacher's background. Make sure your teacher is actively involved in writing for publications. You want a teacher who is current with publishing trends and isn't just another wanna-be writer. I was lucky enough to find two experienced teachers, and I must say I owe a lot of my success to them."

- "The writing field is wide open with opportunities. You can specialize in any area that interests you. A friend of mine and mentor enjoys history. Not only does she have a great excuse for attending reenactments, but she also gets paid for writing about a subject that she really loves."

Pat's Advice

DON'T DO *all your work for one company. I have made that mistake. I was doing all my work for one major newspaper and lost all my work within a two-month period [when the paper downsized].*

Recommended Resources

ORGANIZATIONS

- Women in Communications, Inc.
  1-904-841-2260
  This organization has been around for eighty-six years. Its focus is women who work in the fields of journalism, radio, television, and other forms of communication. It holds monthly meetings—a great way to network.

BOOKS

- Mark Garvey, *The Writer's Market.* Cincinnati: Writer's Digest Books, 1997.
  A national listing of publications that uses freelance work.

MAGAZINES

- *Writer's Digest.* Trade magazine for the freelance writer.

- *The Writer.* Trade magazine for the freelance writer.

SOAPMAKER

Name: Melody Upham
Location: Jackson, Michigan
Family Facts: Married, three chil-
    dren—Michael, 15, Bryan, 14,
    and Parker, 7
Business: Rainbow Meadow Soaps
Web Site: http://www.rainbowmeadow.
    com

Why She Started Her Business

ONE YEAR Melody Upham thought she would create homemade soaps for Christmas gifts. But once she starting making her goats' milk soap, she was having so much fun that she couldn't stop. She says, "I had such a great time that soon my family had more soap than they could use in a lifetime. They started to pass on the extras to friends, who passed it on to their friends."

Melody never dreamed that her Christmas project would turn into a full-fledged home-based business. But around the tenth request for a brochure, she decided that she was on to something, and Rainbow Meadow Soaps was born.

In the past few years Melody's business has changed a bit. Although she still makes a little soap for a few of her faithful customers who will not buy their soap from anyone else, Melody stumbled on a new aspect of business. When she went to purchase her essential oils for her soap she found she had to buy large amounts and because of that had to spend a bit of money. Basically, the products being sold were not intended to be purchased by a small or home-based business. That's where Melody's idea for her next home business came from. She decided to go directly to the growers and distillers for her oils and sell them to the home-based owners at a price they could afford. Her customers include soapmakers, candle-makers, and aromatherapists.

Melody soon plans to open a shop where customers can buy bath and body products. She will also be giving soap and aromatherapy classes there as well.

Start-up Costs

IT TOOK Melody several months and about $300 to perfect various soaps and find recipes she really liked. Then she spent another $700 for supplies, which included shelving for the finished soap to cure.

When Melody started her business four years ago, she made her soaps in the kitchen and dining room areas—although, she ad-

245

"The Internet has put me on an equal footing with the bigger companies out there."

mitted, "We were getting a bit tired of eating off TV trays because every available surface, including the dining room table, was covered with soap." She has since moved her business out of her home and into a warehouse in another state, where she has five employees, including her mother, sisters, and friends. However, Melody is still a stay-at-home mom, and still is able to work out of her home running the other parts of her business.

Marketing

WHEN MELODY first started her business, she put her soaps in craft malls where she paid rent to display them. On occasion, Melody will attend craft fairs to get her name out locally. But she finds she would rather be making her soaps instead of sitting at a booth all day. She now is concentrating more on the retail mail-order part of the business, as well as wholesale, specialty shops, and bed and breakfasts.

Melody says, "What makes you or breaks you in the soapmaking business is the marketing." She is in the process of finding a sales rep to work with. "Selling is not my strong point, so I'm looking for someone to do that for me." Finding a sales rep is

not easy. Usually, they find you. The best way for this to happen is to get your name out there.

Melody also sends out brochures to various businesses. With every brochure she includes a small sample of soap. "I have sold more soap since I have started to put samples in because they smell it and go, 'Wow, this is great.'" She also gives out samples at craft fairs and gets many customers this way.

Now that Melody is considered a retailer of soapmaking products, she is starting to get listed in the back of soapmaking/candle-making/aromatherapy books as a dealer for the ingredients needed to make these products. She also writes for publications and is spotlighted in many magazines as well.

Melody has also found the Internet a wonderful way to get a business known. Because of her Web site, she explains, "The Internet has put me on an equal footing with the bigger companies out there."

Finding a Mentor

MELODY FEELS it's important to network and find other soapmakers who can help you. Melody read an article about

Barbara Bobo of Wood Spirits and was intrigued by her. She was fortunate enough to spend some time with Barbara, who has given Melody a great deal of insight into the soapmaking business. Melody also has contact with other soapmakers through different online services.

When Melody first started out, she received much help from other soapmaking experts. She wants to reciprocate that help and is more than happy to help other soapmakers get started.

Tip

ALTHOUGH MELODY loves soapmaking and is even more thrilled that she can make money from it, she has found that if you want to run a home business you have to be very disciplined. "You have to deliberately set aside time to do the business. You need to set a rigid schedule for yourself even if that means working while your child is napping." Some nights Melody just wants to flop down and watch television, but she knows she has to go out to the kitchen and make soap. That's the difference between a hobby and a business.

Mixing Kids and Business

MELODY FEELS very lucky being able to work from her home. "The idea of running a business from home and not having to put my child in day care is very appealing. This way I have the best of both worlds—time with the kids and a business that I love. Plus I don't have to wear pantyhose or drive through nasty weather, and I can be there for my kids and husband."

Rainbow Meadows Soap is a family business. Each member has a job to do. When Melody first started out, she never made a batch of soap without her husband. Once the soap was ready to be cut, Melody's husband and father-in-law would cut it. Her eldest son, Michael, hand-beveled the soaps, wrapped, and labeled them. Her son Bryan got all the samples ready in bags with their appropriate labels, and Parker had the job of separating blossoms from the heads of the calendula flowers. He put the blossoms in a colander and he shook it around. This separates the head from the petals. "I'm fortunate because I have kids who like to help," says Melody, who credits much of the

Rainbow Meadows Soap is a family business. Each member has a job to do.

success of the business to her family's involvement.

Soapmaking is a very serious endeavor. Melody recommends that anyone with small children be very careful in the actual soap-making process because of the lye used in the soap. None of her children were allowed in the kitchen when she made batches of soap. She either made the soap when the children were in bed or when Michael could watch his two younger brothers.

Now that her kids are older the family is still very involved in her business. In fact, her youngest son Parker reminds her on a regular basis that he plans to take over the business someday. Melody has also seen something interesting emerging from her children. Whereas most kids say they want to be a firefighter or nurse—working for someone else—her kids always think about starting their own businesses when they grow up. They want to make lots of money; however, they always mention they want to be able to stay home with their kids, too.

Rewards

WHAT KEEPS Melody interested in making her soaps is satisfaction. "I get tremendous satisfaction at being able to look around at all the shelves of soaps and think, 'I made that with my own two hands.' The nice comments from my customers don't hurt either. This is the first time in my life I have had a job I enjoy getting up for

each morning. Plus I have such a great boss," says Melody with a chuckle.

Melody's Advice

I'VE READ *articles about people who say, "You don't really know how much time a home business takes. If it's going to take away from your kids, they won't have as much of your time, and you're going to have to put them in day care or shove them aside." It doesn't need to be that way. You can incorporate your kids into the business. Little ones love to do anything to help Mom.*

Recommended Resources

BOOKS

- Ann Bramson, *Soap: Making It, Enjoying It.* New York: Workman Publishing, 1981.

- Susan Miller Cavitch, *The Natural Soap Book.* Pownal, Vt.: Storey Communications, 1995. Good for beginners.

- Merilyn Mohr, *The Art of Soapmaking.* Camden East, Ontario: Camden House Publishing, 1989.

- Elaine C. White, *Soap Recipes.* Starkvill, Miss.: Valley Hills Press, 1995. Great for beginners.

MAGAZINES

- The trade magazine called *Soap, Cosmetics, Chemical Specialties* is mainly for bigger companies, but Melody has found lots of valuable information in it. It's free, but you do have to prove that you have a business to receive it.

- *Saponifier.* This is a magazine on the business of soapmaking. Articles are very helpful for the home-based soapmaker. You may even occasionally see an article by Melody in it.

ONLINE RESOURCES

Melody has started her own soapmaking listserv on the Internet. This is a great way to get answers to soapmaking questions and is also a great support group. To subscribe, send e-mail to majordomo@userhome.com. In the body of the message, type "subscribe soap" and your e-mail address.

MEDICAL TRANSCRIPTIONIST

Name: Luci Godwin
Location: Ashland, Missouri
Family Facts: Married, three children—
    Sam, 9, John, 7, and Jessie, 5
Business: Medical transcription

Why She Started Her Business

WHEN LUCI'S husband found himself in the middle of the military downsizing, they decided to move their family to another state. Luci had to find a job to help make ends meet. At the time, her sons were 2 and 5. "This was the first time I had ever put either of them in day care." However, she was lucky enough to find a job in a hospital as a transcriptionist.

Luci had worked at the hospital for about six months when some general practitioners asked Luci if she would like to do their transcription after work. She said yes and was able to work it out so she could do the transcribing at home. She worked for these particular doctors for about six months when her husband received a job offer in another state.

Fortunately, Luci was able to take her medical transcription skills with her. As soon as Luci started working from home, she took her kids out of day care. Her husband was still home at that point, so he was able to help out with the kids. Luci found the job so accommodating to her schedule and was so happy she had found something she could do at home that they decided to have another baby.

Her Work

AS LUCI says, "I'm just not typing. A doctor gives you a medical report and you have to put it into the right order, put the medical words in there, and know how to spell this and that drug. It's a little more in-depth than just typing," she explains.

Qualifications

THE EXTENT of Luci's medical background consisted of working for a pharmacist for six months. She absolutely loves computers, and typing seems to come naturally to her. She says, "I'm really interested in other people, I guess. You get to peek into other people's lives."

Luci advises you do one thing before you start working at home. "You're going to have to invest some time by going out and working. You just can't start at home. That's what turns most people off. They just want to

250

"A doctor gives you a medical report and you have to put it into the right order, put the medical words in there, and know how to spell this and that drug."

start working at home. You might be able to finagle yourself into a job, but you're not going to know what you're doing."

Equipment

LUCI'S INITIAL costs included $1,700 for the computer and $300 to $400 for a transcription machine. Who you work for determines what type of equipment you need to buy. Some hospitals supply everything. When working for nationwide companies, you have to buy special equipment.

There are three different sizes of dictation machines, and over the years Luci has acquired two of the three. She has a fax machine that was given to her by one of the companies she worked for. Luci recommends WordPerfect software for transcribing. "Word-Perfect is really good because there is so much support software that comes along with it. There is *Stedman's Medical Dictionary* software, which you can use instead of the regular dictionary." Luci suggests one other software program. "One of the programs I use and I swear by is called Flash forward. If I wanted to type the word *cardiovascular* (that's a pretty long word), this

program is set up so I just type CD and the space key and it expands the word out. For the word *the* I just type *t* and then the space key."

Rates

WHEN LUCI worked as an independent contractor, she wasn't getting benefits, but she was paid seven to eleven cents a line. Now she receives less per line, but gets a steady paycheck plus benefits.

Marketing

FINDING NEW clients in another state was of concern to Luci. While she was in Alabama, Luci started to work for a company that allowed her to work for them and live anywhere in the United States. She would get the work over the phone and modem it back to them.

"You really have to know what you're doing to work for a company like this," Luci advises, because you'll be transcribing for foreign doctors and completing other challenging work. Luci says, "It's not easy, but it's a good way to be at home if you can't find something locally." And, yes, there are other jobs like this available. If you register with the American Association of Medical Transcription (AAMT), you will receive their journal, which lists such information.

Once Luci moved she also began to look around locally for transcription jobs. "I started out by calling the transcription services in town and telling them who I was, that I had a year's experience, and that I wanted to work at home." One of the women she talked to didn't have any work for her at the moment but told her that she would give Luci a call if work did come in. "I ended up with about five different clients just by word of mouth like that." Her work mostly came from other transcriptionists' overflow.

Because of the craziness of working for so many doctors, Luci decided she wanted one job and one paycheck. It took a bit of maneuvering to get the job she has now. "They didn't want to hire someone to work at home; they wanted someone to work at the office." Luci eventually gave in and said she would work for them part time. "So I went in for three days and showed them what I could do." But after the third day, she said, "You can see what I can do, if you would just let me do this at home, I'll do it for you full time." They finally said yes. "So now I have one job forty hours a week, and it's wonderful."

Tips

- "A lot of people ask me how to get into it. There are two ways you can do it. The first way is to find someone who is willing to train you. It takes a good six months to get trained. People aren't thrilled about training a transcriptionist, because as soon as they get one trained she leaves. I would start at a hospital because this way you are learning the indepth medical terminology and you can always come down from there. You can always go to a clinic." You won't be making the big bucks starting out. You can expect about $6 an hour. Some hospitals will hire someone new.

- "Another way is to go to a community college where they actually teach medical transcription, textbook style. I don't know a whole lot about that because I didn't do it that way, but that is another way to start. But you're still going to have to get trained once you get done with school." It might be helpful to just take a course in medical terminology. You should have a good English background and know [grammar and punctuation]. It helps to be able to spell. You have to be willing to sit at a computer eight hours a day."

- Luci says, "Ideally the way to do this is to get trained before you have your kids. You really need to go out and work somewhere. This is the perfect way to work at home and to be with your kids. You just need to plan ahead."

- Luci sees networking as a very big part of transcribing. "When you're doing

---

"Staying awake is a big challenge. . . . Every three days I crash."

---

really complicated stuff like that, it's really nice to have a network of friends you can call and say, 'Listen to this sentence,' so you can figure out what they're trying to say."

Mixing Kids and Business

WHEN YOU'RE first starting out, you may have to be content with the amount of work you can get until you can grow your business. Transcription takes a lot of time, and typing quickly is how you make your money. If you're having to stop every five minutes to deal with the kids, you're probably going to be frustrated and not make much money. Luci works in the evening from the time her kids go to sleep until about one in the morning. Sometimes she can also get some work done for a few hours during the morning.

Biggest Challenge

I KNEW SOMETHING was eventually going to have to give, and what I gave up was sleep. I don't sleep. I never thought I could be the kind of person who could get five hours of sleep at night, but I'm doing it," explains Luci. "Staying awake is a big challenge. . . . Every three days I crash."

Meeting deadlines is sometimes a challenge for Luci as well. Every three months or so, Luci asks her friends to watch the kids so she can get caught up on work.

Rewards

WE SAVE over $500 a month in child care. I couldn't afford to go to work," says Luci. And her husband really likes the fact that Luci is home.

Luci believes that if you want to do this type of work at home and you want it badly enough, you can do it. "I have had so many people say, 'Oh, that must be the perfect job to have. How do you get into it?' I'll give them the whole spiel, and then they never follow through. I guess they just don't want it bad enough. I didn't graduate from high school and say, 'I want to be a medical transcriptionist.' I chose it because that was the way I could make $10 an hour and stay home with my kids and not pay any day care. I love it and that helps, but it isn't the main reason that I do it. It's because I want to be with my kids."

Luci's Advice

START SLOW, *don't jump in over your head. And if you're going to plan on having your kids at home with you, start small. If it's not work you can do quickly at first, then plan on having them in at least part-time day care. If you're trying to do a big business and have your kids there at the same time, you're going to end up neglecting your kids. Step back and take a deep breath and just remember why you're doing it. Because sometimes it gets really stressful.*

Recommended Resources

ORGANIZATIONS

• American Association of Medical Transcriptionists (AAMT)
  P.O. Box 576187
  Modesto, CA 95357
  1-209-551-0883

    The $150 annual membership includes *The Journal of the American Association of Medical Transcriptionists* (JAAMT). This journal can give you information on businesses that hire transcriptionists.

• Home-Based Working Moms
  2515 Stenson Drive
  Cedar Park, TX 78613-5704
  http://www.hbwm.com

BOOKS/SOFTWARE

• Sifton, David. *1995 Physicians Desk Reference* (PDR). Montvale, N.J.: Medical Economics Data, 1995.

    This lists all the medications that are out. It is published annually.

• *Stedman's Concise Medical Dictionary,* either in book or software form. Luci recommends the software so you won't have to get up to check something in a book; it will just pop up on the screen.

ONLINE RESOURCES

There is a transcription board on American Online in the business strategies forum. Go to keyword "strategies," then click on the message boards.

QUILTER

Name: Tania Osborn
Location: Chapel Hill, North Carolina
Family Facts: Married, two children—
        ages 7 and 9
Business: Avonlea Concepts

Why She Started Her Business

WITH A background as a material science engineer, Tania specialized in metals and ceramics. Before her children were born, she worked for a surgical instrument company doing a number of different things—audits, designing, computer work, and writing software. However, Tania says, "I didn't like it."

She quit her job to stay home with her first baby. "I didn't really have a choice." Staying home with her kids was very important to Tania; she never sees herself going back to corporate America. She is very happy with the way things are now.

Tania spent five years raising her girls and helping her husband start his own business, which helped her learn about starting a business. Tania had a lot of idle time rocking her babies to sleep and wondering what kind of home business she should start. She says, "In retrospect, I'm glad there was some time in there. Who knows what I would be in now!"

Qualifications

TANIA HAS been sewing since she was 3 years old. As soon as she could pick up a needle, she was sewing alongside her mother and grandmother. Today, however, Tania doesn't enjoy sewing by hand and does most of her work by machine. In addition to good sewing skills, you need good organizational skills. When Tania needs help with these, she usually consults with her friends.

Start-up Costs

TANIA'S START-UP costs were $3,500. Although she put her purchases on

Tania has been sewing since she was 3 years old.

Tania has found one of the best ways to advertise is by doing a good deed with her business.

credit cards, in hindsight she would have preferred to have gotten a loan. At the time, however, it seemed like the best way to go. She feels it's very hard for women to get credit. She has her own business account and advises those interested in getting a bank loan to establish a rapport with their banker.

Equipment

TANIA'S EQUIPMENT includes a Bernina sewing machine, a table, and materials. She also has another machine that does embroidery but feels one machine is enough to get started.

Tania keeps all her sewing machines and equipment in her basement. She likes the isolation. She says, "It's also a nice break away from the days that get a bit crazy." This area is pretty much off-limits to the girls, although Tania does have a television for the girls to watch videos if they want to be with her.

Rates

TANIA CHARGES between $50 and $100 for her wall hangings and $500 to $800 for quilts.

Marketing

I THOUGHT there were formulas about doing home business," says Tania. She read as many books as she could on home business until she found an idea she liked. "For instance, I thought catalog marketing sounded great." So she advertised in a large magazine and found she was spending way too much on ads and not making much profit once she paid for the ads. "Then I discovered I didn't like manufacturing the same thing over and over." But she still liked the catalog concept. She now advertises in her local Sunday newspaper. "I don't think I'll ever advertise in [bigger] places."

Tania had tried craft stores on a consignment basis, but felt they took too much money. She has found one of the best ways to advertise is by doing a good deed with her business. For instance, she teaches a free quilting class and also teaches children's quilting classes at local schools.

She says, "I had to move out of my comfort zone and do self-promotion. Quilting is such a business of solitude. I always disliked street fairs, but I did them and got jobs. I also plan to write a press release so I can have a feature article in the paper."

Her Work

FOR A customized quilt or wall hanging, Tania sets up a consultation to decide the size and colors. She follows up with a price quote and estimated delivery time. Each piece can be made out of the child's clothing or other desired material. Tania meets her clients at home or in restaurants. She has even worked with people she has never met who have faxed a drawing and the names of the Crayola crayon colors for her to match.

Tania also acts as a quilt broker. She has a catalog with the pictures and descriptions of more than 300 quilts. The catalog includes four categories: quilt tops, antiques, recent and new quilts (including custom work), and orphan quilts. "I keep this part of the business because I can always get a sale if someone is interested in purchasing a quilt but is not impressed with my work."

Tania says, "A quilt broker is merely a consignment person. If someone would like to dabble in this market, my first suggestion would be to find several sellers to represent. You must know the values of quilts. There is a lot of information out there about quilts. It just takes research. They are much like other antiques."

Expanding the Business

ALTHOUGH TANIA sews many different types of quilts, she has carved her own little niche making memory quilts. They are made completely from children's drawings. Sometimes she even uses the child's clothing in the quilt.

She says, "I've always been fascinated by children's art. They have the purest sense of composition. I also dabble in painting and struggled with this principle that comes so easily to a 5-year-old. When I got my new sewing machine and wanted to put it through its paces, I picked up one of my daughter's drawings. I just continued to reach for them."

Tip

TO MARKET your quilts, hook up with bed and breakfast establishments. Ask them to display your work by either hanging them on the walls or displaying them on the beds.

Rewards

TANIA ENJOYS the fact that each project is different. Her most recent client had her make a double wedding ring quilt on which Tania embroidered all sixteen names of the wedding party.

Tania will soon be teaching a five-hour class called "A Journey with Quilts" in elementary schools. "It is partially funded through the schools and their individual PTAs. When they purchase my class, I then become their artist-in-residence," explains Tania. "The class teaches the history of quilts, and then leads them through a hands-on encounter with geometry, problem-solving, grouping, and pattern manipulation." The children are then able to design their own quilt blocks, which Tania finishes at home. "The quilt the children make in class will hang in their school, be given to their teacher, or be raffled off to provide funding for future classes."

Tania's Advice

D*O SOMETHING you can stick with, because if you don't like it you're not going to do well. Promote yourself by writing an article in the local paper or teaching a class in the area of your business. I have found that the most successful ventures I have pursued are done with an altruistic spirit.*

Recommended Resources

BOOKS

*   Julie Cameron with Mark Bryan, *The Artist's Way*. New York: Tarcher/Putnam, 1992.

    A great book for figuring out what you like to do.

MAGAZINES/NEWSLETTERS

*   *Quilter's Newsletter*
    P.O. Box 59021
    Boulder, CO 80322-9021

    This covers very high-end work and can be quite intimidating to the average quilter, not to mention a beginner.

*   *Quiltmaker*
    P.O. Box 58360
    Boulder, CO 80322-8360

*   *American Patchwork and Quilting*
    P.O. Box 9255
    Des Moines, IA 50306

    From *Better Homes and Gardens*, this magazine is good for beginners and offers good tips.

CRAFTSMAKER

Name: Amy Reiss Levitt
Location: Needham, Massachusetts
Family facts: Married, two children—
    Jonathan, 8, and Rachel, 5
Business: AmyDoodles
Web Site: http://www.amydoodles.
    com

Why She Started Her Business

WHEN AMY started her business two years ago, she didn't go through a long, arduous search for her home business. She says, "It kind of just started." Before everything "just started," Amy had worked for a publishing firm as a customer relations manager. The company had even worked it out so Amy could be home with her son, Jonathan, two days a week and telecommute. They set her up with a computer and modem, and she did this for eight months. But that still wasn't enough. She wanted to be there all the time for her son.

She finally left the company, along with her salary. "We had to cut back on a lot of stuff, like housecleaning and baby-sitting."

Amy started her business accidentally when she found herself painting little things for her kids. "I just started this business by doodling on my kids' sippy cups." It went from sippy cups to jewelry boxes, visors, you name it. Anything small and plastic—Amy painted on it.

Then friends started coming over and wondering if Amy could paint things for their kids. They offered to pay her. Amy would sometimes sit at the park and paint while her children played. Other parents saw what she was doing, and she soon found herself taking orders at the playground.

Start-up Costs

IT COST Amy only $200 to get started, but this was at a time when family finances were tight, and they were doing their best to squeeze by on just one income. She says, "I didn't have money to burn." So she had to start out very cautiously. In her first year she made a little profit, but not much. But it was enough to cover her expenses.

Some friends and family wondered why Amy was starting a business now, when things were so tight financially. As she says, "I just had to do it. I couldn't explain it; it was something I was meant to do. I didn't

Amy has gone from doodling for kids to a line for babies, adults, weddings, housewarmings, and office and teacher gifts.

even have an arts and crafts background. It was just something I wasn't going to give up. It happened at the wrong time, but for me it was the right time."

Rates

AMY CHARGES anywhere from $1.60 to $44.00 for her merchandise. Her line includes items from wooden puzzles with children's names to coat hangers for kids to personalized dog bowls.

Equipment

IN THE beginning, Amy's equipment included her paint pens, and that was it. She already had a computer that she now uses for her business. Her workspace/office is in her basement. Amy first started buying her merchandise to paint on from dollar stores. But after she did a few craft shows, she acquired her business license and resale certificate. She says, "I was then able to start buying wholesale and buying more upscale stuff." She now goes to large gift shows in New York and Boston to find all her items to paint on. Her goal is to find unique items.

Marketing

AMY ATTENDS craft shows and has a mailing list of more than 200 people. She also holds drawings at the craft shows, and she asks those who sign up if they would like to be on her mailing list. The winner receives $10 to $20 toward one of her items.

The AmyDoodles line has grown tremendously. Amy has gone from doodling for kids to a line for babies, adults, weddings, housewarmings, and office and teacher gifts. She even paints dog bowls. Much of AmyDoodles' merchandise can be personalized, such as a ceramic house for a wedding gift with the newlyweds' names on it.

At most craft shows, Amy takes a sample of her products. People can then pick the item and the color they want it done in. "A lot of the time, I'll go there with things already decorated, and all I have to do is put their name on it."

Most of Amy's advertising is through word of mouth. She uses her mailing lists to tell her tried-and-true customers of new merchandise, or she includes a special 10-percent-off coupon with an expiration date they can use to buy her products. All of her mailings are by postcard. Her last mailing cost her $48; from that one mailing she had a 1 percent response and made around $500. She also advertises in a local parenting newsletter.

Amy has her own Web page on the Internet, which functions like an electronic catalog. People can browse and see her merchandise and place an order. For weddings, people can even fill out a form to include their colors, wedding style, and taste along with their budget. Amy takes this information and comes up with several ideas that she can e-mail back to them.

Tips

- Amy's experience in customer relations has really helped her in her business. She finds people can easily come to her booth at craft shows and talk to her without feeling they have to buy from her (although they usually do).

- If you enjoy painting, there are several avenues you can take: Paint murals for storefronts or children's bedrooms. Redecorate rooms by painting borders or using sponge art. Although these may seem like simple ideas, some people don't have the time or patience to get around to all the great ideas they read about in home-decorating magazines or on TV shows.

Mixing Kids and Business

ACCORDING TO Amy, her children enjoy helping out with the business. "Sometimes they will put the labels and stamps on postcards. They like to get involved. If there are tasks you know you need to do, get your kids to do them. It makes them feel they are doing something for the business." It also makes them feel important if they can help you. Her children are getting old enough where they play independently and work on their own arts and crafts projects while Amy paints. But she has worked around nap schedules and late at night when she has needed to.

Biggest Challenge

AMY'S BIGGEST challenge has been competition in her town. "There are a few stores that do personalized gifts. I try not to have a lot of the same things the stores carry. I like to be different."

Amy's biggest challenge has been competition in her town.

Rewards

AMY FEELS very happy about her career choice. "I can be home with my kids and take them to different places. I can be here when they come home from school." Amy sums it up nicely by saying, "I'm fitting my business around my schedule instead of the other way around."

Amy's Advice

DON'T BE *afraid to explore. I had no idea that I was going to be doing this. Think of your strengths and your hobbies. A lot of the time, hobbies can turn into businesses.*

Recommended Resources

BOOKS

*   Paul and Sarah Edwards, *Working from Home*. New York: Tarcher/Putnam, 1994.

*   Martha M. Bullen and Darcie Sanders, *Staying Home: From Full-Time Professional to Full-Time Parent*. New York: Little, Brown, 1993.

MAGAZINES

*   *Parents Magazine:* A monthly column profiles women who have their own home businesses.

ONLINE RESOURCES

Amy finds networking especially easy through the Internet. She has found the following news groups on the Internet to be very helpful: entrepreneur.moderated, craft.misc, and craft.marketplace. Amy also checks out the wedding discussion groups to see what the new trends are.

ATTORNEY

Name: Lisa Ciancio
Location: Huntington Beach, California
Family Facts: Single mom, one son—
    Nicholas, 4
Business: Law Offices of Lisa A. Ciancio

Why She Started Her Business

AS SOON as Lisa passed her bar exam, she began to work with another attorney in his office. Around the same time, Lisa became pregnant. Fortunately, the attorney she worked with was very understanding and let Lisa bring her son, Nicholas, to work with her. She did this for a few months until he started to become more active. From there, Lisa quit her job and moved into a two-bedroom apartment and started working from home.

Lisa has done everything in her power to raise her son herself, even though this meant a cut in pay. She realized that she might have to quit practicing altogether if she couldn't find a way to work from home as an attorney. She knew lawyers often work close to 50 to 70 hours a week, which would leave very little time for her son. Happily, working from home as an attorney has turned out quite

nicely for Lisa. Although it hasn't always been easy, she wouldn't trade it for the world.

Qualifications

TYPICALLY, A practicing attorney must have a degree from college and law school and successfully pass his or her state's bar exam. It is necessary to take continuing-education courses every year after that. Continuing education classes can cost from $100 to $500 a class, depending on how many units the class is worth.

Equipment

FOR HER office, Lisa needed a bookshelf, a computer, a printer, a desk, a file cabinet, and law books. "Law books [you use] in school don't help you with your practice. You need reference-type material," says Lisa. The best way to get these types of books are through continuing-education classes. "I try to take classes that come with books as study guides because it help builds up your library."

Lisa also has purchased three software programs. One is called SmartLaser, which includes judicial council forms. Whereas attorneys in other states have to draft these

---

"I don't [join organizations] just for the networking, but also for the support."

---

types of documents, California uses standard forms for efficiency. Another software program Lisa owns is called CAPS, which is used for creating wills and trusts. The last program Lisa has is called Support-Tax, which is used for calculating child support.

Her Work

LISA'S SPECIALTY is family law and estate planning. People seek her out when they need to draw up a will or a living trust. She also deals with divorce cases.

Lisa is able to use her old office once a week if she needs to meet with a client, but much of her business can be settled over the phone. The apartment complex she lives in also has a clubhouse where she can meet clients.

Rates

LISA CHARGES anywhere from $300 to $2,500 for large estates, which include wills, trusts, and power of attorney. The price depends on how large and complicated the estate is. For family law counseling she charges $125 per hour.

Marketing

LISA HAS done much of her marketing through the organizations she belongs to. She has found that the organization called Mothers of Preschoolers (MOPS) is a great way to let others know about what she does. They hold regular meetings where they discuss being a mom and raising a preschooler. Through MOPS, Lisa has given a talk about estate planning in front of nearly 150 people. She has also submitted an article for the MOPS newsletter. Lisa also networks through Moms at Home Entrepreneurially Minded (MAHEM) and a little through La Leche League. Lisa says, "I don't [join organizations] just for the networking, but also for the support."

Lisa has just started giving seminars that she can advertise for free through her daily newspaper. The paper has a calendar of events where people can place an event at no cost. She charges approximately $10 a meeting and a little more for her estate seminar.

"The idea is not to give away the cow, but to give them a taste of the milk to see what they need," says Lisa about her seminars. In most cases, people attending these seminars are likely to need an attorney at some point. Once they are done with the class, they will know of a very good lawyer they can call.

One of Lisa's classes is called "Property Divisions and Marital Settlement Agreement Pursuant to Divorce." This hour-long class explains how to divide property, defines community property, and so on. Another class is called "Divorce—What to Expect, How to Proceed." This is for couples thinking about divorce and its probable outcome. The third class is called "Estate Planning— Do I Need an Estate Plan?" This class tells you how to protect your assets through wills and trusts.

Working Hours

UNLESS LISA is meeting with a client, she works in the evening and tries not to work on the weekends. Her hours vary, but she doesn't have to put in the 50- to 70-hour weeks other attorneys do.

Mixing Kids and Business

AS A single parent, Lisa feels it's even more important for her to stay home with her son. Lisa knows she could be making a lot more money if she were working for a firm, but she feels it is important to raise her son herself. She says, "A lot of people wonder why I don't put him in day care. Day care for a small child includes more expenses with lots of incidentals. Balance that against what you're making."

When Lisa has a court date or has to meet with one of her clients, she has one of her family members or a friend watch Nicholas. She figures she will use this type of arrangement until her son is in preschool. For now she makes her phone calls during Nicholas's nap times or in the evening. Most of her clients know she is a single mom, so they are very understanding of her work situation.

Lisa admits that she didn't realize how hard it would be to work at home. "I don't get anything done until he goes to sleep." She also finds it difficult to get work done at night, because she can be just as tired as her sleeping son.

Biggest Challenge

LISA'S BIGGEST challenge is "not enough hours in the day. When I have something to do, it's a challenge not to lose my patience with my son and to realize he doesn't know I have a deadline." She also has a hard time finding time for herself. At times Lisa finds herself going stir-crazy and has to get out of the house to go shopping or out to eat.

Rewards

THE REWARDS for Lisa include, "Getting to see all the leaps and bounds of my son's development. As frustrating as it is with all the deadlines, I wouldn't trade it."

Lisa's Advice

WHATEVER YOU *do, don't get discouraged, especially if you've been a professional. Obviously, it's a big change [to work at] home. You're not going to make as much money or have the support from your colleagues. I would recommend plugging into other groups and networking with friends so you don't feel so isolated. It is possible to make a living on your own and to enjoy it, but it's not going to fall into your lap.*

Recommended Resources

ORGANIZATIONS

- MOPS International, Inc. (Mothers of Preschoolers)
  P.O. Box 102200
  Denver, CO 80210-2200
  1-303-733-5353

  This is an organization for moms that meets once a week. Meetings give women time with other moms, whether it's listening to a speaker or making crafts. Child care is available. To find a local organization in your area, call Protestant churches. MOPS tends not to advertise its meetings, so you will have to do a little searching in this case.

- Moms at Home Entrepreneurially Minded (MAHEM)
  P.O. Box 886

Newport, CA 92661
1-714-723-0756

According to its mission statement, this organization is dedicated to "the support and nurturing role in motherhood while strengthening the business role in the professional woman." It meets once a month.

- La Leche League
  9616 Minneapolis Avenue
  P.O. Box 1209
  Franklin Park, IL 60131

  This is a support group for moms who breast-feed or plan to. For a local organization that meets in your area, look in the yellow pages or call 1-800-LA LECHE.

BOOKS

- Jay Conrad Levinson, *Guerrilla Marketing and Attack for Attorneys.*

  This book is not available in stores. To order, call R. W. Lynch at 1-510-837-3877.

- Jay G. Foonberg, *How to Start and Build a Law Practice.* Chicago: American Bar Association, 1992.

MAGAZINES

- *The Nurturing Parent.* A magazine for stay-at-home moms. Available by calling 1-605-399-2990.

RESOURCES

Specific Resources for the Work-at-Home Mom

- Formerly Employed Mothers at the
  Leading Edge (FEMALE)
  P.O. Box 31
  Elmhurst, IL 60126
  1-708-941-3553
  Web Site: http://FEMALEhome.org
  Membership: $24 annually

  A support group for at-home moms, specifically those who have decided to postpone their full-time careers to be home with their children—this includes women working part time or in home-based businesses. This group offers meetings, play groups, mom's-night-out activities, family functions, and more.

- Home-Based Working Moms
  P.O. Box 500164
  Austin, TX 78750
  Web Site: http://www.hbwm.com
  Membership: $39 annually

  National organization founded in 1995 for mothers (and fathers) who are currently working from home and those who would like to. Offers a newsletter, resource guides, and other publications for work-at-home moms, plus opportunities to share information and support one another. For more information, send a self-addressed, stamped envelope to the address above.

- Moms at Home Entrepreneurially
  Minded (MAHEM)
  P.O. Box 886
  Newport, CA 92661
  1-714-723-0756

  According to its mission statement, this organization is dedicated to supporting the "nurturing role" in motherhood while strengthening the "business role" in the professional woman. This group meets once a month.

- MOMS Club
  c/o 25371 Rye Canyon
  Valencia, CA 91355
  E-mail: momsclub@aol.com

  This is a national support group for the at-home mother. There are 375 chapters nationwide. Club benefits include play groups, baby-sitting co-ops, food co-ops, family parties, mom's-night-out programs, and much more. For more information on a chapter close to you, write to the above address and include $2 for shipping and handling charges. MOMS is a non-profit organization.

- Mothers Access to Careers at Home (MATCH)
  P.O. Box 123
  Annandale, VA 22003
  1-703-205-9664
  Web Site: http://www.freestate.net/match
  Membership: $40 annually

  MATCH, which has been in existence for nine years, publishes a newsletter full of valuable information geared to the work-at-home mom. It holds regular meetings the first Monday of each month. Also included with the membership is the Resource Guide published by MATCH (the guide can be purchased separately). The guide is geared for those living in the Washington, D.C., area. However, there is valuable information for all, including small-business resources for those who have or desire to start a home business, computer/Internet resources, a quiz for those thinking of starting a business, and a "do you have what it takes?" questionnaire.

Home Business Help

- American Association of Home-Based Businesses
  P.O. Box 10023
  Rockville, MD 20849
  1-800-447-9710
  Web Site: http://www.aahbb.org
  Membership: $30 annually for home-based businesses; $135 annually for non-home-based businesses

Benefits include discount business services and an application for a credit card under merchant status. It also provides networking support and legislative monitoring for home-based businesses.

- American Home Business Association
  4505 S. Wasatch Boulevard
  Salt Lake City, UT 84124
  1-801-272-3500
  Web Site: http://www.homebusiness.com

  Membership, which right now is free, includes a 24-hour advice hotline, a personalized 800 number for business use, a Visa or MasterCard merchant account, a newsletter, a magazine, and workshops.

- Home-Based Business Tips
  U.S. Small Business Administration
  409 Third Street, SW
  Washington, DC 20416
  1-800-827-5722

  Free start-up guide for your home business from the SBA.

- National Association for the Self-Employed
  P.O. Box 612067
  Dallas, TX 75267-2067
  1-800-232-6273
  Web Site: http://nase.org

  This organization's main goal is to help small businesses become more competitive by providing more than 100 benefits and services to meet its members' business, health, and personal needs. It represents the views and attitudes of its members and offers advocacy as a prime membership benefit. Another popular benefit is a toll-free hot line for small-business advice. This organization offers big savings on resource books that provide information about the many aspects of a home business. For information, send a SASE to the address above.

- National Institute of Occupational Safety and Health
NIOSH Publications, C-13
4676 Columbia Parkway
Cincinnati OH 45226-1998
1-800-356-4674

This organization publishes tip sheets and a newsletter on how to avoid on-the-job injuries, including common home-based business ailments such as eye-strain and repetitive stress syndrome.

- National Business Association
5151 Beltline Road
Dallas, TX 75240
1-800-456-0440
Web Site: http://www.nationalbusines.org

This is a nonprofit organization for small-business owners, entrepreneurs, and professionals. The association continuously provides its membership with vital support programs, cost- and time-saving products, and health, education, business, and life-style services.

- Postal Tips
National Customer Support Center
6060 Primacy Parkway, Suite 101
Memphis, TN 38188-0001
1-800-238-3150

The post office offers a free disk called The Mail Flow Planning System that helps evaluate the most cost-effective way to send your mail.

- Service Corps of Retired Executives (SCORE)
Web Site: http://www.score.org

This Small Business Administration program provides free individual sessions with seasoned business veterans who will advise you about your venture. Call the SBA at 1-800-827-5722 for more information.

- Small Business Administration (SBA)
409 3rd Street, SW, Room 6400
Washington, DC 20416
1-202-205-6665
Web Site: http://www.sbaonline.sba.gov

Get the facts on starting a home-based business and receive free marketing or accounting advice. The SBA also has a public phone number that provides detailed information about small business. Look for a local number under the U.S. Government section of your telephone book or call 1-800-8-ASK-SBA.

- Small Business Development Center
These programs operate in forty-

seven states and are partially funded by the Small Business Administration. Free or very inexpensive benefits include individual business consulting and seminars on special topics that are important to small businesses. Call the SBA at 1-800-827-5722 for more information.

• Superintendent of Documents
U.S. Government Printing Office
Washington, DC 20402
1-202-783-3238
Cost: $2

Contact this organization to get the publication *Starting and Managing a Business from Your Home.*

Home Business Publications

• *101 Best Home-Based and Small Businesses for Women Updates: The Latest Facts, News, and Tips for Women Entrepreneurs*
Box 286
Sellersville, PA 18960

This publication is written by Priscilla Huff (author of *101 Best Home Based Businesses for Women*). For a one-year subscription, send $15 ($18 in Canada) to the above address.

• *Bootstrappin' Entrepreneur*
8726 S. Sepulveda Boulevard, Suite B261
Los Angeles, CA 90045

This is a quarterly newsletter devoted to helping people run a business on a small budget. For more information, send a self-addressed, stamped envelope to the address above.

• County Cooperative Extension Service
6707 Groveton Drive
Clinton, MD 20735
1-310-868-9410

If you're interested in starting a child-care business in your home, this service provides free copies of *Child Care and Running a Child Care Business*. It includes information needed to run your business. Videos on starting a child-care business include information about nutrition, health and safety, and business management and can be obtained for a modest fee or on a free-loan basis through many County Cooperative Extension Service offices around the country.

If you plan to work as a word processor, the free publication *Women and Office Automation Issues for the Decade Ahead* may be helpful. It discusses work quality, training and retraining, home-based clerical work, and health and safety issues.

Running your own business can cause a lot of added stress to your life—in your family and your marriage—especially if your business isn't doing well. The pamphlet Healthfinder includes stress information resources that list and describe several government agencies and private organizations that offer publications and resources on work-related stress and stress management. Cost: $1.00

- *Scams, Swindles, and Rip-Offs*
  Gold Shadow Press
  P.O. Box 687
  Littleton, CO 80160.
  1-800-844-7532
  Cost: $14.95, plus $3.00 shipping and
    handling
  This pamphlet by Graham M. Mott is a good source of information that aims to prevent you from becoming a victim of scams. It has been featured on *Oprah, Donahue,* and many other television and talk radio shows. To order, call the number listed above or write to the address.

- The Whole Work Catalog
  1515 23rd Street
  P.O. Box 297-CT
  Boulder, CO 80306
  1-303-447-1087
  This free publication features books and periodicals for purchase on alternative work styles and careers.

Mentoring Programs

- The Clairol Mentor Program
  c/o The National Women's Economic
    Alliance Foundation

1440 New York Avenue, NW, Suite 300
Washington, DC 20005
1-212-684-6300
  This program matches career women with leading professionals. To enter, send a typed statement of 100 words describing how a mentor could play an important role in your career success.

- National Association of Women Business Owners (NAWBO)
  1413 K Street, NW
  Washington, DC 20005
  1-301-608-2590
  This organization comprises members who range from corporate to home-based business owners. There are sixty NAWBO chapters throughout the country. Membership benefits include help with facilitating your networking skills, national conferences, financial opportunities such as loans, and education and leadership programs.

- Office of Women's Business Ownership
  U.S. Small Business Administration
  409 3rd Street, SW
  Washington, DC 20416
  1-202-205-6673
  This organization supports women entrepreneurs and helps you find a successful role model who has already gone through what's facing you as a female entrepreneur and who is willing to share her expertise at no charge. Also, if you feel a legislative change needs to be made

in the area of women in business, you can contact this organization.

• Women in Communications, Inc. (WICI)
60605 Judical Drive
Fairfax, VA 22030
1-703-359-9000

This is a professional organization for women in the fields of journalism, radio, television, graphics, and other forms of communication.

Financial Assistance

• Women's Opportunity and Resource Development, Inc.
127 N. Higgins, 3rd Floor
Missoula, MT 59802
1-406-543-3550
Contact Person: Barbara Burk

This company offers intermediate loans up to $15,000 (2 to 5 years) and training for women—particularly rural women—interested in creating home-based successful business enterprises. This service is provided by the U.S. Small Business Administration.

• Women's World Banking
North America Office
P.O. Box 2125
Charleston, WV 25328
1-304-345-1298
Contact Person: Trina Newell

This company offers loans up to $10,000. It also provides technical assistance and support groups that consist of lawyers, bankers, accountants, and business people who provide their services free of charge.

BIBLIOGRAPHY

Agonito, Rosemary. *No More "Nice Girl."* Holbrook, Mass.: Bob Adams, 1993.

Attard, Janet. *The Home Office and Small Business Answer Book.* New York: Henry Holt, 1992.

Barillo, Madeline. *The Wedding Sourcebook Planner.* Los Angeles: Lowell House, 1997.

Bear, John. *College Degrees by Mail.* Berkeley: Ten Speed Press, 1993.

Bird, Caroline. *Enterprising Women.* New York: W. W. Norton, 1976.

Brabec, Barbara. *Homemade Money.* Cincinnati: Betterway Publications, 1994.

Bramson, Ann. *Soap: Making It, Enjoying It.* New York: Workman Publishing, 1981.

Breathnach, Sarah. *Simple Abundance: A Day Book of Comfort and Joy.* New York: Warner Books, 1995.

Bryant, Jane. *Make the Most of your Money.* New York: Simon and Schuster, 1997.

Bullen, Martha M., and Darcie Sanders. *Staying Home: From Full-Time Professional to Full-Time Parent.* New York: Little, Brown, 1993.

Burg, Bob. *Endless Referrals.* New York: McGraw-Hill, 1993.

Burkett, Larry. *Women Leaving the Workplace.* Chicago: Moody Press, 1995.

Cameron, Julie, with Mark Bryan. *The Artist's Way.* New York: Tarcher/Putnum, 1992.

Cavitch, Susan Miller. *The Natural Soap Book.* Pownal, Vt.: Storey Communications, 1995.

Chase, Sarah Lee. *Cold-Weather Cooking.* New York: Workman Publishing, 1990.

————. *Nantucket Open-House Cookbook.* New York: Workman Publishing, 1987.

Covey, Stephen. *The Seven Habits of Highly Effective People.* New York: Simon & Schuster, 1989.

Culp, Stephanie. *How to Conquer Clutter.* Cincinnati: Writer's Digest Books, 1989.

————. *How to Get Organized When You Don't Have the Time.* Cincinnati: Writer's Digest Books, 1986.

————. *Organize Closets and Storage.* Cincinnati: Writer's Digest Books, 1990.

Drew, Bonnie, and Noel Drew. *Fast Cash for Kids.* Franklin Lakes, N.J.: Career Press, 1995.

Edwards, Paul, and Sarah Edwards. *Making It on Your Own.* New York: Tarcher/Perigee, 1991.

————. *Working from Home.* New York: Tarcher/Putnam, 1994.

Ernst, Robbi, III. *Great Wedding Tips from the Experts.* Los Angeles: Lowell House, 1999.

Fields, Alan, and Denise Fields. *Bridal Bargains.* Boulder, Col.: Windsor Peak Press, 1998.

————. *Bridal Gown Guide,* 3rd edition, revised. Boulder, Col.: Windsor Peak Press, 1999.

Foonberg, Jay G. *How to Start and Build a Law Practice.* Chicago: American Bar Association, 1992.

Frazier, Shirley. *How to Start a Home-Based Gift Basket Business.* Old Saybrook, Conn.: The Globe Pequot Press, 1998.

Fuller, Cheri. *Home Business Happiness.* Colorado Springs: Alive Communications, 1996.

Garvey, Mark. *The Writer's Market.* Cincinnati: Writer's Digest Books, 1997.

German, Mario D. *301 Legal Forms and Agreements.* Dearfield Beach, Fla.: EZ Legal Books, 1993.

Gibaldi, Joseph. *MLA Style Manual and Guide to Scholarly Publishing.* New York: The Modern Language Associations of America, 1998.

Godfrey, Joline. *Our Wildest Dreams.* New York: HarperBusiness, 1992.

Hahn, Fred E. *Do-It-Yourself Advertising: How to Produce Great Ads, Brochures, Catalogs, Direct Mail, and Much More.* New York: Wiley, 1993.

Hoff Oberlin, Loriann. *Writing for Money.* Cincinnati: Writer's Digest Books, 1994.

Jacobs, Betty E. M. *Profitable Herb Growing at Home.* Charlotte, Vt.: 1976.

Jessup, Claudia, and Genif Chipps. *The Woman's Guide to Starting a Business,* 3rd ed. New York: Henry Holt, 1991.

Kelley, Linda. *Two Incomes and Still Broke?* New York: Times Books, 1996.

Kursmark, Louise. *How to Start a Home-Based Desktop Publishing Business.* Old Saybrook, Conn.: The Globe Pequot Press, 1996.

Lemay, Laura. *Web Publishing with HTML 4 in a Week.* Indianapolis, Ind.: Sams, 1998.

Levinson, Jay Conrad. *Guerrilla Marketing Excellence.* Boston: Houghton Mifflin, 1993.

Mastin, Robert. *900 Know-How.* Newport, R.I.: Aegis, 1996.

McCormack, Thomas. *The Fiction Editor.* New York: St. Martin's Press, 1998.

McFedries, Paul. *The Complete Idiot's Guide to Creating an HTML 4 Web Page.* Indianapolis, Ind.: QUE Education & Training, 1997.

McQuown, Judith. *Inc. Yourself.* New York: HarperCollins, 1993.

Melnik, Jan. *How to Start a Home-Based Secretarial Services Business.* Old Saybrook, Conn.: The Globe Pequot Press, 1994.

Milano, Carol. *HERS.* New York: Allworth Press, 1991.

Mohr, Merilyn. *The Art of Soapmaking.* Camden East, Ontario: Camden House Publishing, 1989.

Monaghan, Kelly. *Home-Based Travel Agent.* New York: Intrepid Traveler, 1999.

Moran, Patti. *Pet Sitting for Profit.* Pinnacle, N.C.: New Beginnings, 1992.

Moriarty Field, Christine. *Coming Home.* Grand Rapids, Mich.: Fleming H. Revell, 1995.

Mulvany, Nancy. *Indexing Books.* Chicago: University of Chicago Press, 1994.

Nelsen, Jane, *Positive Discipline.* New York: Ballantine, 1987.

Ogg, Joanie, and Tom Ogg. *How to Start a Home-Based Travel Agency.* CITY: Tom Ogg and Associates, 1997.

O'Neill, Pierre George. *Too Good to Be True.* Barrie: Ontario: Factfinder Publications, 1990.

Pilzer, Paul. *Unlimited Wealth*. New York: Crown, 1991.

Pinkola-Estes, Clarisa. *Women Who Run with the Wolves*. New York: Ballantine, 1992.

Robbins, Anthony. *Awaken the Giant Within You*. New York: Summit Books, 1993.

———. "Power Talk" (audiocassette). CITY: Audio Renaissance, 1996.

Roney, Carley. *The Knot's Complete Guide to Weddings in the Real World*. New York: Broadway Books, 1998.

Rosso, Julee, Sheila Lukins, and Sarah Lee Chase. *The Silver Palate Good Times Cookbook*. New York: Workman Publishing, 1985.

Rugge, Sue. *Information Brokers Handbook*. New York: McGraw-Hill, 1997.

Ryder, Judy. *Turning Your Great Idea into a Great Success*. Princeton, N.J.: Peterson's/Pacesetter Books, 1995.

Schofield, Deniece. *Escape from the Kitchen*. Cincinnati: Writer's Digest Books, 1986.

Sears, Martha, and William Sears. *The Baby Book*. New York: Little, Brown, 1993.

Sears, William. *Creative Parenting: The Complete Guide to Child Care*. New York: Everest House, 1992.

———. *Nighttime Parenting*. Franklin Park, Ill.: La Leche League International, 1995.

Shenson, Howard L. *The Contract & Fee-Setting Guide for Consultants & Professionals*. New York: Wiley, 1990.

Sher, Barbara, with Annie Gottlieb. *Wishcraft*. New York: Ballantine, 1979.

Sifton, David. *1995 Physicians' Desk Reference*. Montvale, N.J.: Medical Economics Data, 1995.

Sinclair, Carole. *Keys for Women Starting and Owning a Business*. New York: Barrons, 1991.

Stedman's Concise Medical Dictionary. CITY, Canada: Macmillan General Reference, 1987.

Strunk, William, Jr., and E.B. White. *The Elements of Style*, 3rd edition. New York: Macmillan, 1979.

Sturdivant, Lee. *Herbs for Sale: Growing and Marketing Herbs, Herbal Products, and Herbal Know-How*. Friday Harbor, Wash.: San Juan Naturals, 1994.

Tolliver, Cindy. *At-Home Motherhood*. San Jose, Calif.: Resource Publications, 1994.

University of Chicago Press. *The Chicago Manual of Style*, 14th edition. Chicago: University of Chicago Press, 1993.

Wellisch, Hans H. *Indexing from A to Z*. Bronx, N.Y.: H. W. Wilson, 1996.

White, Ellen C. *Soap Recipes*. Starkvill, Miss.: Valley Hills Press, 1995.

Williamson, Marianne. *A Woman's Worth*. New York: Ballantine, 1994.

Willins, Michael. *Photographer's Market*. Cincinnati: Writer's Digest Books, 1996.

Winter, Barabara J. *Making a Living Without a Job*. New York: Bantam, 1993.

Zobel, Jan. *Minding Her Own Business: The Self-Employed Woman's Guide to Taxes and Recordkeeping*. Holbrook, Mass.: Adams Media Corporation, Forthcoming.

INDEX

About the Author

LIZ FOLGER works full time as a mom, wife, author, columnist, and public speaker. She has two daughters, ages 4 and 5.

Her book, *The Stay-at-Home Mom's Guide to Making Money from Home*, has been featured in national publications, including *Forbes, Business Start-Ups, Working From Home*, and *Woman's Own*. She has appeared as a guest on many radio shows and regional television, as well as on ZDTV (part of Ziff Davis). Liz was also a guest on Lifetime's Television for Women *Our Home*, where she reported on how to avoid work-at-home scams, and on PBS's *Internet Cafe*.

Before the birth of her first daughter, Liz struggled with how she could stay at home with her child and still contribute to her family's income. Falling prey to a scam and sinking a lot of money into a dealership that didn't work out, she finally figured out that the key to success was to find a business she loved that didn't actually feel like work. After this realization, her writing career took off.

Liz Folger is considered the work-at-home mom expert and runs a resource on the Internet called Bizy Moms (www.bizy-moms.com) for moms who want to work at home and for those moms who already have a home business. She also publishes a weekly syndicated column that can be found on a number of Internet sites.

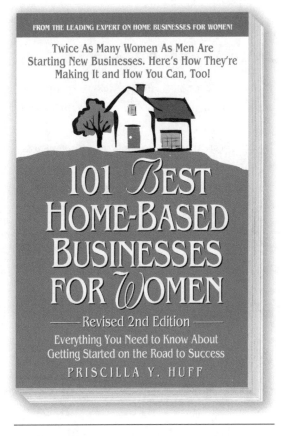

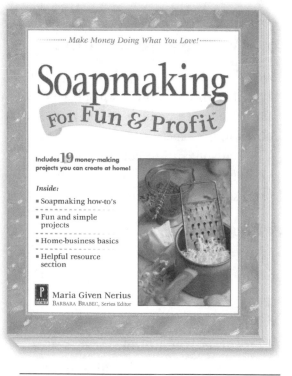

To Order Books

Please send me the following items:

Quantity	Title	U.S. Price	Total
_____	101 Best Home-Based Businesses for Women, Revised 2nd Edition	$ _____	$ _____
_____	101 Best Home-Business Success Secrets for Women	$ _____	$ _____
_____	I Love the Internet, but I Want My Privacy, Too!	$ _____	$ _____
_____	Soapmaking For Fun & Profit	$ _____	$ _____
_____	_____	$ _____	$ _____
_____	_____	$ _____	$ _____

Subtotal	$ _____
7.25% Sales Tax (CA only)	$ _____
7% Sales Tax (PA only)	$ _____
5% Sales Tax (IN only)	$ _____
7% G.S.T. Tax (Canada only)	$ _____
Priority Shipping	$ _____
Total Order	$ _____

FREE
Ground Freight
in U.S. and Canada

Foreign and all Priority Request orders:
Call Customer Service
for price quote at 916-787-7000

By Telephone: With American Express, MC, or Visa,
call 800-632-8676, Monday–Friday, 8:30–4:30
www.primapublishing.com

By E-mail: sales@primapub.com
By Mail: Just fill out the information below and send with your remittance to:
Prima Publishing ▪ P.O. Box 1260BK ▪ Rocklin, CA 95677

Name _____

Address _____

City_____ State _____ ZIP _____

MC/Visa/American Express# _____ Exp._____

Check/money order enclosed for $ _____ Payable to Prima Publishing

Daytime telephone _____

Signature ._____